A Teenager in the
Chad Civil War

A Teenager in the Chad Civil War

*A Memoir of Survival,
1982–1986*

Ésaïe Toïngar

McFarland & Company, Inc., Publishers
Jefferson, North Carolina, and London

Frontispiece: A 1993 photograph of the author in Algeria, where he was attending school.

LIBRARY OF CONGRESS CATALOGUING-IN-PUBLICATION DATA

Toïngar, Ésaïe N., 1968–
    A teenager in the Chad Civil War : a memoir of survival,
1982–1986 / Ésaïe N. Toïngar.
        p.   cm.
    Includes bibliographical references and index.

    ISBN-13: 978-0-7864-2403-0
    softcover : 50# alkaline paper ∞

    DT546.48.T65   2006
                                    2006044941

British Library cataloguing data are available

Cover photograph: Ésaïe N. Toïngar 1986

Manufactured in the United States of America

*McFarland & Company, Inc., Publishers
    Box 611, Jefferson, North Carolina 28640
    www.mcfarlandpub.com*

I solemnly dedicate this book
to those I cherish,
some of whom, alas,
are no longer in this world

Acknowledgments

To my fellows in the Green CODOs (Commandos-Verts), National Chadian Army Forces (Forces Armées Nationales Tchadiennes, FANT), my father, cousins, brother, aunts, granduncles, grandfathers and grandmothers — you who are not any more here to see the end of the tunnel, you might have appreciated this work which brought out to the world our sufferings. You helped me, and I now want to help you in return but cannot.

To villagers whose houses and churches were burned and whose property was destroyed or stolen, those who were tortured, or tortured and then killed later, to widows, orphans, and innocents who were subjected to inhuman conditions.

To the Evangelical and Baptist Mid-Mission churches in Chad, the First Evangelical Free Church of Cedar Falls, the Central Baptist Church of Sioux City, the TRIO program of Western Iowa Community College, Student Support Services and Academic Services of the University of Northern Iowa, John Georgio, Nick Sullivan, Dawn and Tim Glass, Harlan Hough's family and Rachel, the Schram family, Barbara and the Reverend Tim Blanchard, Bob McCue, Eddy Nicolas' family, Nanadoum's family, Nodjigoto Jean Baptiste, Koumandôh's family, Sanabé's family, Mbaïlemdana's family, Mbaïlemou's family, Tolmbaye's family, the family of engineer Maïna Domtiné, Dingamta Daniel, Ngarnadji's family, Odingar Doumrô, Mordjimngarti's family, my uncle Jean Rabbi, and my mother Ngambaye — never forgetting my lovely and beloved wife Brigitte and daughters Jeany Adoua and Joyce Dénénodji Toïngar. Thank you very much for your support and prayers.

Jean Ann Schram, you have my special love for making me what I am today. Dr. Karen Agee, I do not have appropriate words to express my thanks to you for making a great effort to understand my limping English and make me successful academically at the University of Northern Iowa. Dr. Agee, without you, the world might not read clearly my voice in print.

Have here the expression of my filial attachment.

Table of Contents

Preface

I AM A CHILD OF CHAD, an African country that has known internal and external war for years since its theoretical independence from France in 1960. I am a child of Chad who was born and has grown up in deadly war. After a bitter youth and many near escapes from death, I survive today to share with people of the world my experiences. The period covered by this account could be called Chad's *Black Septembers*. In this book I tell about the years from 1982 to 1986. Fighting was especially atrocious in the months of September. Septembers for some reason were the worst months of these years, and of these five Septembers, September of 1984 was the very worst. In this one month the South lost nearly all of its intellectuals, businessmen, and villager farmers. In addition, its many resources were pillaged and taken away.

Ngarlejy Yorongar, also a child of Southern Chad, has written a book about the man who is now President of Chad but was an agent of death during the awful years of this memoir. Yorongar calls his book, *L'Accusé Idriss Déby, Levez Vous (Defendant Idriss Déby, Stand Up)*. One chapter of Yorongar's book makes reference to "Black September" (Septembre Noir), by which he means September of 1984. I experienced other "Black Septembers," as well, and write about them here.

This book traces the path of my survival, and I believe God traced this path for me. I believe I may have been intended to pass through the dangers I experienced in order to let people know —

1

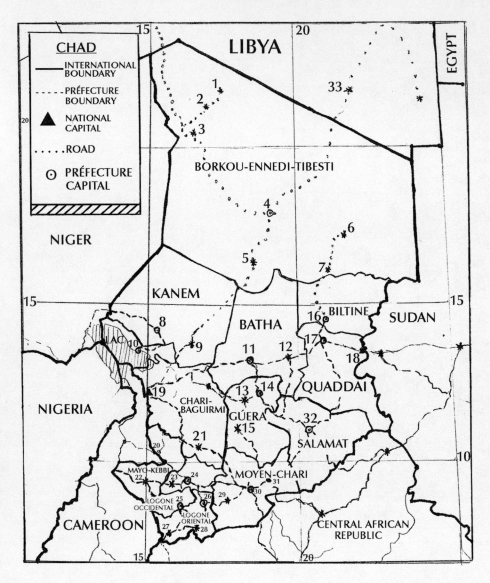

1. Aozou; 2. Bardaï; 3. Zouar; 4. Faya-Largeau; 5. Koro-Toro; 6. Fada; 7. Oum
Chalouba; 8. Mao; 9. Moussoro; 10. Bol; 11. Ati; 12. Dum Hadjer; 13. Bitkin;
14. Mongo; 15. Melfi; 16. Biltine; 17. Abéché; 18. Adré; 19. N'Djaména; 20. Bon-
gor; 21. Bousso; 22. Pala; 23. Kélo; 24. Lac; 25. Moundou; 26. Doba;
27. Mbaïbokoum; 28. Goré; 29. Koumra; 30. Sarh; 31. Kyabé; 32. Am Timan;
33. Ma'jan as Sárah (Libya)

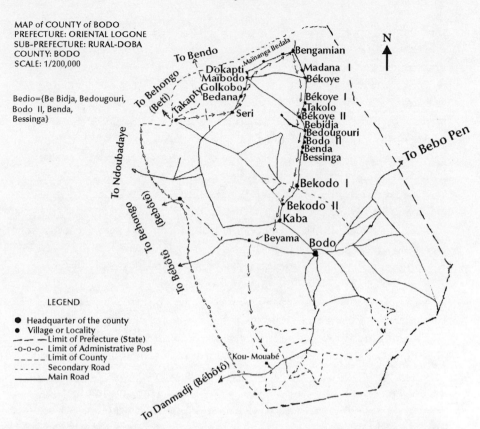

MAP of COUNTY of BODO
PREFECTURE: ORIENTAL LOGONE
SUB-PREFECTURE: RURAL-DOBA
COUNTY: BODO
SCALE: 1/200,000

Bedio={Be Bidja, Bedougouri,
Bodo II, Benda,
Bessinga}

To Bendo
To Behongo (Beti)
Mainanga Bedala
Bengamian
Dokapti
Maïbodo
Golkobo
Bedana
Takapty
Seri
Madana I
Békoye
Békoye I
Takolo
Békoye II
Bebidja
Bedougouri
Bodo II
Benda
Bessinga
To Bebo Pen
Bekodo I
Bekodo II
Kaba
Beyama
Bodo
To Ndoubadaye
To Behongo (Bébôtô)
To Bébôtô
N
Kou- Mouabé
To Danmadji (Bébôtô)

LEGEND

● Headquarter of the county
● Village or Locality
–·–·– Limit of Prefecture (State)
-o-o-o- Limit of Administrative Post
– – – – Limit of County
· · · · · Secondary Road
———— Main Road

Map of the county of Bodo in Chad. The arrows moving from Bengamian in the north to Kou Mouebe in the south indicate the road that I followed to join Codo in the Maquis. The arrows moving from Takapty in the northwest to Bengamian show the route I took to escape the fighters bent on torturing and killing me. In the text I mention a place called Bedio. This is a name that locals gave to a cluster of five villages: Bebidja, Bedougouri, Bodo II, Benda, and Bessinga.

especially the people of Chad—what transpired in Chad during the rule of Hissène Habré. Under Habré, Idriss Déby and his cousin Itno subjected the country and especially the South to pitiless murder. In these years, the uneducated controlled the intellectuals, the blind guided the sighted, and military officers turned papers this way and that before trying to sign, not even knowing how to read. In these years, reason kept quiet.

This is primarily a sad story without a happy ending. The same events recur today in the Sudan, where thousands of Southerners are being displaced and killed by their Northern oppressors. The ruler of the Sudan, Omar al-Bashir, helped the current ruler of Chad to attain power, sending some of his officers from the region of Darfur and granting permission for Sudanese of the Zakhawa tribe to join their fellow tribesmen of Chad to overthrow the government of Chad. In addition, in 1994 Idriss Déby used the army of Chad to help al-Bashir to put down the John Garang rebellion in southern Sudan. Now Déby is attempting to overthrow the government of Sudan by supporting Zakhawa officers who want al-Bashir's power for themselves. My story is just one small part of this larger tragedy in central Africa.

In fact, not only the current distress of the Sudan but even the genocides in Rwanda, the Central African Republic, Ivory Coast, Sierra Leone, Liberia, the Congo Republic, and the Congo Democratic Republic derive from this same misfortune, and the misfortune does not originate in Africa. An external power misled the people of Chad. African people cannot by themselves solve a problem caused by others. What I say in this book is happening to many countries now. My story is similar to the stories of many who have suffered and currently endure all kinds of suffering in many other countries of Africa.

This book is derived primarily from my own memory, but it also utilizes my conversations with people who had been scattered by the events and whom I met again a few years later. Their testimonials I found to be vivid portrayals of what had happened to them or to others. I found out ten years later when I visited my region that what I had learned from them was true. Even now in some villages there are marks of the events of this book. Skeptical readers I refer to the burned homes and human bones that still attest to these cruelties.

The other testimony that I found trustworthy is a videotaped documentary filmed in 1991 that I first viewed in 2003. Shortly after the departure of Hissène Habré from power, the Truth Commission instructed Chad Television to film this documentary, showing how Hissène and his disciples had tortured people before killing them. The websites of human rights organizations also contain accounts that support what I write in my memoir.

This memoir is an honest testimony and an honorable report. I cannot give the exact dates of many of the events herein not only because I was so young but also because I lost my mind and had no expectation of living to tell anyone about these events. Chad has lost so many of its greatest people, its most capable children, and though the precise dates have slipped my mind, the horror remains. I am able to recount the months when most of the events occurred. I know all the areas where the events of this book happened. If someday I could take the reader to investigate what I talk about in this book, I would be able to point out the precise locations of events. Right now, though, there is no way for us to travel to Chad for an investigation of murders and massacres in the South. Right now my country continues to be oppressed by many of the very murderers and killers themselves. Photographs of torture victims and film clips of piles of bones in mass graves would show you the viciousness of the war in Chad. Unfortunately I cannot present those here. Instead, I will try by words to show you Chad's "Black Septembers" of sorrowful memory.

Prologue

"RUN QUICKLY," MY AUNT WHISPERED urgently, with great agitation.
I shot out of my hut toward the bush that surrounded our village.
"May God save you, my boy," she called, and I knew the man with his
rifle was right behind me. Taking the shortcut through my aunt's part
of the compound, I gained some time, because the armed man had to
skirt the fence to reach the back of the compound. As I dashed to the
brush under fire from the man behind, bullets whizzed past my left
ear. I saw another armed man on my left, shooting as he ran in, trying
to cut me off. I swiftly took cover behind some trees. Right then a
friend of mine, Élie, who had apparently also taken to the bush some
distance ahead of me, took off running — and the man on the left
swiveled his rifle toward the boy and fired. Élie dropped dead, taking
the bullet meant for me, and soon the armed men left, maybe nervous
about being so far from their comrades. I remained on the ground,
huddled amidst the shrubs. How had it come to this, that strangers
would drive into our village on a sunny morning, kill us, set fire to our
homes, and leave? This was the spring of 1983, I was 14 years old, and
I was terrified.

1

From Rebellion to Presidency

THE CIVIL WAR—THE NORTHERN REBELLION led by Goukouni Oueddei against the government of Chad—was brought by co-revolutionary Hissène Habré (Hissein Habre) on February 12, 1979, to the capital city of N'djaména and then extended throughout all of Chad. By this time the country was divided into two blocs, the South and the North. People from the South, mostly Christians, who were living in the capital quickly returned home for their safety to the southernmost area, known as the Meridional Zone. This was because people from the north, east and center of Chad were in control of the rest of the country, each area with its own rebel warfare. The Organization of United Africa (OUA) quickly summoned the leaders of OUA states to a second conference at Kano in Nigeria. Within one week, the Kano II assembly had chosen Goukouni Oueddei to lead a new government in Chad, to be named the National Union Government of Transition. That government faced a multitude of problems. It was beset by many political, economic, social, and military crises from the very start.

Hissène Habré, apparently with the assistance of the government of France, took advantage of these problems facing the National Union Government of Transition in Chad and triumphally arrived in

N'djaména on June 7, 1982. In the Meridional Zone in the South, meanwhile, the regular army of Chad, the Chad Army Forces, was dealing with internal political problems. They accused their leader, Kamougué Wadel Kader, of using for his own profit the resources that should have gone to defend the people. Some officers joined a few members of the administration against Kader, while others defended him. This rebel group — led by politicians Mbaïlaou Naïmbaye Lossimian and Nguanguibé Kosnaï and by Army Commandant Galium and Captain Demtita — used paratrooper companies 5 and 2 and other military police to attack the residency of Colonel Kamougué Wadel Kader early in the first week of June, 1982, in Moundou, the capital of the South.

Divided forces, however, led to failure. Because the leaders of the forces against Kader were unable to rally a majority of the people and army behind them, the politicians and officers implicated in the rebellion, unless they escaped, were arrested and jailed in Mbaïbokoum in the deep south of Chad. Among those held in jail was Captain Mindidéal N'djéber, who would later become a serious danger for his own region.

Kader's victory was not without problems, however. The army forces who came from the prefecture of Moyen Chary to support Kamougué Wadel Kader pillaged all the shops in Moundou. Sacked and looted by its "liberators," Moundou became the first victim of the conflict between its children.

On their way back to their headquarters in Sarh of Moyen Chari, the army troops who had helped (and then helped themselves to) Moundou stopped in Doba for while. It was there that my cousin Ngarnadji asked the soldier renting quarters from our family to take me with them to Sarh to visit his sister Massal. In fact, our family had rice for me to sell in Sarh. It was the first time for me to travel with army forces. The first three hours, I was afraid of their guns and munitions, but later I was fine and ate the sardines and other kinds of food that they had pillaged in the shops of Moundou. The second day of our trip when we arrived at the bridge that connects Balimba and Sarh, the soldiers started shooting their guns in the air. I was very afraid, thinking that it should be my last day of life. For them it was a great joy because nothing had happened to any of them during their mission in Moundou, and their mission had been well accomplished.

They brought me to the army's compound and the villa where my cousin Massal lived, and some of them gave her some spoons, plates, and other utensils that they had pillaged in Moundou. Most of them were friends of her husband. After they left, I told my cousin Massal that I did not want to travel any more with army forces. She just laughed at me and said, "Maybe one day you could shoot guns just as they did." I said to her that this was not at all my wish.

A month and a half later, a few weeks after I returned to Doba atop a truckload of bagged sugar, Kamougué Wadel Kader officially arrived in Doba to thank the people of Doba for their support during the trouble that he had encountered with the rebels in Moundou. In addition, he said he was determined to keep the peace in the Meridional Zone by keeping the authors of that trouble, who were at that time in the prefecture of Mayo Kebbi, out on the borders of the Meridional Zone until they had suffered under the rain of August, and then he would forgive them and let them return home. People applauded, and I also did so, but without understanding what he was saying because he spoke by microphone and in his native dialect of Mbaï. I was only about fourteen years old at that time and politically naïve, so I learned what he had said from conversations with family afterward. At the end of his speech, Colonel Kader promised to pay soldiers and civilians when he went back to Moundou.

While Colonel Kamougué Wadel Kader was studying the case of the rebels to reintegrate them back into our society, the rebel leaders signed an agreement with Hissène Habré in N'djaména to give them some of his rebels to come and kick Kader's army out of the South. Hissène Habré, who had failed lamentably to take over the South in 1981, agreed with the Southern rebels led by Commandant Galium and Captain Demtita to send his troops once again to the South to see if with their help he could control all the country of Chad. The two groups of rebels included army forces of the North (the FAN) and paratroop companies Five and Two of Galium and Demtita. These, with a few other soldiers and military police, formed a new coalition army, piled into the troop carriers supplied by Habré, and drove off in a cloud of dust toward Moyen Chari.

During that time Colonel Kamougué Wadel Kader allowed a group of rebels of the late Mohamed Acyl to cross the Meridional Zone with their staff, families, and belongings on their way from the

North to Batha in their home territory in the East. He specified the roads they should take and the dates of their travel. Meanwhile the coalition army was moving to attack Sarh. The two armies collided near Moyen Chari. After four days of fighting, the new rebel coalition made a tactical retreat to Kanu, forced out of Guéré by Acyl's CDR, the *Conseil Democratique Revolutionaire*. The CDR troops, needing reinforcements and munitions, sought them from the civilian and military authorities in Sarh, but the military officers in Sarh were conniving with Commandant Galium and Captain Demtita against the Meridional leader Kamougué and refused to help them. The CDR then folded back to Balimba, where a day or two later the coalition rebels, reinforced now from N'djaména, attacked again. The CDR, though lacking in munitions, was not easily defeated.

Among the coalition rebels, however, were many from Moyen Chari, who knew very well the strategic features of Sarh. And they knew that the only way to get into Sarh was to destroy the heavy automatic guns that the CDR rebels had mounted at the Balimba end of the bridge to protect access to Sarh. Four or five of the coalition soldiers disguised themselves as civilians and took boats across the Barh Kô River. From there, behind the CDR defenders, they surprised the men manning the automatic guns and killed them. A few hours of fighting later the road was open for the coalition rebels to march into Sarh. In the meantime, the CDR rebels gathered their families, made it out of Sarh to the east, and crossed the Moyen Chari River to continue their way to Salamat. The coalition rebels, in control of Sarh, now looked to taking the two major cities in the Meridional Zone — Doba and Moundou.

2

Events in Oriental Logon

O N THE BRINK OF THE REBEL ATTACK on Doba, my cousin Sanabé
Abel, who was the head of the customs officers in Mayo Kébbi,
arrived in Doba with some of his bodyguards around ten o'clock at
night. I stayed awake to help my sister-in-law Moueba cook for them.
We went to bed around two or three o'clock in the morning, but
before 7:00 Moueba and I awoke and started to make breakfast for the
bodyguards of Sanabé Abel. Around 8:00 that morning, Sanabé went
to visit his family, who were living with his mother-in-law, Yellôm,
and took with him his bodyguards and his cousins Mouaromba and
Jacques Tôlngar.

After they left, I prepared myself to go to school (*lycée*) because
our first year in high school had been extended into September on
account of the troubles. We saw an airplane coming from the direction
of Moundou. I found out later that it was Colonel Rôasngar, who
came with some money to pay the army forces of Kamougué Wadel
Kader. Within a few hours after their arrival, the coalition rebels surprised Doba with an attack.

At the sound of artillery and rifle fire, Doba was in stampede. As
I ran from school to home, I saw that the military unit stationed for
the summer in the elementary school at the heart of Doba suddenly
disappeared. And at the military police station, located between the
central market and the elementary school, the military police officers
disappeared, too. I found out later that Commandant Djimtôloum,

whose army unit was in Béraba, the western section of Doba, could not do anything because the garrison and police station of Doba had been almost instantly seized by the coalition rebels.

Colonel Rôasngar, who had been welcomed at the airport by Préfet Job, the governor of Oriental Logon, and taken to his residence, ran out of the palace with Job and down the slope to the Oriental Logon River to escape. They took off running when they reached the Congo side and did not return.

Commandant Djimtôloum, surprised in the middle of Doba very close to the capitol with three or four of his bodyguards, refused to be arrested by the rebel coalition soldiers. He ordered his bodyguards to resist. He himself took control of his Jeep and roared away with his bodyguards as passengers. They were pursued by the rebels until they were outside Doba. There they exploded their Jeep and crossed the ricefields of Doba, eventually finding their way to Congo Republic.

The townspeople and villagers who were in the market did not know which way to take to escape from death. In the southwest part of Doba, people who knew how to swim saved their lives by crossing the river. Those who did not know how to swim were at the mercy of the deep and swiftly flowing river. People told me later that in the river floated bodies of those who drowned and those who were shot. In the southeastern and northern sections of town, people took advantage of the tall grass and fields of millet to run away to the villages and the bush.

From the high school, I ran under the bullets of Kalashnikov, DCA, A52, and many other guns to reach home. I wanted to protect the family of my cousin, because he was out of town and his wife had two babies. When I arrived, nobody was at home. I saw only

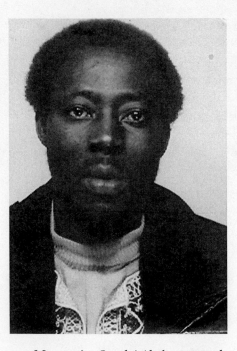

My cousin, Sanabé Abel, as a graduate student in Paris in the 1970s.

my cousin's new Land Rover. I called for the wife of my cousin, "Moueba! Moueba!" Nobody answered. The other people who were running away toward the northeast urged me to follow them because the rebels were coming. We ran about twenty kilometers before I met other people from my canton (county), and we decided to veer to the south to head for our villages. It was so hard for us to choose a direction that would lead to safety. None of the people that I was among knew the right direction. All of them had grown up in the towns and did not know how to reach our canton. I could not discuss the question with them because they were all my seniors, to whom it would be rude for a child to give advice. From village to village we asked for help, and the villagers gave us some directions until we reached our respective villages.

It was a great joy for the people of my village to see me safely among them. They asked me about the family of my cousin Ngarnadji. I told them that I had been in school when the fighting started. I had risked my life to return home and look for them, but they had left the house before me. Probably they had gone to seek safety somewhere in the bush or village. The day following my arrival in the village, I decided to go back to Doba and look for my cousin's wife and children. Some of my relatives advised me not to go back again. But I said, "No, Ngarnadji and his family took good care of me in their home. If today the circumstances become dreadful, I have to suffer with that family. I will be ready even to die because of them instead of leaving Moueba alone with the two children."

People were surprised to see me as a boy of fourteen making a reasonable speech like that. I left the village for Doba, and with me were two other relatives had apparently been shamed into accompanying me. In the middle of the road right outside Doba, we decided to take different directions to see if one of us could find the family of our cousin. We gave ourselves three days to meet back in the village, whether we got them or not. I was the first to find Moueba with her two children very close to Doba in the village called Damala. I remember that it was around 5:00 p.m. on the second day. We slept there that night, and early in the morning we continued our way to the village. It was there that people in my village said that, though I was a small boy, I was greater than the men in the village. From that time on, when there were any similar problems, people said to others, "act like Toïngar."

The people of our village, not knowing the precise location and situation of Sanabé Abel and others, knew only that they were in grave danger. We feared they might have stopped at the house of his mother-in-law, which was on the road that the coalition rebels had taken to reach Doba. Finally we heard that Sanabé and his colleagues had arrived in Babo without encountering any problem on the road. It was from Sanabé that we heard the frightening news that Corporal-in-Chief Mouaromba, a cousin of ours, might have been arrested. When the coalition rebels started shooting in Doba, Sanabé Abel had asked him not to go to the camp, but Mouaromba said he had a duty to join the others. As we found out later, in fact Mouaromba was arrested, compelled to join the coalition forces, and taken to Moundou with the first unit of coalition rebels. But a week later he escaped from the enemy and joined us in the village. Mouaromba confirmed that Moundou was totally controlled by the coalition rebels and that when he was with them he had been among the first unit that attacked Moundou. He said Kamougué Wadel Kader had just left the airport at Koutou when they arrived. After the fall of Moundou, the Meridional Zone was totally under the control of Hissène Habré. Thus the former prime minister became the self-styled "President of All Chadians" two years and some months after the start of his second revolution.

On the national radio station of Chad, politicians and journalists asked people to join with the new president, Hissène Habré, to reconstruct the country. Every day, journalists transmitted the voice of Hissène Habré, who was asking people to join him for the new Third Republic. No one in the South wanted to join him, because they knew that his rebels and he himself had killed and tortured many people since the civil war had begun in February of 1979. Most of his rebels were uneducated, lacking in religious scruples, and quick to kill people. The only language they knew was Gourane, which was spoken by few people in Chad. When they asked you a question and you answered in Arabic, if by chance they could find among their ranks someone who spoke both Gourane and Arabic, he could interpret for them. But if you answered them in French or Sara (the major dialect of the South), you would be tortured or killed. It was a grim situation and a hard life we had in that time, when Hissène Habré wanted his men to control the South by killing off the people, especially the educated class.

Ten days after the rebels took Doba, my cousin Ngarnadji asked me to go with him back to Doba. We took with us the key to Sanabé's new Land Rover. When we arrived in Doba, we met another cousin of ours, the tailor Bouyobé Tombaye, who was the elder brother of Corporal-in-Chief Mouaromba Tombaye. We found all of our belongings in the compound safe and untouched. The Land Rover also was not stolen. To avoid drawing the attention of the rebels to ourselves, we moved the Land Rover by pushing it instead of running the motor, to hide it in the tall sorghum behind the house and covered it with shrubs and sorghum stalks. In fact, we hoped to protect it from both rebels and thieves, in case they visited the periphery of Doba.

Then we needed to return to the relative security of the village until the situation became safer. Bouyobé Tombaye asked my cousin Ngarnadji to leave me with him so I could carry his sewing machine to his workshop in the morning and take it back home in the evening. In the current situation it was not wise to leave his machine at the workshop overnight. I stayed with Bouyobé Tombaye, and every day people came to his workshop and talked about people that the coalition rebels were killing and throwing into the Oriental Logon River.

3

The Murders Continue

A MONTH LATER, THE SOUTHERN REBELS were asked by Hissène
Habré to join him in N'djaména. The South was in the hands of
the northern rebels at this point. The situation became very bad for
the residents of the South. If the northern rebels saw you on your
bicycle or motorcycle and stopped you to take it, you could thank God
to have escaped with your life. Most of the people the fighters encountered were tortured or killed before their property was taken. Doba,
which never before had lived in the darkness of fear, started living very
dark days indeed. To go to the market or anywhere in town, it was
important not to look to the right or left, even if the rebel troops
called to you. If you responded to their call, they might accuse you of
belonging to the enemy. On the other hand, if you did not respond,
they might see this as a sign of rebellion. Either way, you could be tortured or be killed.

In the face of that intolerable situation, many Southern civilians
and former troops of Kamougué decided to run away from the cities.
They fled to villages within Chad and to the Central African Republic,
Cameroon, Nigeria, or the Congo Republic. Some others preferred to
stay in the bush and resist the government of Hissène Habré.

Sublieutenant Koulengar, who was originally from Doba, went to
rebel headquarters in that city to join the coalition rebels. Unfortunately, the rebels wanted to arrest and kill him as part of their general
program of elimination of educated people in the South. He escaped

from them that day. The following night, when rebels surrounded his house, the young officer jumped over the property wall and ran away. They pursued him with vehicles but could not catch him. Koulengar joined the new bush rebels in the South.

A week later, one of the northern rebels saw Adjutant Ngarkada (became sublieutenant later) in Doba and arrested him. He was tortured, beaten with rifle butts until his head was a bloody pulp, and thrown into a Jeep. They made the mistake of leaving him alone in the vehicle without stopping the engine while they went to capture and beat another man very close to the central market of Doba. Ngarkada took advantage of this lack of sophistication and, getting behind the wheel, drove the Jeep toward the road to Bodo. He broke the gate blocking this road and continued on his way. The northern rebels pursued him with other vehicles, so when he got about ten miles (16 km) from Doba, he abandoned the Jeep and escaped in the bush. In this way, Adjutant Ngarkada Japania saved his life from the rebels and chose the path of rebellion. He arrived in Bégada late in the night, and a villager named Nambétingar took him to the clinic of a healer, Masbé, who took care of him. Two weeks later, when the coalition rebels heard that it was Masbé who had taken care of Ngarkada, they came to arrest him. Fortunately for Masbé, he was able to escape before his house had been completely surrounded by the coalition rebels. Thereafter Masbé could not return to his village, which was terrorized by the coalition rebels. Three days later young Masbé joined the group of new southern rebels who called themselves "CODO," meaning "commando force."

Since the northern rebels became the new masters of the South, we lived in a world of darkness. The northern rebels were helped by the northern civilians who had grown up in Doba — and especially by the smiths and artisans — to arrest the intellectuals and other people who had money. The rebels tortured their victims and tape recorded their cries of pain before killing them. During the day, when they were lying under the mango trees, they replayed these recordings and laughed cruelly at their victims' screams.

Late in November of 1982, the few teachers still remaining in Doba and the new students that had just received their baccalauréat were asked by the government of Hissène Habré to reopen the Lycée Bernard Dikoa Garandi of Doba. We students were small in number in each class until early January, 1983, when the number increased a little bit in each room. During that period a new rebellion against Hissène Habré started in the North. The rebels, who called themselves the National Government Union of Transition, was led by its former president, Goukouni Oueddei. These new rebels in the North were strong and well equipped by Libya. In every battle early in this conflict, they always defeated Hissène Habré's forces.

The rebels in the North had established a variety of systems that made them successful: communication, army forces, logistics, and military materiel. They had their own radio station in the extreme North (in the city of Bardaï) to shape national and international opinion about events in Chad. They explained how France had shaped Chad's current crisis: how France and the Organization of United Africa (OUA) had provided information to Habré's forces in the Sudan, how France's strategic military information had enabled his fighters to take N'djaména easily, and how this had helped Hissène Habré to overthrow the legitimate Union Government of Transition in 1982. The rebels had sources of information among Hissène Habré's collaborators in N'djaména who communicated to Bardaï news of the government's plans and strategies. This information proved to be helpful for all Chadians living inside and outside of Chad. Later we learned that the United States, France, Egypt, and Sudan were all supporting Habré's attack on Goukouni's government.

In Chad if the authorities caught anybody listening to Liberty Radio of Bardaï, they might torture and kill him. But people developed a strategy for listening to broadcasts without getting caught. When it was 9:00 p.m., the time every evening when the broadcast would be transmitted in Sara, the language spoken by most in the South, there was someone inside each home who was listening to Liberty Radio of Bardaï while others stayed outside as guards. Later, news from the broadcast would be shared with those who had watched and waited outside. Hissène Habré's government snarled the transmissions of Liberty Radio of Bardaï by creating interference on their frequency, but it did not help his government. It was through those radio broadcasts that people in the South heard about the plan of Hissène Habré's government to arrest them and send them to the North as troops to fight against the new rebellion.

A month after this anouncement by Liberty Radio of Bardaï, President Habré asked the authorities in the South to arrest young and middle-aged men to send them to the North. In the oppressive heat of the month of March, the army came with military transport vehicles, trucks, and trailers to the Lycée Bernard Dikoa Garandi of Doba. We were surrounded by the army. But all at the same moment, the staff and we students of the school came running out at top speed. We scattered, and the soldiers started shooting in the air. I do not know how many people they succeeded in arresting that day. For me, I was lucky to have chosen the right direction to run, and in less than twenty hours I reached our village. My cousins Odingar, Dangar, Kouladoumngar, and Béngar reached their own villages, also. Two days later, the authorities announced that the soldiers were looking for the area boys and not the students. They promised that nothing would happen to the students and the staff of the Lycée if they returned to school. Little by little, we returned to Doba and started our school again.

In the middle of May, there were a lot of pressures on Hissène Habré's forces by the rebels of Goukouni Oueddei. The soldiers tried to arrest us again at school, and we escaped from them. None of us were captured, but we decided not to risk a return to school any more. Béngar and I helped other cousins in the village in their fields of cotton, sorghum, and millet. Our older cousins started preparing their own fields.

Late in the month of May, the CODO sent a message to many different villages in the South of the country to plow under the cotton. Cotton is grown only in the southern part of Chad and is a major source of income for the government of Chad. To weaken the power of the government, production of cotton had to cease. Anybody who refused to execute their order would be punished. It was a serious problem for the villagers, because growing cotton was the only way for them to get money to provide their families with clothing, medical care, salt, and schooling. In that situation, they did not know what to do. They did not have the power to say no. Their only option was to agree — to prevent reprisals.

When the fighters of Hissène Habré heard that CODO had ordered people not to cultivate cotton, they told villagers to ignore the CODO and to raise their crops of cotton as usual. If they failed to do so, they would not be permitted to cultivate their fields of sorghum, millet, rice, or other crops. Hissène Habré ordered the fighters to attack the CODO whose presence had been signaled in the South. These fighters were led by some of the politicians and traitorous officers who had been jailed by the permanent committee of Kamogué Wadel Kader in June after their failed coup. Among them were people like Captain M'ndidéal N'djéber and Commandant Ndoubatôg, who were natives of our region who had been working against the CODO and against their own people.

The villagers were under serious pressure. We were between the anvil and the hammer of the smith. Habré's fighters who were supposed to go to Kou to confront the CODO were afraid and turned instead to the villages in the opposite direction. First they pillaged the villages and tortured the people. A month later they came out with another strategy, which was to bring with them trucks and trailers they had "acquired" and to steal all the property they could, torturing the villagers before putting them into their houses and burning them down or tying villagers by the neck with long ropes and bringing them to the public places. There they slit the throats of these villagers as if they were goats or sheep to be butchered. If the fighters found themselves in an area that seemed dangerous, they just shot the villagers quickly and drove back to their base.

I remember an event (though not the precise date) in June 1983 when I came to Békôdô 1 to visit my grandfather, Mbaïlemdana. Early in the morning the fighters came from Doba and attacked us.

On that horrible day, a blind man named Jules surprised me greatly. Jules had been blinded by disease by the time he was five years old. About forty years old, Jules was a man who had much experience of darkness. Jules could do all things that the sighted can do. He did not need a guide to go from one place to another or from one village to another to visit people. God had given him a miraculous power to sense things even without sight. He had his own fields of rice, millet, sesame, sorghum, and cotton to cultivate. During the hot season, Jules went to the bush to look for tall grasses to use for fences and roof thatching.

When fighters attacked Békôdô 1, we ran in every direction except the direction from which the fighters had come. I was among the people who had chosen to run north toward the bush. Jules came running at a very high speed. I had left people behind me in my rush, but Jules' speed was even greater than mine. He left me behind, too. When we were less than a hundred meters from the protection of the bush, the blind man apparently tripped on something on the ground and fell down. The others and I thought that one of the fighters' bullets had felled him. He quickly stood up, though, and ran safely to the bush. It was a real surprise for me to see Jules responding so capably to danger. I would not have believed he could defend his life like that.

The fighters claimed as a pretext for this attack that because CODO means "commando," then Békôdô 1 (which really means "the village of smiths, number one") signifies "the first village of CODO." From afar they started shooting guns in the direction of the village. None of us were killed, and immediately they continued their journey to Békôdô 2. I do not know how many people they killed over there, but probably people ran away before the fighters' arrival because they heard the noise of their guns.

The same day I continued on my way to Béngamia, the village of my father's family, by way of the villages of Bédio and Békôï. In these two villages lived relatives of my maternal grandmother, and I wanted to inform them about what was going on in Békôdô 1, but no one was home, and I realized that they had been informed of the danger by the noise of guns before me. As I knew the bush and their millet fields well, I went there and joined them for awhile to get something from them to eat and drink before continuing on my way to Béngamia. To avoid traveling on the roads, I continued by bush. By evening of the same day I arrived in Béngamia to join my relatives in their millet field.

A week after the attacks on Békôdô 1 and Békôdô 2, Hissène Habré sent reinforcements from the regions of Occidental Logon, Moyen Chari, and N'djaména to help the fighters attack all the prefecture of Oriental Logon and a part of the region of Moyen Chari. The areas most badly destroyed were the villages around the towns of Gôré, Bébôtô, Bodo, and Bénjondô. Many people were killed. The fighters' strategy was to strike quickly at a village, kill as many men as possible, burn down the houses, and then move on before the CODO could be alerted. After each attack we lived like animals in the bush for several weeks. To get water to drink was not easy. The ropes and buckets needed to get water from the well had been consumed by fire. Women waited until the middle of the night before carefully entering the village from the bush and looking for water for their children and families.

Béngamia is completely surrounded by trees, and mango and other fruit trees are planted closely among the houses. One morning, fighters came through the woods from the north, and about one mile (1.6 km) from the village they left their vehicles and came on foot and surprised us. When they were still 100 or 150 meters away on the other side of the village, my aunt felt their presence and knocked on my door. When she said urgently, "May God save you, my boy," we had already been seen by one of the fighters, who shouted, "Don't move!" Already I was fleeing out of my hut toward the bush. I had not waited to consider the alternatives: my choices were to be shot immediately while I was fleeing, or to put my hands up and be tortured before being killed within the hour.

While the attention of the fighter was on me, my aunt escaped by running in a different direction. I heard the whizzing noise of several rounds of ammunition very close to my ears as the fighter pursued many of us into the bush, but I continued my flight to the southwest until another fighter came from the south to help his colleague by heading me off. I was tired and dropped to hide myself among the small trees to catch my breath. Before this second fighter reached my position, I saw a villager named Élie who had hidden himself between me and the fighter who was looking for me. Apparently in a panic that the fighter might reach his position before mine, Élie leaped up and started running again. He was immediately shot in the back. The fighter probably assumed he was shooting me. Immediately the two soldiers turned back and joined the others. It was perhaps thirty minutes later that we heard the noise of their vehicles leaving for Doba. After Béngamia, Békôï, Bédio, and other many villages buried their dead, I chose the road to the *maquis* (scrub) to join the CODO.

4

Choosing the *Maquis*

B Y THIS TIME, LIVING IN THE VILLAGE was more dangerous than living among the CODO. Many people wanted to join the CODO in rebellion, but they did not know how to find them. I wanted to be among the men who joined the CODO but could not let my relatives know. This was for two reasons. First, I was under fifteen years of age, so they might think I could not walk for 100 miles (160 km) to reach the area of CODO, which might be as far away as the border of the Central African Republic. Second, as Christians we were not supposed to kill others. I told myself that my goal would be to join my cousin Sanabé Abel with the CODO where I might be safer — but not to kill.

Early in one morning in June, I left Béngamia and informed my cousin Doudjim that in case my relatives asked about me, he should tell them that I went to Békôdô 1 to visit my grandfather. Heading south, I reached Bédio mid-morning and went to say hello to some of the brothers and sisters of my grandmother. Everybody was in the bush except one of my aunts. When she saw me, she said in surprise, "My son, Toï, who brought you here?"

I replied, "Mother, I came by myself. From Béngamia to Békôï I took the bush, but from Békôï to here I took the road and did not see anybody on the road."

She said, "Let's join your granduncles, uncles, and aunts in the bush, because they heard that the fighters were going to come again very soon."

I could not tell her the real reason I was traveling, so instead I said, "Thank you, Mother, but I would like to continue on my way to Békôdô 1 to see my grandfather Mbaïlemdana."

She said, "Do not worry, one of your uncles will take you over there through the bush."

I said, "Mother, I can reach my grandpa's area without any problem. Even from Béngamia to Bédio I arrived safely. Why are you worried about the smaller distance between Bédio and Békôdô 1?"

She replied, "I am not talking about the distance but about the situation, which is critically dangerous." As my aunt, she was responsible for my safety.

I tried to reassure her, saying, "Mother, I promise you that I will reach my Grandpa Mbaïlemdana without any problem."

Then she took me about two miles (3 km) outside the village toward Békôdô 1 and showed me the direction I should take to reach the fields of my Grandpa Mbaïlemdana. She wanted to take me all the way there, but she could not because her parents were waiting for her to bring water from the village. She said, "N'gônum (my son) Toï, may God protect you on the road."

I said, "Thank you, Kôm (Mother), and say hello to everybody for me."

She said, "I will be in trouble with our relatives for letting you go alone, but I hope nothing will happen to you on the road. Give my greetings to your grandfather's family when you reach there, and tell them that except for the houses and animals we lost in the fires set by the fighters last week, we are all right."

Near Békôdô 1 my cousin Jospa had been set as lookout in a tree to signal our relatives in case the fighters were coming. From afar he saw me and recognized me. He scrambled down from his post, ran to me, and embraced me warmly before climbing back up to his post in the tree. My relatives in Békôdô 1 were very surprised to see me, and my grandfather immediately asked about the situation in Béngamia. I told him that the village had lost many people there, but none in our family. I had not seen everybody by the time I left home, but I said that there probably was no emergency. After eating the food that his wife gave me, I started explaining to them what had happened to us in Béngamia.

In my Grandpa Mbaïlemdana's area of the bush, I shared the traditional sleeping mat with my cousin Jospa. Early in the morning

before they went to work in their field of millet, I confided in Jospa
that I was going to the *maquis*. He begged me to inform our grandfather before going. I said I knew already what his reaction would be, so
Jospa should let me go before informing Grandpa. Jospa said to me
that if I had come two days earlier, I could have traveled with some
young guys of Békôdô 1. Jospa was about eleven years old by that time,
but with his knowledge of the direction the earlier group had taken, he
headed me toward the area that the rebels might be. Then I took my
way to the *maquis*, the scrubland, by following his directions.

Arriving between the villages of Kawa and Béyama, I had the
remarkable good luck to meet a group of five young people who were
also on the road to the *maquis*. They were led by one of their number
who had come from the *maquis* and knew where we could join up
with the other rebels.

The CODO had established a base on the border between the
Central African Republic and Chad. Within the previous weeks they
had moved into Chad and installed a base between N'gôwn ("small")
Kou and Kou. Shortly after we had passed through the Protestant sem-
inary named Bé Nyando Kou (BNK) on our way to the village of Kou,
we were suddenly confronted by a CODO soldier who appeared in the
road, shouted, "Halt!" and aimed his Kalashnikov rifle at our small
group of boys. (We found out later that a unit of more than 120 of
these well-armed soldiers lay unseen in ambush in the tall grass around
us.) The sentry called for his chief, who came and took us to the commander of their unit, who sat in front of his crude shelter made from
branches and leaves. The commander, flanked by three bodyguards
nearby, asked us some questions about Hissène Habré's fighters. We
explained the situation and our desire to join his troops. He summoned a soldier to take us away and to write down our names. After
this soldier had registered our names, he told us that we were going to
sleep with them there until the next day, when someone would take us
to the base. It was already too dark that evening to cross the treacherous Kou River.

5

Among the CODOs

ALL THE SOLDIERS' SHELTERS WERE CONSTRUCTED from small tree branches, leaves, and tall grasses. Instead of weaving sleeping mats from palm fronds, the soldiers slept directly on piles of freshly cut fronds. They shared their huts with us, and none of us was surprised about their "mats"and "huts"because thanks to the fighters we had been living that way in the bush with our families before joining the CODO. After spending one night with them, we were led by a Corporal Moutedé to cross the Kou. This is a swampy area, chosen by the CODO because it would be difficult for their enemies, not knowing the area, to sneak up on them through the swamp. In fact, one soldier with a rifle could hold off an entire column of fighters by concealing himself or herself behind a tree and picking off enemies as they moved laboriously through the swamp. To cross the Kou riverbed — more of a marsh than a river — required our following the guide very carefully. We had to travel single file, gripping a tree branch or vine for safety at every step, and if we stepped off the path with both feet, we were warned, we would sink deep beneath the surface of the swamp. Someone traveling alone along this path could slip off the path and be lost forever. Luckily, all of us crossed the Kou safely and in only an hour or so. We arrived at the CODO base in the forest between N'gôwn Kou and Kou. This was the section of the base for active troops. We waited for a while before someone came to take us the seven kilometers farther west to the CODO reserves.

In Kou, the area looked very strange to me. I had never seen a place like that in my life. We saw different kinds of monkeys, snakes and birds than in my home area. Kou looked heavy and gloomy all day. The trees were dense and tall. Under the trees was some thin grass, easily parted by hand when we wanted to move about. The ground was damp under the trees. When we looked toward the sky, we could not see it because the branches of the trees high above the earth made so dense a network as to block the sun. This made the nights long and the days short.

We stayed at the command post with the reserve officers until the CODO reserves came back from their training. After that we were presented to the training instructors, who took our names and histories. Then the officers asked people from our different villages from among the troops to take care of us for a few days and share their small shelters with us. During that night I was surrounded by people from Béngamia, Békôï, Bédio, Békôdô 1 and Békôdô 2. They asked me about the situation in their villages and about their relatives. I talked for a while, but I was tired, and then the oldest of the soldiers from my village, Djimnguengar, asked them to leave because he realized that I was exhausted.

Early in the morning we were taken to the bush for our training. It was very hard for most of us, but I was able to keep going because I had started with the martial arts when I was a young teenager and had already earned my blue belt in taekwondo karate when I joined them. That same day the two instructors of our section talked about my skill to their colleagues.

The second day, they started teaching us how to drill without weapons — to make half-left and -right turns, full turns, turns backward and forward. I did them without problems because in taekwondo karate we did those same kinds of movements. After that day they used me as a model for the others the rest of that first week of training before we moved on to other sections of training. After that, they were always especially nice to me, and in response I paid more attention than the others to what they were teaching us.

After two weeks of practice, we started with lessons in military discipline, such as saluting and immediate execution of orders. I had the advantage of learning these things more quickly than other men that were my elders and with more seniority in training. It was not because I was cleverer than they, but because most of them were not fluent in French, and instruction was given first in French and then in Sara. The only two people in our section that were almost as skilled as I were Béta Poïrô and Valentin. Both of them had completed primary school and knew some French but had failed qualifying exams for high school.

During my fourth week in the reserves my maternal uncle from the active CODOs was deployed to the reserve CODOs as our unit commander. During his first meeting with us, he was surprised to see me. After the training he asked me to see him in his hut. There he started asking me about our relatives in the villages. My uncle had not been to the villages in more than six months, but he had more information about the villages than I did. He dismissed me to join my friends in our hut after saying that the next day he would take me back across the swamp to Kou village to visit some of the relatives of my grandfather Mbaïlemdana.

The following day, my uncle Mbaïorndjam took me to Kou village as he promised. When we first arrived, my uncle did not introduce me, so the relatives of my grandfather Mbaïlemdana (who at this time was back in Békôdô 1) assumed I was my uncle's bodyguard. It was after the evening dinner that he introduced me to them as their grandson and nephew. My great uncle Édouard Kéïkam asked him, "From which side of our family is he our grandson?"

My uncle answered him, "The first son of your niece N'gambaye Mbaïlemdana."

My great uncle stood up, lifted me up off my feet, and hugged me with great joy. His two wives, all his sons, daughters, and other relatives who were there for the dinner joined him and celebrated my presence among them. They told others in the compound, too. To celebrate, those who were Christians drank tea, and others drank *argué* (local alcohol). This was just to honor my presence among them, because few of them had seen me since I was five years old, and some had never met me before. But the most important reason for celebrating my presence among them was probably that they had a special love for my grandfather Mbaïlemdana and took him as their advisor and leader in the county of Bodo, and I was his first grandson.

After this introduction to my grandfather's relatives in Kou village, I no longer slept in the camp for the rest of my training. My great uncle and his sons always asked me to come back to the village each evening after our daily training. Every day the other commandos and I with relatives in Kou village carefully crossed the Kou marshes to spend the night with our relatives. Conditions were much better for us in the village than in the reserve camp. The only days I could not travel to Kou were when I was on guard duty. I always gave my great-uncle 24-hour notice of my service days, and he asked one of his wives or daughters to prepare food for me to take with me for dinner the next day. I felt guilty that other new commandos lacked the good food and comfortable sleeping quarters that my relatives provided me, but guilt did not prevent my appreciating what I had.

Early in the month of August, the CODOs' authorities received information that the commandos of the Democratic Republic of Congo, formerly Zaïre, had just joined Hissène Habré's fighters and were moving against us. Rather than attacking us directly by moving through the Central African Republic, Congo troops were said to be flying into the airport at N'djaména. We were on alert and were not allowed to leave our base except for those who were to take up ambush positions. I felt bad that I could not go to Kou village, because it was always fun to be among my great uncle Édouard Kéïkam's sons. But I had to stay in camp because it was the order given by our authorities, and it was for our own safety.

We waited for the Congolese fighters for two weeks, but they did not come. If they had come during that period, it would have been a great opportunity for us to get weapons from them, because they did not know our area very well. We soon found out that instead of sending them south to fight us, Hissène Habré sent them north to fight the new Gunt rebels, and later Bardaï's radio announced their defeat in the North. Almost all of them were killed. The radio announcement, in fact, changed Mobutu's name from Sese Seko to *Cessez, c'est trop*, meaning "Stop, it's too much." This indicated resistance to Mobutu's sending any more troops to their death in the North.

When we heard on Bardaï's radio that Moboutou's soldiers had been destroyed by Goukouni's forces, for the next few days the CODOs did not worry about being attacked in our areas of the South. All our units went on patrol missions far from Kou and from our base. The only remaining unit was that of Captain Guerngar, which for strategic reasons was not allowed to participate in attacks but stayed behind to guard the camp.

Hissène Habré's fighters took advantage of the absence of CODO troops from Kou and entered the area of Bodo. They were led by the former prisoner of Colonel Kamougué Waddel Kader, Captain M'ndidéal N'djémber, who had been liberated from Kamougué's prison by Hissène Habré's forces and was a native of the area of Bodo. There were other men from Bodo, like Timothé Dédjimbaye (a relative of Captain M'ndidéal N'djémber) and David Belmbaye, who were also among them. They divided the canton of Bodo into three sections and started killing people, burning their houses and the goats, sheep, pigs, horses, and cattle who were tied in their huts during the rainy season. All the property in the area of Bodo was stolen or destroyed on that day. Many villages smelled of burnt flesh, human and animal. N'djémber, Dédjimbaye, and Belmbaye — children of Bodo whom one would expect to protect their homeland from harm — instead destroyed it themselves, even their own villages.

When we in the reserve CODOs got the news of Bodo's devastation, we were not allowed to cross the Kou. Only some of the officers had orders to cross the marsh and investigate the villages. My Uncle Mbaïorndjam and his colleague Corporal Miki were the investigators selected to go to Kou village. My uncle asked his cousin Allahtoïngar and me to accompany them. After crossing the Kou, we carefully approached Kou village. From 100 meters away we saw the unit of CODO Sublieutenant Abdoulaye Fall, who had returned from their mission and arrived there, too, just then. We thought they were enemies and hid ourselves. When my uncle identified them clearly with his binoculars, he said we should join them. As we approached, they took us for enemies, too, and would have shot us, but my uncle signaled the password, and immediately they recognized us as their friends.

In Kou we saw only dead animals and burned homes and churches. Villagers had already buried some of their dead relatives. My uncle conversed with Abdoulaye Fall for five minutes, and afterwards we left Fall's CODOS in the village while we ourselves joined the former residents of Kou in the bush. The villagers told us that the enemies had arrived around 11:00 in the morning, by which time most of the villagers were already working their fields of millet and ground nuts. As a result, the fighters were not able to capture and kill many people. After the leaders of each quarter had time to regroup, the villagers told our CODO officers that Kou Village had lost fewer than ten people but nearly all of their homes, churches, and animals, which had been burned and destroyed completely by the fighters.

We continued our mission to the bush to search for more villagers. I suspected that Abdoulaye Fall and his CODOs might be staying near the village to allow the people to come and carry away any of their belongings still remaining and then would continue their patrol of the area. We were lucky enough to meet my great uncle Édouard Kéïkam's family right away. My uncle Samson and his younger brother Toïdé hugged me, and Nadjirôm brought a sweet, fresh root of manioc to eat. My Uncle Mbaïorndjam asked people to go that very night back to Kou village and look for whatever they thought might be helpful for them, because CODOs might be there to provide protection for only twenty-four hours.

They left me there with my great uncle and continued their mission with Miki to investigate other villages. I was in the bush with my great uncle and uncles for four days before my Uncle Mbaïorndjam and Miki came back from their mission and took me back to base. Two days later the officers that had gone on investigative missions also returned. It was then that the base commanders realized what traitors had been behind that catastrophic destruction of the villages. Little by little most of the traitors were arrested and interrogated. Those who were guilty ended their lives there, and others were released. N'djémber, Dédjimbaye, and Belmbaye themselves were not apprehended in this sweep, but all three passed away within a dozen years.

Even before that catastrophic destruction, we knew that some girls in Bodo county had boyfriends among Hissène Habré's fighters. Two local girls, Taonmbayal and Naelmbayel, were arrested by the CODOs and interrogated. Apparently they had been used by their boyfriends as a source of local information and now feared for their lives. The CODO authorities kept the girls with them and made them their girlfriends. Later Taonmbayal and Naelmbayel became CODO girls and fought against Habré's fighters.

Certain men also were suspected of collaborating with Hissène Habré's fighters. Mbaïnanbé, a relative of my grandfather, had been arrested about a month before the attack on suspicion of collaborating with the enemy and taken to the CODO base. Mbaïnanbé would have been executed, but with the intervention of Yawaye, his sister (who was the former wife of Mita, the traditional chief of Bodo) he was released with a warning not to go anywhere near Habré's fighters in Bodo. Unfortunately, after the surprise attack by the enemy, Mbaïnanbé made the mistake of going there again, perhaps to give information to Hissène Habré's fighters. He was arrested and interrogated. I was in the area at the time, on my way to deliver a message from our reserves to the command post of the active CODO troops. The command had determined that Mbaïnanbé was to be executed. His legs were tied, and he was lying under a tree. He called to me to say farewell and let his family know his fate. It was the end of his life. I assume that he was executed in the usual way, by being suddenly struck on the head along the trail, with a stout stick about the size of a baseball bat.

After the attack by Hissène Habré's fighters, Tédjim was arrested and taken to the base. This man was known locally as a thief and in his youth had been punished for his crimes by the traditional chief of Bodo by having his feet held to a fire heated by a bellows. When he was arrested by the CODOs on suspicion of having communicated with the enemy, after some interrogation, he was released and became a useful person on behalf of our rebellion. Armed only with bow and arrow, he guided CODO troops on missions to arrest suspected enemy sympathizers.

Another local man arrested after the surprise attack was Baoupolo, the son of Belmbaye David. David had guided the enemies to the area of Bodo to kill people and burn their properties. Baoupolo, David's son, went to where the active CODO troops were stationed. Pretending to sell drugs to the CODO, he was really spying for the enemy. Before he arrived at our position, we were informed. When he walked into our patrol area, strongly-built members of the correctional brigade arrested him. To elicit answers to their questions, the correctional brigade jammed burning wood here and there all over his body. After being questioned so incisively, he recognized his errors and begged for pardon, which was not granted. The torture was so painful that before he was executed he probably regretted having come into this life.

After the technical mistake of leaving Bodo unprotected, the CODOs no longer sent out all the units, nor did they send them so far on their patrol missions. We always had at least two units around the areas of Bodo and Bébôtô to take action against any other agression in that region.

During that time the base of Kou was the main strategic area for all the CODOs in the South. It was there that the messengers made connection between us and the other forces, both in the North led by Goukouni Oueddei, and in the Moyen Chari led by Tokinôn Pierre. Tokinôn Pierre was a former military commando who had earlier been arrested in Sarh by Hissène Habré's fighters for being a CODO sympathizer and taken to N'djaména to be killed. By a dramatic leap from a fast-moving Toyota, however, he escaped from the dead to join the CODOs and became one of the great fighters during the period of the rebellion. In addition, we also had a special cleared area near N'gôwn Kou that could serve as a big airfield, to be used in case we got some external help in the form of weapons and other matériel.

6

Foreign Aid in the Form of Weapons

B Y LATE SEPTEMBER, OUR TRAINING at the base was very acceler-
ated because we had to be prepared to use the matériel soon to be
sent from Libya. All the reserve CODOs on vacation were asked to be
back for a special exam of physical and military skill. They needed the
best fifty of the troops from that exam to be sent on a special mission.
About two or three thousand of us took that exam. My colleague, Béta
Poïrô, and I were among the best fifty people.

The two men sent by Sublieutenant Abdoulaye Fall to take us to
that special mission saw that I was very young and slim. They asked
the reserve CODOs to give them another person in my place. Some of
the reserve officers disagreed, because the order from Actives headquarters had specified that they should send the best fifty men, and I was
in fact among the best twenty. The messengers of Sublieutenant
Abdoulaye Fall said they had their own reason not to accept me right
now, but they might be in need of at least three hundred men soon,
and they were sure that I would be among that group. Only later did
we realize that they wanted someone sturdier to go to Kan with them
because Kan was so far from our base, perhaps as far as 62 miles (100
km) away. And all the movements of CODOs were on foot because we
did not have vehicles. The second reason for them not to take me,

despite the good standing I had earned, was that purpose of the mission turned out to be carrying heavy loads as fast as possible from the border of the Central African Republic into Chad and then from our border all the way to our base. They did not think that at 14 years old I was strong and sturdy enough to be of much assistance.

Two days before my colleagues from the reserve CODOs left on this mission, all of the active units left the area in various directions on missions unknown to us in the reserves. Our main leaders apparently had made arrangements for meeting up later. The fifty reserves and many more active troops reached the border four days later in the area appointed by Sergeant Djimiel Pen, who led the Libyans to drop the matériel for us. When the CODO units arrived not far from Kan, they did not come close to the appointed area, which was located by a big tree, nor did they go close to the villages. This was to prevent any traitor among them from signaling their positions to the enemies.

The Green CODOs, the branch to which I belonged, were considered the main force of the rebellion and were headed by Sublieutenant Koulangar, seconded by Sublieutenant Abdoulaye Fall. The main inspector of customs, my cousin Sanabé Abel, was their general secretary. Captain Ndilnodji was the coordinator between the Green CODOs and Red CODOs. Sergeant Djimiel Pen, the son of Pastor Moussa Pen (who had been buried alive for maintaining his Christian faith during the 'Yo-ndo' period of the revolution, by order of the first President, François N'garta Tombalbaye), was the coordinator between Goukouni's forces and the Green CODOs. Sergeant Djimiel used to travel from Libya through the Congo Republic, and sometimes Gabon and the Central African Republic, before reaching our base to give us some information and then carrying information from us to the northern base led by Goukouni. This brave sergeant succeeded in sending us the war matériel on a huge cargo airplane flanked by fighter planes all the way from Libya, over northern Chad, to our position in the South. This was early in the month of October, 1983. Despite his heroism, he would later be killed by our CODO leaders only a few weeks later because of his opinion that the CODO should not rally with the government of Hisséne Habré.

The war matériel was dropped from the transport plane along Chad's border with the Central African Repuiblic. Arriving at the appointed area, Sergeant Djimiel Pen and his companions located the big tree and the sign that the CODOs had made on the summit of the tree. A Chadian parachuted down from the transport airplane close to the tree with special communication equipment and a password to inform the crew of the plane if it was the right place and to verify that the CODOs were there to receive the goods. When this man landed, three CODOs who had hidden themselves close to the tree came out to welcome him. Later Sergeant Djimiel and another man also parachuted from the plane and confirmed that the units of CODOs were in the area. Then the transport airplane started dropping equipment both in the territory of the Central African Republic and Chad. The two fighter planes continued to protect the transport while it was dropping the crates.

Among the matériel dropped were at least two generators, which would allow us to produce AC power. (Unfortunately, we needed DC power for the radios we used to communicate with the new Gunt forces in the North.) I was later told that there were hundreds of Kalashnikov rifles dropped, along with mortars, bazookas, lance-grenades, A52 rifles, and other weapons I could not identify, in addition to great quantities of food. Each category of those weapons had some thousands of boxes of shells and ammunition. Among the equipment dropped were also some receivers and transmitters and even communications jamming equipment.

The population on both sides of the border were willing to help the CODOs, because the fighters of Hissène Habré had tortured their people. Many residents of the northern part of the Central African Republic had relatives in Chad who had suffered from torture. Some Chadians and people of the Central African Republic who had escaped from Chad in the previous year to hide themselves in the Central African Republic had marks of torture on their bodies that attested to their suffering. So it was that the people on the border were very eager to help the CODOs to transport the materials to our base.

Women, men, young boys, and girls joined the CODOs to transport these heavy loads. They put some crateloads of goods on ox carts and boats. The women arranged cloth into cushions for the traditional platters they use to carry heavy loads on their heads. Quickly and efficiently they helped the CODOs to take all the matériel into the territory of Chad. The French soldiers who were encamped near the town of Boar in northern Central African Republic were informed of our activity and arrived in the area of the Central African Republic where some of our materials had been dropped, but they had arrived too late, because the materials had all been carried away. These French soldiers immediately informed their base in Boar about the materials received by the CODOs. The command at Boar informed the government of Chad and asked if they could cross the border by reconnaissance aircraft. The authorities of Chad gave their okay. When the French flew to the direction of the CODOs in our territory, one of our technicians simply switched on the communications jamming apparatus sent from Libya. The aircraft could not continue its mission to the CODOs' area because the apparatus muddled the aircraft's communication with its airbase. The aircraft went back to Boar and never came back to the CODOs' area in Chad.

The villages on the way from Kan to Kou were happy to help the CODOs. Just like the residents of the border territory, they used their ox carts and other means of transportation to relay the load to Kou. The CODOs also sent word to headquarters of our reserve troops to ask for help. Many of the bigger and stronger reserve CODOs headed off and made themselves very useful. Before bringing the materials to Kou, CODO troops cached some of the boxes of ammunition in case either they were attacked along the way or our base was attacked later. The ammunition was hidden in three different areas on the way back to Kou, and the location of these reserve stashes of ammunition were known to only a few CODOs who could be trusted with the information, because it was a military secret. About 60 percent of the ammunition was brought to Kou. About two thirds of this ammunition was kept at our base, and one third was distributed among the units for their immediate use.

While the second team from the CODO reserves set off in the direction of Kan to help the others with transport duties, General Secretary Sanabé Abel asked the head of the reserve CODOs to send me to him. I joined the main base in the morning and found out then that he was planning to go on leave to Babo and needed to take me with him or suffer the accusations of our relatives for not having brought me along. Twenty-four hours later, Sanabé Abel and I left the base for Babo. We spent about three days walking from the base before reaching our village. From Kou to Babo, we passed at least ten villages, and in each village where we had relatives we tried our best to meet them and at least say hello. All the people that we met had abandoned their villages and were living in the bush for their safety. It was very easy for us to meet them, because the population knew by our faces that we were Southerners and by the speed of our walking that we were CODO. When we reached Babo, our uncles came from the different villages to gave us their traditional blessings and asked God to protect us wherever we went.

While we were in Babo, all the units involved in matériel transport had returned to Kou, and about a week later the leaders at the camp near Kou were in need of cousin Abel for a special meeting. They sent Jacques Tôlngar to inform him that they had an important meeting and his presence might be necessary. Jacques Tôlngar met up with us at Bengamia. Sanabé Abel asked him to go back and inform them that we might be there in about three days. When Jacques Tôlngar headed back to Kou, we immediately followed him, but we took a shorter route to reach Kou.

In Bengamia, our aunts did not want me to go back to Kou. They said I was too small to be in the *maquis*. They preferred that I stay with them in the village. It would have been disrespectful of me to contradict them. Though I wanted to rejoin my unit, I could not comfortably leave without their approval. A person who does not show respect for elders will not have a good future.

Abel, even with his high military rank, had to speak with diplomacy and skill. He spoke respectfully to my aunts, referring to them politely not by name but by their status as mothers. "I understand your point of view, Kôn Moal (Mother of Moal) and Kôn Mara (Mother of Mara). But you have to understand that in Kou my cousin is safer than he is here. How many times have Hissène Habré's fighters tried to kill us in this region, and particularly in this village? Please, pray for us, and we too will pray for you so God will be with us."

My aunt Kôn Moal said, "I know that Toïngar has escaped more than three times already from the enemy fighters, but he is still too young to be so far from us."

Sanabé Abel replied to her, "My aunts, I take to heart what you are saying, and I promise you that all the cousins — including our youngest, Toïngar — and I myself will return to this village. Even if our enemies totally destroy this village, we will be back to rebuild it."

Finally our relatives agreed with Sanabé and gave their approval for me to go back with him. But we were ordered by our eldest aunt, Kôn-mara, to eat the special traditional porridge before leaving. Different porridges are concocted with different properties, and I believe that the porridge she prepared for us was to protect us from poisoning.

Instead of arriving back in Kou on the third day, as Sanabé Abel had promised Tôlngar, we joined the CODO leaders in less than three days by traveling more quickly than we had departed. When we walked into headquarters, we were welcomed by Sanabé's friends, the other leaders. The men exchanged their diplomatic words of greeting and finished by exchanging some jokes. In the evening of that the same day, Sublieutenant Koulangar invited Sanabé Abel into his hut. They spent about three hours meeting in Koulangar's hut. Some hours later, Koulangar convened a meeting of all the leaders. I believe that they talked about the ceasefire and the negotiations proposed by the government of Hissène Habré.

In my own opinion, I could say that there was good reason for Hissène Habré to ask for a reconciliation after having neglected the South for more than one year. At the beginning of the rebellion, his commanders used to mock our lack of matériel by saying that we could not do any damage to them with ammunition tied in handkerchiefs, which is all the ammunition we had in the first year or so of the rebellion. They would continue to make our men live in the cold and the rain. They promised suffering to our women and death for all our men in the South. But after the matériel arrived from Libya and the government fighters had been informed of this by the French soldiers in Boar, there was a big change. They started sending helicopters and fighter jets against us. These battle helicopters — Jaguars — were not able to locate us because the trees of Kou provided superb cover and all CODO actions were taken very far from the base. Thus Habré may have seen the need to deal with rebellion in the South in some other way. In addition, he had surely been informed of our new military equipment, which made us less helpless than before.While the leaders accepted the ceasefire and reconciliation requested by the government in N'djaména, an incident occurred. Someone at general headquarters violated one of the traditional laws imposed on the CODO by the traditional chief of Kou. Before the base had been installed in Kou, the chief came and performed a special ceremony for the protection of all people who ran away because of persecution and needed to hide themselves there in the forest. He blessed some of the top leaders to be successful in their actions against their enemies. He promised to them that no animal, whether beast, snake or insect, would bite or kill any of us in Kou. During the period that we were in Kou, none of us had been sickened or killed by any creature of the forest.

We had lived in the bush for many months without electricity. I do not know why, but one night Sublieutenant Koulangar and others needed the generator to be switched on. Unfortunately by using the light during the night they had alerted any enemies flying over us in Jaguars or war helicopters to our position. The trees were not so dense that they could conceal from the heavens a bright light below. Enemies could locate and mark the area and investigate later. In addition, not only had the officers possibly given away our position, but they also violated the law of the Chief of Kou (N'gar meen Kou). By using the generator to produce light, the men inadvertently attracted insects, which brought in their turn toads hungry to eat the insects, and even worse, attracted a kind of snake that eats toads and is also particularly dangerous to humans, a boa. In fear, Koulangar ordered his bodyguard to shoot the snake without consideration for the blessing provided by the chief of Kou. That blessing had been as much for the creatures of the forest as for us.

The chief, who was living in the village of Bémbaïtada about fifteen kilometers from our base, felt by his traditional powers that something had happened in Kou. Early in the morning, he crossed the Kou River and came to Koulangar. He said to him, "My son, you have violated my law." His eyes were red as he spoke, as if he wanted to cry.

Sublieutenant Koulangar answered him with deep humility, saying, "*Baba*, I am sorry. We thought ourselves in danger when the snake tried to attack three times in succession. It was then that we defended ourselves."

The chief of Kou asked him, "Why did you not turn off your white-men's light or call me? Did you not know that it was only because of a strange thing or action that my snake challenged you? Did you forget my instructions that I gave you the first day of our meeting? More than one year you have been living here in the forest. Who among you passed away from sickness or was killed by beasts, snakes or insects in this area?"

Sublieutenant Koulangar answered, "Nobody, *baba*."

"But why did you kill me?"

Koulangar answered, "*Baba*, I am sorry and give you my word of honor that we will not make that mistake again."

The chief of Kou said, "I forgive all of you. I wish you good luck and pray that nothing bad will happen to you in my area. But you have to realize that you are no longer protected as before, because you have made an irreparable mistake. And there is nothing I can do for you." He left Kou and went back to his village.

The following day, Koulangar went with some leaders of the CODO to the house of the chief of Kou to beg forgiveness of him with some money, distraught that they had violated his law. He said to them, "Thank you for coming into my house, my young men. I understood your problem, and it was for this reason that I forgave you yesterday in Kou."

Then he gave each of them some traditional onions to eat for their personal protection and others to use in Kou for the protection of all the CODO. He told them, "My young men, I now restore everything for you. But you have to be careful, because when a bowl of sesame seeds falls to the floor, there is no way to pick up again every single seed." They left Bémbaïtada, not completely satisfied, to go back to Kou. All of this I learned from Sanabé Abel.

7

Period of Reconciliation

DURING THE CEASEFIRE PHASE, THE LEADERS discussed the possibility of their reconciliation with the regime in N'djaména. Nobody among them wanted to give his own real opinion on the reconciliation, for fear that the group would later make a decision in the opposite way. A few days later, Hissène Habré sent to Bodo a man named Mbaïwikeyal, a former administrator of Chad who was originally from Bodo and who had relatives in the CODO. He was instructed to meet with the elders of Bodo and with our leaders to seek a peaceful solution for the South. Our leaders agreed to meet with Mbaïwikeyal between Kou and Bodo. Mbaïwikeyal went back with the message from the CODOs to his president, that CODO leaders were willing to discuss a possible reconciliation with Habré's emissaries. Hissène Habré, in hopes of getting in the South the munitions and people he needed to reconquer the North after so many battle losses in that area, promised to Mbaïwikeyal that if he were successful in bringing CODO into his forces, he would grant Mbaïwikeyal the post of internal (domestic) minister.

Meanwhile former President of Chad Goukouni in Libya and his forces in north Chad were waiting for us to attack and take over a village or town with an airport, somewhere outside Kou. In that event, in order to support us, they could send heavy guns to that airport and also soldiers at the same time to the airport at Kou (so they would not have to transport the heavy guns across the Kou River to the area

44

under our control). Our leaders were busy with their program of reconciliation at Kou, and nobody in the leadership was thinking about the plan of attack. In his eagerness to get his hands on the weapons recently delivered to our CODOs from Libya, Hissène Habré was apparently busy in N'djaména creating a committee and plan of reconciliation. I suspect that our CODO leaders, weary of life in the bush, were very excited about the possibility of collaborating with the regime at N'djaména and sharing its power, despite the fact that this regime had killed many thousands of Southerners for their religion (Christianity) or political opinion. In this respect the plans of our leaders differed from the plans of the CODO troops, who wanted to liberate all of Chad from this hateful government.

When the command in Libya and the leaders of the forces in the North communicated with our leaders, they felt that there was something wrong because the agreed schedule of offensive action in the South was not respected. They sent three emissaries — Sergeant Djimiel and two other men — to come and see what was going on. When the messengers arrived in Kou, our CODO leaders were in full meeting in Bodo with a group of conciliators sent from N'djaména. Because these three emissaries needed to meet with our leaders who were in Bodo, they were taken there. It was there that they lost their lives.

The governmental delegation sent by Habré to negotiate a reconciliation was impressive, staffed by government ministers, technical experts, and Commander-in-Chief Idriss Déby and other officers. It was led by former State Minister Djidéngar Ngarbarim. The delegation was divided into two sections: the civilian body led by Moussa Seïd, and the military body led by Déby (later to become President of Chad). Other delegates were politicians, administrators, physicians, military officers, fighters, and specialists. The total number was possibly one hundred. About thirty of these men were negotiators; the rest were military protection for the delegation.

The delegation of CODOs was led by Sublieutenant Koulangar. Among the delegates we had economists, engineers, administrators, scientists, commissioners, police, and military officers. Members of our delegation tied their heads with strips of green or red cloth, and all the CODO troops used the same symbol. The color green represented the justice and hopefulness that we were defending. The red symbolized the blood of our innocent people who had been killed, and their animals, homes, churches, and other belongings senselessly destroyed by the fighters of Hissène Habré.

Bodo, which received the two delegations from N'djaména and Kou, looked like an area of dense bush and not as it once had, as a big, beautiful village where many trucks and transports came from different cities of Chad — and in the dry season even from Cameroon and the Central African Republic — for their weekly market. The village of Bodo that Chadians used to be proud to call the "granary of Chad" for its rich agricultural products had been totally destroyed. The clusters of thatch-roofed houses no longer existed. We recognized the places we had known only by a remnant of a wall of brick, or a clump of mango, lemon, or guava trees.

The delegation from N'djaména reached Bodo with a large number of well-equipped fighters. Among those fighters they had some regular soldiers and officers who were originally from our area, including Captain M'ndidéal Ndjémber, who had destroyed the area of Bodo some months before. The delegation seemed very fearful, thinking maybe we were going to take reprisals. Not only were they afraid of us, but also they were afraid of the region of the Oriental Logon and particularly the area of Bodo, which usually is dense in trees and grasses during the rainy season. Most members of the delegation had never before seen this kind of lush and luxuriant area of the country in their lives. In the North, people lived in a desert. The center of the country is a savanna area. When they came to Bodo, the fighters took up positions in the east, north and west sectors of Bodo. They all aimed their weapons in the direction of Kou. They must have thought the CODOs were present only in Kou but not in other areas. What they did not realize was that we surrounded the area — and them — with our soldiers.

Before the delegation from N'djaména reached Bodo, the CODO units had hastened to get into ambush positions on the five main roads that had once brought so many people to Bodo for its weekly market. In addition to surrounding Bodo, troops from our base in Kou were sent to guard the area around Kou, especially the T-road that linked the area of Bébôtô to Bodo by crossing Kou village from the west. And another unit was sent to watch the road that originated in Mbaïganda to the northwest of Bodo and ran south to Kou. All the roads into

Bodo were completely secured by our carefully hidden CODOs. One brigade of Hissène Habré's fighters who had been stationed in the northeast section of Bodo for the past year were now being reinforced by more fighters in case of trouble during negotiations. They aimed their weapons to the south, where they suspected our CODO base probably lay. Our CODO unit of Sublieutenant Abdoulaye Fall in fact had taken up position to the north of Bodo, behind the brigade's compound. There was a Catholic mission just south of Bodo near where the CODO mobile camp was usually headquartered. The lush growth of trees in that vicinity provided excellent cover from aerial observation. It was near the mission that our leaders met early every morning before conference sessions and also during the night afterwards to discuss the previous day's reconciliation talks and to plan strategy for the next day. This area was guarded by a special unit with the new heavy weapons from Libya. Our second base was on the road from Bébara about eight kilometers south of the Catholic mission.

8

The Reconciliation
Meeting in Bodo

THE DELEGATION FROM N'DJAMÉNA ARRIVED and was lodged in the palatial residence of the county's chief. Earlier this had been the finest residence of all the counties' chiefs and sub-prefects in all of Chad, but after several years of fighting it now looked wild and overgrown. All the furnishings that had made the residency beautiful had been stolen by Hissène Habré's fighters in the previous year.

The first day of the reconciliation meeting was a delight for us CODOs and a surprise for the delegation from the capital. Before the CODO delegation reached the palace for the first day's meeting, our CODOs took advantage of the long grass inside and just beyond the wire fence surrounding the residency to surprise the enemies in case of foul play. The residency was filled with bodyguards for the delegates from N'djaména and some of their officers. Before our CODO delegation entered the palace, there was one section of thirty-two CODOs who first entered, and then the CODO delegation arrived a few minutes later. The CODOs who had hidden themselves in the grass around the residency suddenly made their appearance in the palace courtyard. The fighters who had been stationed in the northeast section of Bodo with their heavy weapons also were surprised to see suddenly the units of Abdoulaye Fall right behind them. This created total panic for the delegation of N'djaména. They thought perhaps the CODOs wanted to attack them and realized instantly that CODO troops certainly could attack with great force at any moment. They were also surprised to see CODOs with collapsible (and therefore easily concealed) Kalashnikovs. The other guns that we carried also looked totally different from theirs. If we had attacked that day, more than 90 percent of both delegations would have perished.

A rough wooden table from the village had been set up in the courtyard under the mango trees, with bare benches and wooden chairs arranged on both sides for the delegates. There was space all around the table for bodyguards and a few brave villagers to stand or sit on the ground. Before the negotiation started, the delegation from N'djaména put on the table some tea, coffee, and American and Chadian cigarettes for the negotiators of both sides. Everyone was tense. The chief of the delegation, Mr. Djidéngar Ngardoum, greeted the CODO delegates on the east side of the table and introduced his delegation, who sat on the west side. Then he presented the tea, coffee, and cigarettes on the table to both delegations. Speaking in French, he told them to serve themselves at any time when there was a need. He said, "These things on the table are symbols of the love that we have for each other in Chad." He added another sentence, saying that when brothers are together, they love to share the same food. The delegation from N'djaména, elders of Bodo, and the villagers in attendance applauded these words of his.

Djidéngar Ngardoum then read a message from his president, Hissène Habré, which was beautifully expressed but, as we learned later, constructed of devious lies. The message charged Libya with external aggression and spoke of the eagerness of the government for unity of all Chadians to protect the integrity of their territory against any external aggression. It was Habré's intention to develop agriculture in the South, he said, which was a message designed to gain favor with the people of Bodo. The message ended with purported details of Libya's plan to control the entire territory of Chad. Hissène Habré said, "I was with Goukouni in the North, and I decided to leave him. It was because our rebels there had an evil plan against our country, Chad, in collusion with Libya's imperialist dictator, Kaddafi. If we Chadians are not careful, we will become the slaves of the Libyans. They will torture our parents and violate our daughters in our presence.

Kadafi is a slaver and imperialist. This is why I need you, and you need me, so that together we can protect our country and develop it. We need to think about these matters for the future of our country."

The message was very long, but my understanding of spoken French at that time would not allow me to remember everything in the message, so I have provided what I can recall. When State Minister Djidéngar Ngarbarim had finished reading Hissène Habré's message, he made a brief commentary and added his own message of unity to that of his president addressed to the CODOs.

In response, Sublieutenant Koulangar said, "Thank you for your presence among us." The delegation of N'djaména, elders of Bodo, and the villagers applauded him, too. After the applause, he continued reading his message. Koulangar, the voice of the CODOs, explained point by point the irresponsibility of the government regarding the Chadian armed forces who deprived businessmen, civilians, and particularly the villagers — who had nothing to do with politics — of their goods, their homes, and their lives. He said, "If today we are in a state of rebellion against the 'government' of Chad, it is because the government has brought us to this point." The public applauded loudly.

After the reading of the messages by both leaders of the delegations, the dialogue started. Members of the CODO delegation mentioned on this first day of the talks their anxiety about a number of recent events. First was the robbery of livestock, merchandise, cars, vehicles, and other property in areas where the population had been victimized by the fighters of Hissène Habré. Next was mentioned the arbitrary arrest, torture and killing of artists, engineers, businessmen, Christians, officers, villagers, and administrators by his fighters. Finally, complaint was made of the illegal taxes demanded by the fighters' authorities or by people of Hissène Habré's clan.

There were other important issues that the CODO delegates mentioned on their first day of the meetings, but I am not able to remember them all. The delegates from N'djaména, comprising primarily staffs of various government ministries, tried to answer diplomatically each of the points mentioned by the delegation from Kou. Both of the delegations agreed that these atrocities should never have occurred. In many cases, however, Habré's ambassadors said they needed to inform competent authorities in N'djaména, who then would surely study these charges and work with us to solve these problems Although I knew their comments were insincere, later I realized that they were obligated to say these things, because with Hissène Habré, any mistake on their part would result in dismissal, torture, or death. The severity of their punishment by this cruel man would depend on the size of their mistake or the seriousness of their diplomatic breach.

On the second day, negotiators discussed the intentions of Libya and particularly of its president, Moammar Kaddafi. The delegates from N'djaména explained point by point Khaddafi's plans not only to control Chad but also to take over most neighboring countries. Their thinking was that once Khaddafi had control over this part of Africa, we would all be subject to Muslim rule and serve as slaves to the Libyans. One member of their delegation reminded us of Hissène Habré's words: "Libyans are worse than imperialists. They are truly barbarians. Their intention is to enslave and oppress us. We Chadians must take them as they are — and say no to their ambitions."

Most of the N'djaména delegates were originally from the North and particularly from Borkou Ennedi Tibesti (B.E.T), the prefecture located in the extreme north of Chad that shared a border with Libya. These natives of B.E.T. explained how the Libyans took advantage of Chadians' political naivete to create the rebellion in the North. The Libyans even considered the Aozou band — the far northern portion of the B.E.T.— to be their own territory. Today, these ministers said, Libya controlled all the B.E.T. It used people like Goukouni, Cheik, and others to deceive both Chadians and international governments. Rather than liberating Chad, the leaders of Libya intended to enslave it. These delegates insisted that Libya was not merely supporting the rebels in the North. If that were so, why then was it creating secret military airports in our territory and using thousands of Libyans and other mercenaries from Eastern Europe to kill our people and destroy our country?

One of the delegates said, "Yesterday Libya established social cooperation with us in the B.E.T, but before long it had occupied the Aozou band. Today, it is using Goukouni and other Chadians who do not care about their parents and children to bring Libyans into the B.E.T. and control it. If we do not pay attention to or think about the intentions of Libya, tomorrow all of Chad will no longer exist. The Libyans — and some of us know them very well — will show us the law of life. We and our future generations from tomorrow to infinity will not forget that tragic lesson. In brief, we will be their slaves. Our situation will be worse than in that time of slavery when our ancestors crossed the Mediterranean Sea and Atlantic Ocean. Dear brothers, I ask you to think about and analyze the presence of Libya in our country. It is very important for us Chadians to stay together in love and unity. This way we will have the unified strength to protect the integrity of our territory and allow our people to live in peace. It is only in this way that we can end this suffering from so many years of war, our blasted economy, and these social problems."

Then both delegations talked a long time about these points. There were many arguments mentioned and discussed during the second day of the meeting, primarily about the intentions of Libya in Chad, but I did not comprehend them all because of my lack of fluency in French and my lack of familiarity with political discussions at that time.

Then the chief military leaders of both the government and the CODOs, six to eight of them, withdrew to a small building adjoining the meeting area, saying that their discussions could not be public, for reasons of military security. Both Déby and Koulangar took notebooks with them. After only 15 to 20 minutes, these men emerged from the building. Koulangar now carried a document with his notebook. I assume that, although civil negotiations might continue, a reconciliation pact had already been signed by the military leaders.

The second day of the meeting was finally over that evening. The meeting was followed by a number of ceremonies featuring cultural performances. The CODO delegation needed to consult their leadership and discuss certain points in their camp before the next day's meeting. The other delegation also tried to discuss certain points among themselves. They informed the authorities at N'djaména and particularly their president, Hissène Habré. Normally the head of a delegation is supposed to send a daily report of the meeting to their president and discuss with him the strategies to use. But with the dictator Hissène Habré this was not the case. He demanded reports from each member of the delegation. In addition, he interviewed each of them every day after the meeting, using military radio communication. And the following day before the meeting began, he would give his approval or orders with regard to requests made by the CODOs. Every speech the ministers would make had to be read, corrected, and approved by their president before it could be delivered. On some points, Habré's ministers were so afraid of doing the wrong thing that they deferred to him completely. He insisted that CODO leaders should go meet with him in N'djaména to work out resolutions of their concerns directly with him.

The third day of reconciliation meetings in Bodo focused more on the previous points enumerated: security in the South from government forces and social problems in the areas where the fighters of Hissène Habré had burned the villages. When the two delegations were on the topic of security, one of the villagers of Bodo stood up and asked for permission to address the delegates. When this was granted, he spoke in French from where he stood, briefly and persuasively. "Where the elephant and buffalo face off, it is the grass that suffers. But the way that we suffer in this area as a result of the fighting is even greater. The fighters of the government have accused us of being supporters of CODO, without any evidence. They have done so many cruel things to us in this area. When they come, they surround the villages and order everybody to go to the marketplace for a meeting. Then they use long ropes to tie us together by the neck before stabbing us or shooting us to death. Baby boys are killed together with their fathers. When they see people in church worshipping God, they burn the church with the congregation inside. Some of us are arrested and tied in 'arbatacha,' the worst method used by Hissène Habré and his fighters to torture people. They use a strong rope to tie the victims' forearms behind them and press them until the elbows touch each other. They tighten the rope little by little as they interrogate their victims. By the time the victim's elbows touch each other, he is either dead or crippled for life. In the towns, a fighter or group of fighters may arrest us and ask us questions in Gourane or Arabic, and we try to let them know that we speak only French or Sara. They ask us if we are French or Kirdi [a term used by the Muslims in Chad for those who are not Muslims]. We automatically become targets of persecution because of our speech. When Habré's fighters see us with any Christian object, such as a Bible, they ask why we are not Muslim. Nonmuslims are immediately beaten and arrested. We are not allowed to grow millet, rice, and other kinds of foods essential to our own survival and to the economy of our region.

"On the other side, the CODOs accuse us of being supporters of

Habré's fighters, and we suffer from their interrogations and arrests. We also suffer from their recently imposed rule against growing cotton, which would provide the government with funds from our area.

"I could list many more oppressions that we have suffered from both sides, but that would take too much of your time. I would like instead to touch briefly on three last points: (1) What are the plans of the CODOs and the government for the people whose properties have been burned or stolen? (2) Many people's houses or huts have been destroyed, and most of these families have lost their boys and men. What can the two groups do to provide a minimum of their needs to survive? (3) Social problems are very serious. The presence of government forces in the area of Bébôtô, Béti, Bénjondô and Bodo kept our people from cultivating their plots of rice, millet, sorghum and other foods. In fact, those who risked their lives to grow crops in defiance of orders had their fields burned. Now they live in the bush and barely find the food to survive. These people need food, shelter, medicine, and other minimal necessities just to start their new life. What the two groups can do to make this happen is very important. These areas — and particularly Bodo — are the granary of our country. If the CODOs and the government do not find a lasting solution for this crisis, all of Chad may suffer a serious lack of grain for many years in the future. Chad's granary is empty today.

"I would like to end by saying thank you for your attention as I made my requests. And I hope you will think about them to solve the real problems that we villagers face." When this villager sat down, the delegates around the table sat in silence, but the villagers standing in the courtyard who heard this speech applauded long and loudly.

It was very difficult for both delegations to respond to the requests of this young villager who had not been afraid to bring to their attention the many sufferings of the people of the South in general and of the Oriental Logon in particular. Among the delegates at the table were the very killers and torturers of whom the villager spoke. These were primarily the intellectuals and officers, including Idriss Déby (who was in 1990 to become president of Chad), Captain M'ndidéal N'djémber, and others. Delegates from the South knew the truth of these allegations, as well. After a long silence, State Minister Djidéingar Ngarbarim thanked the young villager for letting the delegates know about the suffering of the people. He said the questions the young villager had asked were very important. Each of the delegates would think about them. These requests should be among the first problems submitted to President Hissène Habré.

Every day the delegates ended by signing documents and papers. On this day, they signed the reconciliation agreement. While they were doing this, one of the members of the CODO delegation asked for the retreat of Hissène Habré's fighters in the areas of Bodo and Bébôtô so there might be no incidents between the two groups. Another CODO delegate asked the negotiators to withdraw people like Captain M'n-didéal N'djémber, Commander of the zone of Oriental Logon, and other fighters who had killed a lot of innocent civilians in that region, before CODO troops arrived in Doba. They were still furious at the atrocities committed by these men on their friends and relatives in the area and warned that fights and revenge killings would surely occur if these men were permitted to remain in the area. State Minister Djidéingar Ngarbarim said the delegation agreed with them about their anxiety for peace in Chad. But the CODO delegates needed to give them time to work on it. He promised the CODOs that his delegation would submit every one of their requests to the President, and he believed the President might be able to give them a satisfactory response.

Thus the second and third days of negotiations gave diplomatic victory to the delegation from N'djaména. The leaders of the CODOs were deceived. They swallowed whole the illusory speeches of Hissène Habré and his followers. The third day had been dedicated to the public signing of agreement papers. For any political problem, the papers were signed before the two delegations and in public. But for any problem concerning the army, apparently a deal had already been struck. Because none of us knew what the military agreements provided, none of us could object when those agreements later were betrayed and violated.

The last meeting of that second day let the public know that the CODOs had already been corrupted by money and government promises. Their diplomacy had collapsed. They were more interested in the stimulant kolas, cigarettes, and flavored teas on the table than the important negotiation they had before them. The various members of the government delegation from different departments of N'djaména had submeetings with the other CODO delegates in their government

departments. After those submeetings, we who were close to the
CODO delegates started seeing them spend large amounts of money —
in large bills — around Bodo. While the CODO troops were thinking
about how to win a war to deliver our people from the heavy yoke of
Hissène Habré and his hired killer, Idriss Déby, our "leaders" were
apparently thinking about their future places in the army and government offices.

On the fourth and last day, the delegation from N'djaména social-
ized informally with people in the palace courtyard, mentioning members of their bureaucratic divisions who might be able to provide
assistance in various ways. At around noon the Minister of State, Mr.
Djidéngar Ngarbarim, made a brief speech wishing good appetite to
the people who were present for the ceremony of reconciliation at the
residency in Bodo. Both of the delegations shared food and drink —
meats, sandwiches, chicken, beer, Coca-Cola, Fanta.

Our CODO leaders forgot to think even for a moment about
their martyrs and about the poor population who had been innocently
killed because of their war. Without a word of apology or regret, they
began to eat with the governmental delegates. Even if they did not
have a long memory, they should have been able to recall the adjutant
Almbaye, originally from Bodo, who was their first martyr in Bémbaïtada after the attack on Bodo. Unfortunately, dubious beliefs about the
future built on apparently false promises made by governmental delegates emptied their minds of all thoughts of the past.

The evening dinner was followed by a performance by a cultural
theatre troupe of Bodo quickly assembled and led by the griot Téra.
The group presented the traditional and French songs of reconciliation
to the two delegations. I remember that some of those songs were for
unity, love, and peace. Even though the fighters who were bodyguards
of the N'djaména delegates did not understand the Gor language of
Bodo nor the French language, they seemed so moved by the final performance of the young griots of Bodo that they forgot their weapons
and their employers. One bodyguard's Kalashnikov actually fell onto
the ground as he swayed to the music (though luckily the weapon did
not discharge, and no one was harmed), and the rest of us were
amused to see his movements toward one of the female dancers. Most
of the members of the two delegations themselves stood up and danced
with the young griots. It was not because they knew how to dance, but

they were moved by the message of the young griots and their performances. We forgot that day that we were in a war zone. For a while, nobody thought about death or enemies. We were inflamed with joy by the traditional music and dancing of these talented young griots of Bodo.

(The griot Téra was so skilled at creating just the right mood and singing the praises of the delegates that he was noted that day by the authorities of Chad. A few months later, Téra was taken to Doba to be the regional griot of UNIR [National Union for Independence and Revolution], the political movement of the UNIR party of President Hissène Habré. Two or three years later, Téra brought out other songs in praise of Hissène Habré. Very happy with his songs of praise, Habré gave him another promotion to Presidential Griot of the UNIR Movement for Young Men and Boys, named RAJEUNIR, until the end of his presidency.)

A few months later, it was apparent that we had been fooled. The private meeting rooms that some of our CODO officers shared with the delegates of N'djaména had been filled with lies. When they joined the government troops, none of the CODOs received the positions and promotions promised by the delegation. Habré emissaries had given them hope that they would be zone commanders in the military or high authorities of some kind, but those hopes and promises became evil coffins of death.

While we were in Bodo for negotiations, on the second day of the talks, the CODOs' coordinator of international support, Sergeant Djimiel Pen, and two of his companions arrived secretly in Kou. They were to meet with our leaders and were surprised to hear that the CODO commanders were in Bodo, chatting with the enemy. CODO troops brought Sergeant Pen and his companions to Bodo, hosting them at our base in the area of the catholic church. They were insistent on meeting with Captain Guerngar (CODO war advisor) and the two sublieutenants Koulangar and Abdoulaye Fall, respectively commander and second commander of the CODOs. When they heard that Sergeant Pen was in Bodo, before receiving them, the CODO commanders had a private meeting regarding the North's forces and their messengers, who had been key to our receiving the matériel from Libya. Then the three CODO leaders had a private meeting with the three messengers from the North. As I heard later from bodyguards and others, after exchanging the traditional greetings, Sergeant Pen said, "We are surprised to hear that you are meeting a high-powered delegation coming from N'djaména."

The three CODO leaders acknowledged that they were in fact meeting with the enemy, but for strategic reasons. The messengers from the North said they would need to inform the North's forces and, more precisely, the former President of the Chad Republic, Goukouni Oueddei, and his vice-president, Kamougué Abdel Kader, who had deployed their resources to send to them the weapons and ammunition from Libya. The sergeant reminded them about the risk to their lives they in the North had taken to get the materials. He thought right now was the best moment to kick Hissène Habré out and give hope to our people who were suffering. This was the moment to give our families an opportunity to come back home out of the bush and bury the rest of those innocents who had been murdered — stabbed, burned to death, or shot. This was the brief moment to allow our parents to rebuild their houses and cultivate their fields to feed themselves instead of living in the bush under the rain, suffering from cold, and eating only the roots of trees to survive.

Sublieutenant Koulangar responded to Sergeant Pen that CODOs were indeed negotiating with government agents, but it did not mean that they were joining Hissène Habré's fighters. He said the CODO leaders at headquarters at the Catholic church could show the emissaries the CODO strategy at the next morning's meeting.

The messengers said they had an arranged to be in radio communication with forces in Bardaï at the GUNT base. The base leaders might ask to know the time that they planned to attack, so forces in the North could make an offensive there at the same time.

The three CODO leaders said they would be making those plans that very night and would meet with them again the next day to let them know what they had decided.

Sergeant Djimiel Pen and his companions were not pleased. After all they had done to aid us against our enemies, they were aghast that our leaders were now dealing with those enemies. Moreover, our leaders had betrayed earlier plans they had made to coordinate attacks with forces in the North. Pen and the others apparently talked to officers at Bardaï using their military communication radio. They informed the GUNT leaders about the communication that Kou might have with them the next day.

The messengers' reaction to this news turned out to be fatal. I suspect their reminders of all they had suffered for our cause elicited some guilt in the hearts of our CODO leaders. Sublieutenant Koulangar and his team decided immediately to liquidate the messengers to avoid any divided purpose among the CODOs. In the middle of the night the three envoys from the North were arrested. A few minutes later, they were taken to the bush between south Bodo and Bébara to see their last stars. This injustice took the place of justice, mindlessness dominated mindfulness, the slaves of money finished off the messengers of support: Koulangar and his companions had killed Djimiel and his comrades.

Once again the Southerners betrayed themselves through cowardice and deceit. Officers at Kou who were supposed to call Bardaï to let the forces of the North know about their plan of action failed to make the call. Even though Bardaï eventually that morning had the courage to call Kou, Koulangar and his team refused to take the call not only because they had liquidated the envoys from Bardaï but also because they were ready to go to N'djaména to sign an agreement that all our CODO troops would rally from the bush, join the government forces, and turn our weapons against the North.

9

On the Way to N'djaména

THE MORNING FOLLOWING THE CLOSING CEREMONY, all the members of the delegation from N'djaména were driven by Land-Rover, Land Cruiser, and Toyotas back to Doba. Some were scheduled to leave Doba that same day for N'djaména. Others had to wait to go together with the CODO delegation. But before leaving Bodo, they left behind them two or three Land-Rovers for the CODO delegation, as a gift.

After the departure of the delegates from N'djaména to Doba, some CODO delegates had to follow them twenty-four hours later in one of the Land-Rovers. Instead of going with our delegation, Sanabé Abel let his colleagues know that he and I were going to join them in Doba because he needed to retrieve some documents from Béngamia. His objective was not really to get his documents from the village but to let his father, Pierre Waïtôloum, know what was going on. Waïtôloum had been a politician before and immediately after the independence of Chad, until the first president of Chad was assassinated. Then he became a forestry agent in various locations in Chad. Sanabé Abel and I left Bodo on a Honda C75 motorcycle around 7:00 in the evening and arrived in Békôdô 1 twenty minutes later. We drove to the home of my grandfather Mbaïlemdana.

When we stopped the motorcycle under the mango tree outside my grandfather's house, which was still roofless from the attack more than two months before, I caught sight of my grandfather through the tall grass as he and other family members worked to put the compound to rights. I called out, "Kaka," which means grandpa, "we are lucky to catch you at home." My cousin and I had expected everyone to be in hiding in the bush.

Kaka laughed at me. He said, "We heard that you were in the process of reconciliation, so we tried to come back home and arrange some of our property. Early in the morning, though, we will need to go back to the bush, because the attacks still tend to come in the morning."

Sanabé Abel said to my grandfather, "The CODOs just signed a ceasefire agreement with the government. Right now we are on the road to Doba to catch an airplane for N'djaména, where we will meet Hissène Habré. So I do not think that the fighters are going to attack here now. If we are not ambushed in Doba or N'djaména and the ceasefire holds, then perhaps there will be no more attacks here."

Because the wife of my uncle Mbaïngomal knew that my cousin liked to drink the local alcohol, she brought him a bottle of the local *argué*. While Sanabé Abel was taking his *argué*, I took tea with my grandfather. Then before we left Békôdô 1, my grandfather prayed with us and asked God to be our protector. We left the village around 9:00 that night and reached Bédio twenty or twenty-five minutes later. Our uncles in Bédio were very happy to see us. Most of their children had returned to the village. They were taking advantage of the period of negotiation talks to come back home and see what property had survived the burning and looting. Many of them did not know my cousin Sanabé.

Sanabé Abel had studied far away from home in big towns in Chad and, after graduation, he had traveled to Senegal in West Africa for a degree in philosophy. Then he studied economics at the University of Paris for five years. After his DEA (Diplôme d'Études Approfondies), Sanabé Abel studied at the School of Neilly in Paris for one year, where he attained the highest degree for customs officials. He came back home to serve his country and became the head customs inspector for all of western and southwestern Chad. But very soon the rebels of Hissène Habré took control, and this man — trained in

philosophy, economics, and international affairs — found it necessary
to hide in the bush. As a result, he was not known well by our cousins
of my generation, who were some years younger than Sanabé.

While we were surrounded by some of our cousins and uncles,
others quickly went back to the bush to look for chickens and goats to
prepare for us. Sanabé Abel told them not to bother, that we had to
go, and he hoped we would be back soon to spend more time with
them. One of our uncles said it had been more than fifteen years since
they had last seen him, so this night was a great opportunity for
them — and particularly for our cousins — to see him.

Sanabé said, "We would like to stay for a while with you, but we
have to go because the airplane will be in Doba tomorrow to take us to
N'djaména." One of our cousins asked me if Sanabé Abel could at
least take time to drink tea. I said, "If you can get *argué* for him, he
would drink that."

My cousin was surprised, because he thought that people who
came from Europe did not like our drinks and foods any more. In less
than five minutes he has found two bottles of *argué*. By taking the
argué, we lost about two hours there, and by that time the roasted goat
and chicken that we did not want were ready for us. We finally left
Bédio — one of us full of food and the other full of drink — and arrived
in Béngamia after midnight.

Despite the late hour and the fact that we were not expected, we
knocked on the door at the home of our uncle, Jean Rabbi. He came
out and, both surprised and pleased to see us, embraced us warmly.
While Sanabé Abel was with him, I went to see one of his sons, Doudjim, who was only a few years older than I and lived in the next hut.
When I knocked on his door, Doudjim saw me through the small
window of the door. Because I carried a Kalashnikov, he was afraid
that I was one of Hissène Habré's fighters and did not open the door. I
went back and asked my uncle where Doudjim was.

My uncle said, "He probably is inside his house."

I said, "No, I called him and heard a little bit of noise, but
nobody answered me."

He asked me to go back and try again to see if he was there. I
returned to Doudjim's house, knocked at the door again, and called,
"Doudjim ngoloba, ngoloba (son of my father), it is I, Ésaïe, calling
you."

Doudjim came out from his house in a rush and gave me a warm embrace. He said he had seen me through the window. "I took you for a fighter of Hissène Habré. I was so afraid that I thought today would be my last day." He gave me another hug and wanted to put my Kalashnikov inside his house.

I said, "Ngoloba, no. You are my senior cousin, and the Kalashnikov is our Benjamin (our precious youngest brother), so it has to be close to us."

Despite the late hour, Doudjim hurried to our junior aunt Kôn Moal to inform her that Sanabé Abel and I had just arrived from Kou. Doudjim went to other relatives, too, and informed them also that we were back from Kou. In under twenty minutes we were surrounded by our relatives and their neighbors. While Sanabé Abel and other uncles and cousins were drinking *argué*, the women whose sons were with the *maquis* rebellion in Kou asked me questions about their sons. If I told them that I had not seen their sons, they might worry that something terrible had happened to them. To prevent their needless worry, I just told them that their sons were all doing fine. I apologized for not having brought messages from the boys and men, but I had not known that we were coming to Béngamia, because Sanabé Abel told me that we were going to Doba.

My aunts and other relatives were so happy to see me back in the village with my cousin Sanabé Abel. But their happiness disappeared when Sanabé informed them that we were going to go to N'djaména that evening. They wanted to know how we could reach N'djaména in one day. He replied that an airplane would come to pick us up at Doba.

Our senior aunt, Kôn Mara, said, "In the army, people do not know their last hour of life. Death comes to them as to a chicken which can be slaughtered at any time by its owner. I have a special love for Toïngar. He was well named High Chief. I need him to be the pillar and mainstay of our next generation. The white men took Sanabé from us for many years. I do not want Toïngar to be in the army, nor in the country of white men. We need him to take care of and preserve the wisdom of our generation." I was amazed to hear that I was the one chosen for this honor. Ordinarily the announcement would not have been made until after years of training. Kôn Mara's anger over Sanabé Abel's plans must have caused her to speak in this way.

Our cousin Philemon spoke respectfully to his aunt, "Mother, please do not talk like that. You know that Toïngar is not in the army. He went to Kou to protect himself because we did not have peace at home. All of our young boys are in Kou for the sake of their security. Toïngar has escaped from the dead three times, and you yourself know the matter better than we do. They will go to N'djaména to see Habré, so give them your blessing so that God will bless Toïngar for our generation. Nothing can happen to them. And only one of them will go to see the killer Hissène Habré."

Sanabé Abel said, "My aunt, I understand your concern. We have signed the paper for peace with Habré's fighters, so we need to go meet Hissène Habré to talk more about it. If you see Toïngar always with me, it is because I do not want to let him be away from me. I want him to be with me now, and I want him to be someone, a respected man, tomorrow."

Our aunt, Kôn Mara, replied, "Do you want him to be someone for us or for the white men like you?"

To end the discussion, Sanabé Abel said, "I want him to be a man for our future generation."

Kôn Mara concurred, saying, "If that is the case, I give you my approval."

Sanabé said, "My aunt, as you give me your approval, I hope we are free to go to N'jaména now, yes?"

Kôn Mara responded, "Yesterday, you talked about Kou. Today, you talk about N'djaména. Tomorrow, you are going to say you will take Toïngar to Europe. We have lost you, Sanabé, because the white men have changed your thoughts. We do not want to lose Toïngar as we have lost you. You may go to N'djaména. When you return, you will take him back to Kou."

Our uncle, Jean Rabbi, said, "My senior sister, with all respect, I would like to make a suggestion. Please, let Toïngar go with his cousin to Doba because Sanabé has a motocycle. If there is any problem on the road, Toïngar can help him. When they reach Doba, Toïngar will stay with Sanabé's wife, Dandé, until Sanabé comes back from N'djaména. It makes sense for both of you, Sanabé and Kôn Mara?"

Our aunt finally accepted the suggestion of her junior brother. She quickly prepared the traditional porridge for our blessing and wished us a nice trip to Doba and N'djaména.

We left Béngamia at 9:00 a.m., but we had to be in Doba before 2:30 p.m. to catch the plane to N'djaména at 3:30 p.m. Instead of taking the short way through Babo to save time, Sanabé Abel took the road through Bénjendouli. This detour was intended to avoid our relatives in Babo who might not let us depart without going before the Bainda.

The Bainda are the gods of our ancestors, the spirits of the bainda tree, which are said to give certain members of my family the strength of lions and also protection from certain kinds of danger. Particular men and women in my family are said to be able to create downpours of rain when necessary and can walk in that rain without getting wet. My grandfather from time to time was asked to use his powers on behalf of friends to settle disputes ; apparently he could terrify enemies with a loud roar and attack with such speed that he was always successful. Two lion men could defeat the men of an entire village. Lion men also appear in the village every time a member of our family passes away. My father, who was supposed to have become the Bainda leader because he was the Benjamin of the family, refused to take on that role after he became a Christian. He always said his children were not going to use the supernatural power of their ancestors. To avoid the delay that Bainda ceremonies would require and to prevent any trouble with my extended family, Sanabé Abel chose a longer route to Doba that would not take us before the gods of our ancestors.

From Béngamia we passed by Bénjedouli on our way to Bégada, where we stopped at the house of my uncle, Sanabé Abel's father. When Sanabé had told the rebel leaders in Bodo that he needed to gather important materials from his home before traveling to N'djaména, that was not the truth. In fact, he wanted to consult his father about recent events and seek his advice.

My uncle, Pierre Waïtôloum, was the only man left in the big village of Bégada. All the others had fled to the bush, but because of his broken leg he had determined to stay in his home. When we visited him, he was tended by his young granddaughter. He told us that he preferred to be killed at home rather than to be in the bush. Recently the village of Bégada had been burned by Hissène Habré's fighters, but for some reason his house had not been burned. We stayed only about five minutes with him and asked our niece to bring a glass and a jug of *argué* beside his bed for us.

It was there that Sanabé Abel tried to explain point by point the CODO meeting in Bodo with the delegation of N'djaména. Sanabé explained that he was not ready for reconciliation, but he himself could not do any thing to stop it. He told his father that he wished to cross the border into the Central African Republic and return to France, because he was sure that the CODOs were going to N'djaména to rally the regime of Hissène Habré. He said that he did not want to work with that regime, explaining that most of those with important posts were ignorant men, not even able to write their names. Men from the South with knowledge and education had to serve as advisors to those ignora-muses, who had risen through the military and had no real knowledge. He finished by saying, "Working with uneducated people is killing me!"

My uncle, Pierre Waïtôloum, said, "Do not leave your country. During the period of colonialism, slavery was very hard, but we per-sisted to achieve our independence in those days. It will change one day. You are the most educated person in our family. If you go away because of the current situation, what will be the future for your chil-dren, younger brothers, and cousins, who place their hope in you? Go with your companions in N'djaména, and when you return from this trip, we will make the final decision."

Sanabé Abel responded, "What you say was not my wish, but I respect your will, Father."

My uncle spoke again: "Thank you for taking into consideration my words. You are my blessed son, and nothing can happen to you because you are protected by my word of blessing."

Sanabé responded, "I love you, Father."

Pierre Waïtôloum asked, "What about Toïngar? Are you going to leave him in Doba, or is he going with you to N'djaména?"

When Sanabé said that we would be going to N'djaména together, his father retorted, "Toïngar must not go to N'jaména with you, for two reasons. First of all, he is chosen by our family to be the mainstay and pillar of the future generation. You cannot take him out-side of our area without the approval of your aunts and especially that of Kôn Mara. Secondly, it is not good for people from the same family to go on this kind of trip. I prefer that you leave him here with me, and when you come back, you can take him with you."

Sanabé explained, "Aunt Kôn Mara gave me her okay for Toïngar to go as far as Doba, but I need him to go with me to N'djaména."

His father advised him, "Respect the word of your aunt, Kôn Mara. If you do not, you will be in big trouble."

Sanabé finally agreed, "Well, I will leave him with my family in Doba until I come back from N'djaména."

In conclusion, his father said, "You and I do not share the opinion of your companions, but when the masses applaud, reason keeps quiet. You have to be very careful in your discussions with the CODOs and with Hissène Habré. Remember that however high a military man's education or skill or wisdom, he is still just a killer."

I said, "You are right, my uncle. Sergeant Djimiel Pen, who helped to get us the materials from Libya, was killed about two days ago between Bodo and Bébara by our leaders." My uncle was saddened at the news.

A few moments after our conversation, Sublieutenant Tôlngar and his two bodyguards appeared. He said they were on a mission to Kokat, and he wanted to come and salute Sanabé's father before continuing on their way. As was the custom of the CODOs, while their boss was in the village, they ambushed roads leading to Bégada. Other leaders of the CODOs were waiting for Sanabé in Doba. I suspect they were worried because Sanabé had not yet arrived there. His presence might be important because he was the general secretary of the movement.

We finally left Bégada with almost enough time to make it to Doba. Because Sanabé had drunk a lot of *argué*, he had difficulty driving the motorcycle properly. Not only was he a bit drunk, but the road also had a lot of sand on it. So between Bégada and Béango, we got into an accident, slipping suddenly on a patch of sand. Sanabé fell on the moto, I fell on him, and my Kalashnikov fell on me. Luckily, I had locked the trigger, or it might have been the end of our lives. I was the first to stand up, then Sanabé. He quickly switched off the engine of the vehicle and then asked me if I were all right.

I said to him, "I was worried about you, because you were between the moto and me. As for me, I feel fine."

The motorcycle was not badly damaged, so we continued on our way, more slowly this time. When we reached Béango, we went to the back yard of our uncle, Moyebé. He had hidden himself among the banana plants, but when he recognized us, he came out to welcome us. Sanabé asked him to hide the Kalashnikov, probably because he himself did not need it and our uncle could use it for his family's protection. Then we continued on our way to Doba.

When we reached the outskirts of Doba, Sanabé did not trust the officials manning the control post on the main road, so he asked me to remove his insignia, the strip of green cloth, from his head. I removed mine, as well, and hid both in my sock. Sanabé then took a minor road to enter town.

When we got to his wife's house, it was a great joy to his family. A few minutes later, his wife let him know that Sublieutenant Koulangar had sent someone three times to look for him. Very quickly, Sanabé took my pistol and his own and gave them to his wife to hide in a secure place. He gave me orders not to visit anybody, nor to join the protection force of Sublieutenant Koulangar until he and the other CODO leaders returned from N'djaména. I did not reply to him.

He said, "Did you hear me?"

I said, rather sullenly, "Yes." I was not happy about having to stay in the house, without seeing any of my friends or relatives. It was some years later that I realized this arrangement was for my own security, not to shame me.

A few moments after his words, someone came with a password from Koulangar, and then Sanabé left to join them. Thirty or forty-five minutes later, his wife and I stood in the yard to see the airplane take off, circle once, and head to N'djaména.

In three or four days, the CODO delegates returned to Doba from N'djaména. They were met at the airfield by their bodyguards, the civil authorities of Doba, and those N'djaména bureaucrats who had not accompanied the CODO leaders to meet with Hissène Habré. Two hours after arrival, Sanabé Abel joined us at his wife's house. That evening, Koulangar's relatives organized a traditional dance — known in the South as "Saï" — in the back yard of Koulangar's mother's house. I wanted to go to see the dancers, but I was worried that Sanabé would disapprove. There had been very little security in Doba while the CODOs were gone, and Hissène Habré's fighters liked to arrest young men arbitrarily in the evening or during the night, whether on the streets or outside our own houses. They customarily imprisoned, tortured, or killed those they arrested. This night, however, the CODOs had returned, and I knew that reconciliation had been achieved, so I was not worried about my safety.

At about 10:00 that night, when the xylophones, drums, and other instruments were making lovely music from half a kilometer away, and the dancers were singing sweetly, I left the house quietly. I was prepared to excuse myself by claiming I had to urinate, but no one woke up, and I slipped out undetected.

I made my way to the dance. Watching the dancers, I could see Koulangar and his bodyguards, but I was careful to stay away from them so they would not report my presence at the dance to Sanabé the next day. Koulangar seemed to be doling out large amounts of cash, both to dancers and observers. Every time people came into the circle to dance, Koulangar brought out money from his bag or pockets and threw it to them. As he distributed the money, even people who did not know how to dance very well came into the circle to dance and get some of that money. I do not know how many thousands of CFA-francs he spent that night. People really enjoyed their alcohol that night — a local beer made from sorghum and a commercial beer known as Gala. Judging from the crowing of the neighborhood roosters, it was about 5:00 a.m. by the time I returned to the house, slipped back inside, and went to bed.

Two days later Koulangar and his bodyguards returned to Bodo with some of the CODO delegates. They had to report to the other officers at headquarters about their mission to N'djaména. They asked Sanabé to accompany them, but he demurred, saying that he had driven the motorcycle to Doba and needed to drive it back. We left Doba that same day and drove via a different route from the one taken by Koulangar and the others.

When we reached Bengamia, our relatives were overjoyed to see us once again. Because they were living in the bush, they could not organize the traditional feast and party, but we stayed for almost a day and then drove on toward Bodo.

The next day, one of Koulangar's bodyguards, Octave, told me of the stirring event that occurred as their motorcade traveled through Béti the previous day. Apparently the local people had heard about the reconciliation and had such great hopes for peace that they sang out with sounds of celebration, stopped the motorcade, and praised the CODOs for returning peace to the region. Koulangar handed out even more CFA-franc notes to the residents milling around his car. A griot woman produced a song bemoaning the events that had forced these

residents from their homes to sleep in the bush like animals, like chimpanzees. Now, she sang, the chimpanzees would be driven out, and the
people would regain their homes. In grateful response, Koulangar took
a Kalashnikov from his bodyguard and shot three times into the air.
The motorcade then continued on to Bodo, heartened and rejoicing.

When they reached Bodo, however, the response was quite
different. Bodo had been a combat zone, most of the residents were
still living in the bush, and Hissène Habré's fighters were still there.
There were no parties or celebrations of joy in Bodo. No one felt safe
there.

A few days later, Koulangar began distributing large amounts of
cash to CODO unit leaders. I suppose it was at this time that he presented his report about negotiations in N'djaména. Then he asked two
units to go with him to Doba, the others to follow later. When they
arrived in Doba, they sent Koulangar's sublieutenant, Abdoulaye Fall,
to N'djaména at the request of Hissène Habré. When Abdoulaye Fall
returned a few days later, his pockets also seemed to be stuffed with
CFA-francs of large denominations. To prevent fighting between the
two forces, neither was permitted to patrol Doba, by terms of the reconciliation agreement. In this time of friendship and peace between
military leaders, many dances were held, and whenever Abdoulaye Fall
heard the beat of the tomtoms, he made his way directly to the dance
and gave out large amounts of money to the dancers.

10

Bodo to Doba

AFTER A FEW DAYS IN BODO, WE LEFT for Doba. With the presence of CODOs in Doba, the city was now a little bit more secure than before. People in the zone occupied by the CODOs had had their lives disrupted by terrorism under Hissène Habré's fighters, but now they enjoyed their freedom from oppression by returning to their former lives. Every moonlit evening after work people would get together in open places in the various quarters of the town to dance and talk and drink. Generally at these social evenings people brought local beers, called *bilbil, cochette,* and *boté,* as well as regular industrial beer. Some drank *argué* throughout the day, as well, meeting with friends and talking about events. This was a pleasant time, when all were hopeful of the peace to come.

Sublieutenant Koulangar with some of the officers took advantage of this live-for-the-moment ambiance to enjoy some blessings they had been denied for the past two years. They moved from one bar to another with young women of Doba. Koulangar was very much appreciated for the protection provided by his bodyguards, who ringed the dance area and prevented trouble. All the young women that shared his table in the bars or drank with the other officers would pile into his Land-Rover and go with the men to his residence. Once Koulangar reached his residence, he would choose one girl for himself and make the others available as service benefits to his bodyguards. He did not care whether he had met the girl before, nor did it matter to

71

him what his bodyguards did with the others. From my conversations with Koulangar's bodyguards at his home in the evening, I found that these were nightly events, with even more celebrations on the weekends, when Koulangar would host our soccer teams after the games.

During the CODOs' meeting in N'djaména with Hissène Habré, Koulangar had been promised command of Military Zone Five, comprising the Prefectures of Tanjilé and the Oriental and Occidental Logon. Wanting to gauge the atmosphere in Moundou toward his command, Koulangar asked Sanabé Abel to go with him to Moundou in Occidental Logon. Hissène Habré had agreed in negotiations that his fighters would be merged with CODOs and accept CODO leadership. Koulangar was eager to meet with traditional leaders of Moundou to get advice and information to help with the transition, and Sanabé was skilled at analysis and diplomacy.

I was to travel with the men as Sanabé's bodyguard. In early November, less than two weeks after our arrival in Doba, we left town for Moundou in the morning. When we arrived in Bébidja less than an hour away, the people in the marketplace there presented us with a grand welcome. As is typical in Chad, we were surrounded by silent and smiling men and also by women trilling "youh-youh-youh-youh-youh" to glorify Koulangar. Koulangar in his pleasure at this reception threw five-thousand CFA bills to the women who led the"youh-youh" chorus. Our vehicle was surrounded by the crowd in Bébidja. People continued to come from their homes to the marketplace, summoned by the "youh-youh," and we could not drive on to Moundou because of the press of bodies around the Land Rover.

I remember that one of the five-thousand CFA bills was torn between a woman and a man. The woman told the man to give her his portion of the bill, and the man demanded that she give him her portion of the bill, and they argued loudly. Another man advised them to glue the bill together and change it to two bills of two thousand five hundred CFAs so each of them could have half the money. The woman said she had a bigger portion, so she deserved more than three thousand CFAs for her share. We were driving away for Moundou, and I don't know how they solved the problem of the split bill.

When we arrived in Moundou, people were very happy to see us, but they manifested their joy with reserve because Moundou was one of biggest towns in Chad, and there the people did not know who was who and who was working for whom. That night Koulangar and his men stayed in the residential area in a lovely villa by the river, while Sanabé sent me to sleep at the villa of a friend in the compound of CotonChad, a cotton-manufacturing business, while he and his friend went off to town.

At the time, I resented not getting to share Sanabé's accommodations. Now I realize how by putting me in a separate location he often was protecting me from harm. In the middle of the night, a group of Hissène Habré's fighters opened fire on Octave Radé, one of Koulangar's bodyguards on guard duty at the villa. Without waiting, he opened fire on them with his Kalashnikov. All the bodyguards and their boss, Koulangar himself, were on high alert that night. A very hasty investigation was conducted, and for some reason Octave Radé was suspected and found guilty of trying to start trouble among the "reconciled" troops. As the CODOs did not have a house to use for a jail, Octave Radé was punished that night with fifty *coups de chicottes* (canings) and released. It was not until the next morning, when bullet marks were found on the wall near Radé's post, that they realized Octave Radé's innocence, but of course it was too late to take back the fifty *coups de chicottes*. After our second night in Moundou, Abel and I returned to Doba in a special CotonChad car. Two days later, Sublieutenant Koulangar and his team joined us in Doba.

During that month of cease-fire, all the CODOs with arms — those called "CODOs In Action" — joined us in Doba, the capitol of the Prefecture of Oriental Logon. These troops were placed south, north, and west of Doba. During that time some officers and the CODO troops had hope that one day they would liberate the people, now suffering under the regime in N'djaména. Unfortunately their hope would be reduced little by little and would finally disappear within six months. Some weeks after this initial deployment, the CODO troops west of Doba were taken to Moundou with Sublieutenant Koulangar, while the others remained around Doba under the control of Sublieutenant Abdoulaye Fall. Although I would miss the parties and entertainment we all had enjoyed under Koulangar, I admired Fall's wisdom better than that of Koulangar, and so I was not distressed to be under his command.

During the time we were in Doba, school started again, so I went back to my studies. I stopped spending time with the CODOs. Most people did not know me as a CODO. When I went out with Sanabé Abel, I was assumed to be his son, except by our close relatives and the CODOs who knew me. Sanabé Abel explained clearly to me that the time would come when most of the CODOs might be taken to the North to fight against the new GUNT, the neo-National Union Government of Transition. He asked me not to wear any military clothing but to focus myself on school. He said, "I hope one day Chad will change, and your education will help you toward higher education."

I told him that when we were in Kou some of our leaders said that we would attend military high schools.

Sanabé Abel replied, "There is no proof that CODOs will be invited to attend Habré's military high schools. Even if they want you to attend such a school, I prefer that you go back to a normal high school, because I do not trust this government. The government might take you from military school and use you at any moment for its own purposes." He asked me to think about the previous year when the government used every young man to fight against the new GUNT. It might be better for me to be in a normal high school. If the government tried to arrest us, I could just stay at home for awhile or, if it were possible, run to the village.

I agreed with Sanabé's opinion and thought it safer to attend public school. I also remembered that he had promised my aunts, when he supported my joining the rebels, that I would not be joining any branch of the military.

From November to June, the entire time that we CODOs were in Doba, there was never a month that we did not have a misunderstanding or altercation with Hissène Habré's fighters. Every month the two groups of men-in-arms tried to take positions to fire on each other. I remember the two worst showdowns, but I do not really know the causes.

The first event happened in the morning, probably at 10:00 or 11:00, and ended before 6:00 that evening. For some reason, Hissène Habré's fighters took up a position to one side of Doba, opposite where CODOs took position in their camp. When the civilians saw them taking positions, they stayed in their houses or backyards. That day we were in class, and when other students who were outside saw the movement of Sublieutenant Ngarkada and his CODO troops, they realized that there was something wrong between the CODOs and other fighters. School was quickly dismissed. While the other students tried to leave the Lycée Bernard Dikoa Garandi de Doba, I joined the troops of Sublieutenant Ngarkada. Then Sublieutenant Abdoulaye Fall went to the residence of Commander Ouaradougou, military commander of the sub-zone of Doba, to figure out the matter. They must have solved the problem, because at around 5:00 that evening the two leaders, Sublieutenant Abdoulaye Fall and Commander Ouaradougou, asked their troops to go back to their respective camps.

I left Sublieutenant Ngarkada's CODO troops around 6:00 p.m to go back home. When I reached the house, Béngar told me that Sanabé Abel was looking for me. I went to his wife's place but did not find him. Then I went to the house of our uncle Ngakoutou, where I met him. Sanabé Abel asked where I had been. He had been looking for me because Doba had been on alert all through the day. I told him that rather than run home or to the bush, I had preferred to join myself to Sublieutenant Ngarkada's troops that were near the school.

Sanabé Abel said that he appreciated what action I had taken, but next time when I found myself in this kind of situation, I should go home and try to be in a safe place where I could quickly find my way to the family village instead of joining other troops, because he wanted me to focus on my schooling rather than fighting.

I thanked him with respect and said that I would try next time to get home if I were outside the area, or if possible I would find my way to the village in case there were fighting between the two groups. Later that evening he asked if in the camp they had told us the cause of the problem. I said no. Then I said everybody was nervous, even Ngarkada, so we did not know the cause of that incident. I suggested to Sanabé that he was in a better position to know the cause than I. He replied that I was right about that, but he did not want to join the leaders and figure out the cause because military officials were generally quite stupid, and he preferred to let them decide or take action however they liked.

I told Sanabé Abel that I wanted to go home and study my lessons a little bit. He told me that the situation was still unclear, so his girlfriend, Béatrice, sent her niece to the evening market to find some fish and cook for me. Later in the evening, Abel said that I would spend the night there, and I would not be going home that night. If there was any fighting during the night, we would know where we could go. (By this, I assumed he meant that we would join the CODOs in the fight.) So I slept there in the compound of our uncle Ngakoutou.

The following morning, I went home and then to school. Some instructors and students showed up, but others did not. It was two days later that the high school was back to full attendance. I guessed that some instructors and students had left Doba on the day of the showdown to go to the villages around Doba.

There was a second major conflict in Doba. A fight broke out between two CODOs and a few of Hissène Habré's fighters in a bar. It was during the evening that the conflict took place. One of the CODOs was arrested and jailed at the *gendarmerie* (military police station) of Doba. When the fighters of Hissène Habré and CODO troops heard about the conflict, both groups put their troops on alert. All public activities in Doba were stopped. Doba was perfectly quiet that night. No one knew when the CODOs would fight their way to the *gendarmerie* to rescue the prisoners. There were no lights on in the town, nor could one hear the noise of any engines. The CODO troops of Lieutenant Rônaïmou and those of Sublieutenant Abdoulaye Fall took advantage of the darkness to control the entire border of Oriental Logon from Bédôli to Béraba. The troops of Sublieutenant Ngarkada took position on the north side of Doba. The CODOs were waiting for one of two alternatives to attack. Either one of the enemy fighters would fire his gun or Abdoulaye Fall might give them the order to attack first. Most of the troops, not realizing their CODO leaders had received money from Hissène Habré, looked forward to the opportunity to fight the enemies who had wounded them by murdering their families, for these wounds had not yet healed.

Sanabé Abel came from downtown Doba and joined us at the house of our cousin Ngarnadji, the porch area of which I shared with other student cousins, including Béngar, the half-brother of Sanabé Abel. Inside that house Sanabé himself had one bedroom where he kept some of his own documents and the documents of the CODOs. Sanabé said, "This night there will probably be a fight between CODOs and Hissène Habré's fighters." He tried to give us some instructions, oral guidelines to run to the village in case there were fighting. Because in Chad most people tend to take into consideration what their elders say without contesting it — even when they are wrong — we listened carefully to Sanabé's advice. In addition to being our elder, Sanabé was the best educated member of the family and was the General Secretary of the CODOs, so all our cousins accepted his suggestions. I was the youngest among them at that time. I wanted to give my opinion in response to what Sanabé Abel had said, but I was afraid of the negative response that I might receive from him or others who were older and better educated than I.

A few minutes later I decided to share my opinion privately with Sanabé Abel about what he had said to us. I told him that I had a message for him, if I could tell him inside the house. He agreed, and we entered his room. I said, "Please, *grand* (elder), do not be angry with me about the suggestion that I am going to share with you, and please let me have time to finish it before you respond."

When he gave me permission to speak, I said, "Thank you for giving us some instructions, and I appreciate your advice to run away in case there is a fight. But I wonder if you have taken all the factors into consideration. First, as we know that the CODOs are in the south, west, and north, in case there is a fight I think the only way Hissène Habré's fighters will save their lives is to escape toward the southeast, the very direction you have advised us to run to get to the village. We do not know if our enemies may have informed their colleagues from Bénjondô and Koumra to ambush the axle road that runs from Doba to Sarh, so that route may not be safe for us. And here is my second point. Our enemies know you are General Secretary of the CODOs, and there are many people — I don't know how many — who know that sometimes you are at your wife's house and sometimes you are with us here. In my opinion, if it is the enemies who want to attack first, maybe they will try to attack where our leaders are. You were supposed to ask one section of troops to be here for your protection, but you do not take care for your own safety. I would like to suggest that you find a safe place to sleep tonight, rather than sleeping here or at your wife's house or at our uncle Ngakoutou's home. Many people have seen you in all these places. That is all I want to tell you, but if I am wrong, please forgive me."

Sanabé Abel said, "There is nothing wrong in what you said. You have said something that I did not expect. Even my colleagues did not think about it. Thank you, my brother." Sanabé then said that he took my suggestion of the night's lodging into consideration but that he did not know where to go that night.

I said, "If you want, I can take you where you can be in a safe place and yet, in case of a fight, you can quickly join the troops of Rônaïmou or cross the river and go back to Kou."

He said, "Where is that place?"

I said, "The Bédôli quarter of Doba, and I have many reasons to say that."

He asked me what those reasons might be.

I said, "Well the first reason to be in Bédôli is because of its geographical position in the south and the excellent tree cover, both of which provide good security. Secondly, Rônaïmou's CODO troops are there and could protect the area for a while in case there is a fight. Thirdly, it is just north of the river, and the enemies, being from the North, do not know how to swim, so they will not venture to do their attack near the Logon River. Fourth, in case their reinforcement comes from the southeast, you can just cross the river to the south and go on to Kou. And finally, I know the family at the house in Bédôli very well. They have been the best friends of my grandfather Mbaïlemdana since before my mother was born, and most of my uncles grew up with the men of that family. Even now my Aunt Thamar is with them and has been since the age of three."

It took us about thirty to forty–five minutes to conclude our discussion. When I came out with Sanabé Abel, there were some student neighbors with our cousins outside, so we could not speak freely. A few minutes later Sanabé Abel asked me to accompany him to his friend's house. We left our house to go not to visit his friend but in fact to walk to the house of Doumalta Issac in Bédôli. When we arrived, they were very surprised to see us. A few minutes later I called my Aunt Thamar aside and explained to her the reason I had brought Sanabé to pass the night at Doumalta Issac's house. My aunt spoke quietly to Doumalta Issac and explained this to him. He gave his approval. They arranged one small house for him within their compound. We went inside that house, and I gave him instructions on how to join Rônaïmou's CODO troops or cross the river to get to Kou. Sanabé Abel asked me to stay there with him, but I told him to allow me to go back home, because we had not told others our intention to sleep away from home.

He said that I was right but that it was now too late at night for me to go back alone, since we were so close to the enemy compound. I said, "No, they will worry that something has happened to us if I do not return. And I also have the intention, on my way home, to inform your wife that in case of a fight, your family should not worry about you."

He said, "No, just tell them that I am with other colleagues and I might be at home tomorrow."

I agreed. I reached the home of his wife, Dandé, in about fifteen minutes and delivered the message to her. The food that Dandé kept for him was presented to me and her nephews. After eating the food I continued on my way back home. When I reached the house, other cousins asked me, "Where is our brother, Sanabé Abel?"

I told them, "He met his colleagues and wanted me to tell you that we should leave this house and go to Bouyobé's house nearby for our security."

Miandjingarti said, "Let's go."

I told them that I had a suggestion to make.

Odingar asked, in an authoritative voice, what suggestion I might have to make.

I said, "If we go there in a group, maybe people will notice or ask questions. So let us take different ways and reach there one by one."

Miandjingarti agreed, and we set off singly. As we all knew how to open the gate of Bouyobé's house, Béngar arrived first and opened it. He left it open for us. Odingar was the last to arrive, and when we realized that everybody was there, he closed the gate. Worried about the possible conflict between CODOs and fighters, we had a hard time getting to sleep that night in our cousin's extra house.

The next day, the CODO troops kept their positions and did not allow people in the villages around Doba to come to its daily market because they could not guarantee their security. The CODO troops waited in their positions until First Lieutenant Rônaïmou came to the *gendarmerie* with his bodyguards and broke open the door of the jail by force to release his imprisoned CODO soldier. The enemy troops did not respond to this act of deliverance. First Lieutenant Rônaïmou took his men back to their camp. As there was still no reaction by the enemies, the CODOs went back to their camps a few hours later under the instruction of Sublieutenant Abdoulaye Fall. The troops remained on alert in their camps, with weapons arranged outside to be ready in case of attack. Had there been a fight that day, most of the population of Doba, thousands of people, would have been trapped in the line of fire, unable to escape.

That same day, Sanabé Abel followed the suggestion I had given him and joined First Lieutenant Rônaïmou and others. When the atmosphere became normal between the two camps, Sanabé Abel rejoined us. Two days later, the two of us went to one of the best restaurants in Doba, where CODO leaders liked to meet. He bought one bottle of beer for himself and one bottle of Fanta for me. When we started on the second round of drinks, Sanabé Abel wanted to know who had given me all the clever instructions to avoid danger and asked how I had gotten the idea to help him that day.

I asked him, "Please, what are you talking about?"

He said, "I am talking about the thought that you had to take me to a safe place last week. I have been wondering about the good strategy that you used last week."

I said, "Well, the thought did not come from someone else. I just analyzed the instructions that you gave us and by comparing with the reality of the situation in Doba, I pulled out my logic and shared it with you that night."

He said to me, "You are a teenager, but I prefer to call you a man. Your thoughts are always useful. The others are your seniors in age, but you are their senior in thought. They like only to drink *argué* and *bilbil*, but their heads are empty of thoughts. I really appreciate your feedback of last week. At any time when you have something to tell me, do not hesitate. I am not one of those who are too traditional to allow their children or younger brothers and sisters to give their own opinions."

This was the first time I had ever been invited to give advice to one of my seniors. I said, "I will do that at any time when there is something that seems unclear to me."

A few minutes later Lieutenant Madjidé Bénoît appeared at the restaurant with his bodyguards. We spent about three hours together with them before we left for Dandé's house.

11

Payment Deal —
But with a Catch

S INCE THE *MAQUIS* (REBELLION) HAD BEEN born, each reserve
CODO depended on his own efforts to survive, and active
CODOs survived by their own skill. Without pay or supplies,
CODOs had to scrounge for food, equipment, and weapons. Successful ambushes of Hissène Habré's fighters would net them weapons,
ammunition, and money. They also retrieved goods stolen by the
fighters. CODO troops sought to block farmers from selling their cotton, which would end up enriching the government rather than the
people of the South; they waited until they saw CotonChad buyers in
the market, ambushed them, and "liberated" the CotonChad purchase
money. Some CODO troops sought food from their relatives in home
villages, while others bartered with local farmers for produce. Because
the *maquis* was an anti-establishment movement, there were no pay-
checks. By terms of the ceasefire agreement, the government in N'd-
jaména would provide for the active CODO troops. Perhaps the
money given to Koulangar in N'djaména was supposed to be used for
the troops. No provisions were made for the reserves.

As a result, a few days after the ceasefire had been announced
in October, CODO headquarters asked the reserve CODOs to go
back to their respective villages but to remain always ready for when

headquarters would be in need of them. The reserve CODOs dispersed as requested.

Two months later, the reserve CODOs all heard from an unnamed source that they should gather in Bébôtô because payment would be provided to reserve troops after all. Thousands of CODOs poured into Bébôtô thinking to be paid. Having heard the news, I went, too, though I was not a reservist. Some walked three or four days to get to town. Their number was greater than the population of Bébôtô itself. It was very hard for the resident population to house and feed them all. Those whose home villages were close to the administrative post (A.P.) of Bébôtô took in colleagues whose villages were several days' walk from Bébôtô. After a few days it was clear that neither the CODO leaders nor the government would provide these reserve CODOs with any assistance, neither food nor money. First Lieutenant Manassé, who was in charge of the CODO Reserves gathered in Bébôtô, asked them to go back to their respective villages and when everything was set, headquarters would call them.

Most of the reserve troops were disappointed and disgruntled because they had been expecting some kind of payment for being at alert on reserve duty for the previous two months rather than taking other employment and helping their families, who had suffered many dismal tragedies in the past few years. The reserve CODOs went back home having been greatly deceived and apparently not greatly valued by headquarters.

Three to four months later, perhaps in April of 1984, CODO headquarters sent messengers to Bodo and from there to the villages to ask the reserve CODOs to come to Doba. This time, thousands of *maquis* troops came with confidence that they would get something substantial to help them and their families. After getting into Doba, however, they found that their situation was even worse than in Bébôtô. Because they were very far from their own villages, the men suffered greatly from hunger. To get food and a place to sleep was very difficult. For example, in Ngarnadji's house where the young men of our family stayed when attending school, we had more than thirty persons living with the five of us. As the house was not able to contain all of us, some of us slept outside and others inside. A week later when there was still no pay or provisioning from headquarters, more than half of the reservists went back to their villages. Some of those who persisted in that difficult situation and stayed in town wrote letters to headquarters seeking help. It was then that Sublieutenant Koulangar finally ordered Sublieutenant Mbaïndag-djé, who was in charge of financial affairs, to supply the reserve CODOs in Doba with food.

Mbaïndag-djé and his bodyguards hopped into his Land Rover and drove to the market, where they purchased cooking pots, plates, vegetables, grains, and even an ox to be shared out to various companies of men. These supplies were taken to a central distribution area. Before receiving their share of the food, reserve CODOs were divided into more than ten units of two to three hundred men each. When the couragious men who had stayed in Doba started getting food, the others who had gone home to their villages heard about the new situation and came back. These newcomers swelled the number of units to more than twenty, and headquarters had a serious problem trying to provide enough food for so many thousands. The quantity of their daily ration had to be reduced to feed so many men.

I suspect that CODO headquarters then presented the number and needs of the CODO reservists to Hissène Habré, who now for the first time probably realized that the CODOs outnumbered his fighters. To find out exactly how many CODOs there were, Hissène Habré sent military photographers to take identity pictures of each CODO and assign registration numbers before the government would provide assistance and pay. When the military photographers started taking identity pictures, a rumor got started that anybody who agreed to have his picture taken would have to continue with a military career or the government would arrest him. If he ran away, his family would pay the price. This rumor spread through all the units quickly, and three opinions developed among the CODOs. One was that getting photographed and registered just to obtain a token, one-time payment was too great a risk. The men who held this opinion feared they would not be permitted then to go back home to take care of their families and fields. These men refused to take this kind of risk. A second opinion was that it was worth the risk in order to get financial support. They assumed they could be ID'd and get some payment, and then they could escape and go back home. The third opinion was that a career in the military might be a good deal. Men of this opinion were ready to continue to serve as CODO troops to save their country. Some were even willing to ally themselves with Hissène Habré's fighters if necessary, and if their CODO leaders wanted them to do this.

I was waiting for cousin Sanabé Abel to tell me to join a unit just to get the pay and then go back to school. Though we were together every day, I did not get any news or orders from him. On the third day, I let him know about my intention to be registered, not to embark on a military career but just to get paid and go back to school. He said, "Well, if it is just to get paid and go back to school, go ahead."

When I said to him that I had one more question, he said, "I am listening to you."

I said I had heard that anybody who agreed to have his identity picture taken would have to continue in the army, and if he ran off, the government would arrest him, tracking him via the ID photo.

He said to me, "Who told you this?"

I said, "They said that, and I heard it yesterday and today, too."

He said, "'They said?' In my opinion, 'they said' is information without a source, and I can assert with confidence that 'they said' is the younger brother of a lie. During normal times when there was no trouble in the country, the government sent recruiters to go from village to village, and the village chiefs warned the young men who came voluntarily to be registered that it might be possible for the government to track them down if they left service prematurely. Because the government had complete information regarding them — since everyone had been recruited from the same village — it would have been possible. In the current situation, however, the government would not be able to track all these men, because these thousands of people came from many different villages. The government cannot track you with a photo and a number."

I trusted what Sanabé told me. I went the following morning to the military photographers, and they took my identity pictures and gave me my registration number, which permitted me to go and get payment. I got my pay that same evening. Now I consider this pay to be an "all-inclusive price with poison," but at that time I was ignorant of future events. Since the paymaster's office was not far from our high school, I continued my way to school with great joy.

Some CODOs — those of the opinion that they could get their pay and go home — also were ID'd and paid and then went back to their respective villages. A few days later, the commanders of the CODO units remarked on how considerably the numbers of their troops had been reduced.

Sublieutenant Daniel, who was one of Sanabé Abel's close friends and the commander of Unit #10, put my name on the list of his troops to get me some assistance (soap, cigarettes, food in the general mess) and also to provide me with some pay just until the CODOs were to be allied to Hissène Habré's fighters, at which time he planned to disperse the unit. During the time I was part of Unit #10, I could join them at any time I liked. I did not have to show up for morning and evening roll call like the others, since my duty assignment was to attend school. My name was there just to draw pay and then get out of the military. I suspect that Sublieutenant Daniel informed his section chiefs not to take official notice of my absence nor to put me in service. At any rate, I never was punished for failure to serve during the one month that my name was listed with Unit #10.

While CODO headquarters was preparing the division and assignment of CODO troops to be allied to different units of Hissène Habré's fighters, all the other officers and sub-officers decided to go back to the *maquis*. Their leaders, they thought, had betrayed them to the enemy. Among those officers and sub-officers, we had two leaders of the neo–CODOs. One was Ngarguerna, a chief customs officer in his professional career, but an active fighter for freedom in the Green CODOs. The second was Djobaye, a sergeant-major of the military police, who was with the CODO-Rouge in Moyen Chari but refused to negotiate with Habré's emissaries. Captain Guerngar, Sublieutenant Mbaïndag-djé, and Sublieutenants Adil and Daniel were of the same Sublieutenants opinion.

Sanabé Abel, who was of the same opinion as the neo–CODOs but now considered himself a civilian, was suddenly summoned by the central regime to join them in N'djaména. In less than two days, he received more than six radio messages from N'djaména. I suspect that CODO headquarters, concerned that Sanabé was not fully engaged in their efforts, applied indirect pressure to get him assigned to the capital. Sanabé Abel had no choice but to go to N'djaména. He traveled on an airplane that had brought the official authorities of N'djaména to Doba to pay the CODO troops and arrange for their departure to different units in different areas of Chad as allied forces. It was on the same day that Sublieutenant Koulangar gathered for the first and last time all the CODO troops in the big field between the Catholic primary school for girls and the Lycée Bernard Dikoa Garandi de Doba (public high school). Koulangar informed them that they would be sent to different areas of Chad to serve their country. I was in school and missed this assembly, so I do not know how he started and ended his speech. The gist of his message was reported to me by CODO troops.

The day following the arrival of the officials from N'djaména and after Koulangar's speech, the commander-in-chief of all military police in Chad, who headed the delegation, wanted to visit all the CODO troop units and inform them that they would be paid a salary and then sent to different areas of Chad to serve their country. This officer, whose name I no longer recall, was well dressed in a military uniform with at least three pens of different colors in the top pocket of his shirt, and behind him there were four armed bodyguards. Sublieu-tenant Daniel was there in our camp with his second in command of our unit to welcome him. We saluted him, and Sublieutenant Daniel presented Unit #10 to him in French, because it is the official language of Chad. One of the bodyguards who was close to the military police officer translated into Gourane, his local language, spoken at that time by a small percentage, including Habré's people. When Sublieutenant Daniel tried to say more to the officer via one of his bodyguards, the guard had difficulty understanding Daniel. Maybe it is because Daniel had studied in France for many years and therefore had a French accent, or perhaps the guard had learned only a modicum of French in school. The guard asked Daniel if he could explain himself in Arabic. Daniel said, "It does not matter to me, "and thereafter spoke in Arabic, which the guard translated into Gourane for his boss. So during our meeting the conversation went from our unit's French to Arabic, and then to Gourane and vice versa back into French for Unit #10 to understand. It was during that meeting that the commander-in-chief of military police informed us that we would be sent to Abéché in the north-central part of Chad. I suspected we were to face the neo–GUNT forces there. We did not get paid on that day, and I thought it was because of the lateness of the hour and also because the pay and supply airplane had not yet arrived. I thought that the next day we could get our pay and then leave.

When Sublieutenant Daniel had left camp, I left Unit #10 and went home. I waited until later that evening and went to Sublieu-tenant Daniel's quarters to say goodbye to him, because his unit was going to Abéché without me, and also because he was a close friend to my cousin, Sanabé Abel. When I reached his quarters, he was with other officer friends and was complaining about the situation in Chad. I overheard him say to his colleagues, with a bitter smile on his face, "We suffer in school for many years, we are beaten by our parents and instructors to be good in school and get a lofty education. Yet today uneducated people who do not know how to speak any official language—and cannot even write their names—are going to be our leaders. When I look at my past and especially the test that I took to be among the best students in all the French-speaking countries of Africa and then many years of study in France to learn civil and military law—well, I thought when I returned, I could better serve my country. Today, I face a man with many pens in his pocket who is able neither to write nor to speak an official language, and yet he is my superior officer and commander-in-chief of the military police. If this man holds the highest rank in my department, I can only imagine what his subordinates will be like. And I am going to work under them?" Sublieutenant Daniel was furious that day. Because it sounded as though he might not in fact be traveling with his unit to Abéché and to avoid adding fuel to the fire of his anger, instead of saying goodbye and wishing him *bon voyage*, I said, "I come to give greetings to your family."

He said to me, "If tomorrow you get your money, do not forget what my friend told you, okay?"

Knowing that he was referring to Sanabé's advice to take the pay and immediately leave military service, I said to him, "Yes, *grand*," and then I returned home. It may have been that same night that Sublieutenant Daniel went back to the *maquis*. I do not know if he received any pay before he left.

As many officers and sub-officers knew me through Sanabé Abel, the following day instead of going back to Unit #10, which would travel to Abéché after getting paid, I looked for units that might stay in Oriental or Occidental Logon, to join one of them. I was looking for three units whose commanders and troops I knew. By this time the authorities had noticed that most of the troops that got their money soon disappeared. The paymaster devised a new formula: no pay for the troops until they arrived at their destination. We who had intended to get our pay and go back home were thrown into confusion by the new rules. Some of us decided to go back home without pay. Others decided to go to their new post for the payment it would provide, and then make their way back home.

It was very hard for me to make a decision. I went to several units that were supposed to be stationed in Oriental Logon. I found one unit scheduled to be sent to Bébidja. Bébidja is about thirty-five kilometers from Doba, and I reasoned that I would be able to leave immediately after payday and return to my studies in Doba with the September semester. The bodyguard of the adjutant of the company for that unit was a friend of mine named Élias. He asked his boss, who was also his uncle, if there was a way to include my name among them, and his uncle agreed to add my name to their unit. On the day scheduled for our departure, the trip was cancelled because our ration was not ready. This delay in our departure gave us time to rethink our decision, and some of our friends decided that evening not to go to Bébidja after all.

During that night I met Michel, my cousin, and asked him to join the unit traveling to Bébidja. I explained to him my plan — that once we got paid, we could come back to Doba and then continue to the village. He wanted to refuse, but I told him, "Michel, my cousin, listen to me. Our region has suffered a lot from Hissène Habré's fighters. They have burned down our houses, destroyed our property, and killed our relatives and livestock. They did not allow us to cultivate our crops this year. The government was supposed to help us after the war, but it does not. This is our opportunity to get our pay. That 15,000 cfa cannot cover what we have lost, but it will be better than nothing." Finally that night Michel was convinced.

Early in the morning, we went to the Independence Plaza of Doba to wait for our unit's ration of food and supplies and then continue to Bébidja. We waited from morning to evening before our leaders got our ration — and also got the money to pay us once we reached our destination. We arrived in Bébidja at around 5:00 p.m. and were put up in a public primary school facing the market of Bébidja. Immediately our two leaders — one of whom was a Northern fighter for Hissène Habré and the other (a First Lieutenant) in the regular military — started paying us. When they called the name of one of my friends who had deserted, Michel answered in his place and got that man's 15,000 cfa. Because I had only recently been added to the unit's roll, I was the last to be paid. We were hungry because we had not eaten since morning. Michel and I went to the market and bought grilled meat with bread and ate them greedily. When we went to the place where sleeping mats were sold, I bought one mat for us to share. Michel wanted to buy his own mat, but I told him not to, because he had only one night to spend in Bébidja. Early in the morning, Michel left Bébidja for Doba.

As for me, I was not worried about getting back to Doba right away, partly because that town was a little bit insecure at the time but also because the results of our exams at the *Lycée Bernard Dikoa Garandi de Doba* were not yet ready. Usually it took the school about two weeks to give us the results, and I hoped to take my scores with me when I went on from Doba to the village.

The second day after our arrival in Bébidja, Élias's uncle rented a house and invited me to join them. Two days later our unit was moved from the public primary school to the high school of Bébidja, which was about two kilometers from town. We had to assemble twice a day. The first meeting was at 7:00 in the morning and the second at 5:00 in the evening. Our unit was divided into four sections of 50 or so men, and I belonged to the third section. Our schedule in that unit was that the entire section must be on duty for twenty-four hours, and the next day would be the turn of the next section, and so on.

When it reached the turn of my section on the third day, I had sentry duty in the morning. After someone replaced me, I asked our section chief to allow me to go downtown for an hour. He permitted me to go, and I came back about three hours later, after a pleasant time with my friends. He was angry with me because of the rule that I had violated by coming back later than promised. He said if we had a jail at headquarters, he would put me there for some days. As there was no jail in the high school of Bébidja, he ordered me to cook for the unit for three days. The unit gave me two men to help me. First we prepared the sauce of legumes, beef, tomatoes, herbs, and seasonings. I tasted it and thought the salt was insufficient, so I wanted to add just a little bit more. Because of my inexperience with the ladle, too much salt went into the sauce. I did not know what to do. I thought maybe by adding more water I could reduce the saltiness of the sauce, but adding the water only made the sauce worse—I was making brine rather than sauce.

When I finished with the unsuccesful sauce, it was time to start the *boule* , the flour of millet, rice, or sorghum stirred into the boiling water until it becomes almost solid, like a bread, and then is ready to be eaten with sauce. When the water was nearly boiling and I wanted to add the sorghum flour, one of my two assistants suggested that I reduce the quantity of water, because the quantity of the flour was not enough for that pot of water. I told him that the quantity of the flour was indeed sufficient. When I dumped the flour into the water, I discovered that I knew less about making *boule* than my colleague did. Our bread was more like porridge.

Most of the men in our unit were very angry at the low quality of the food that noon dinner. Some of them wanted to beat me up, because this was the only meal provided for twenty-four hours. I said to them that I was sorry. Nobody wanted to accept my excuses, except a few of the men who knew me. And I am grateful that these men not only argued in my defense but also tried to protect me later.

I was reported to our section chief, who came and tasted the *boule* and sauce, neither of which was pronounced edible. He said instead of decreasing his anger by my actions, I had increased it. He said the seriousness of what I had done was so great that only his superiors would be able to adjudicate the problem. He therefore referred the matter to the unit's adjutant.

Luckily for me, the adjutant of the company knew me, and knew me well, in fact, because I lived with him and his nephew, Élias. On the following day when the section chief had brought my case to him, the adjutant ordered the sergeant to call me in so he could interview me himself. When I faced the tribunal, the sergeant explained my dreadful mistake once again. The adjutant ordered me to stand at ease and to explain myself.

I told the adjutant that I was sorry about what had happened the day before. I told him that it had been the first time I ever had prepared sauce and *boule*. And I had not intended to ruin the meal for my unit. As the adage says, "Ignorance is the mother of evil" — that is why my colleagues treated me like someone evil.

The adjutant said to me in the presence of my section chief that he forgave me because it had been the first time for me to cook, but next time if someone asked me to cook for others, I had to let that person know so that he could find someone with experience to help me.

I was very happy to hear that I would not be severely punished. I stood at attention and saluted him. I took three steps back and saluted him again. He said to me, "I return you to the disposition of your section chief." The problem was solved that day, just like that. My mistake set me free from the remaining two days of kitchen duty. The men who had expected me to serve some time in prison were as surprised as I to see me among them without any punishment.

That evening, we heard that there was a faction of CODOs who had gone back to the bush and attacked Hissène Habré's fighters between Gôré and Mbaïkôrô. All of Hissène Habré's fighters in Bébidja were on alert. Koulangar figured that the new peace between CODOs and the government was at risk if these CODOs resisted reconciliation, and he suspected they might be getting their ammunition from the secret cache of Libyan matériel that he and others had helped to hide a few months before. Therefore, two days after that attack on Habré's troops, Koulangar mixed his CODO troops with the fighters stationed in his area and conscripted the drivers of three trailer rigs to travel with them between Kan and Kou to unearth the cases of ammunition hidden there. He hoped to get the ammunition before it was taken by the new CODOs.

When they arrived in the area, Koulangar discovered that he was nearly too late. Most of the ammunition had already been unearthed by the new CODOs led by Master Sergeant of Customs Ngarguerna. Koulangar and his troops and fighters gathered the remaining cases of ammunition, loaded them into the trucks, and headed back to Moundou. On their way back, they stopped for a while in Bébidja. When I saw Koulangar's bodyguards, I hid myself, fearing that they would want to take me with them to Moundou for military service.

That day, I remembered the bitter reflection of Sublieutenant Daniel that someone who did not know how to write his name had become his boss. I then suspected that Daniel, who had apparently gone back to the *maquis*, might be the leader of these new CODOs.

The following day, I left Bébidja for Doba. The situation was becoming more violent, and I was ready to leave behind the military life and return to my village. When I reached Doba along the way, I heard that Captain Guerngar and Sublieutenant Daniel might be in the *maquis*. People in Doba were worrying that the fighters would once again oppress them because of this new rebellion. I did not want to tarry in Doba because I might be arrested if the fighters knew of my relationship with suspected CODO leaders Guerngar and Daniel — and also because I was young, male, and a Southerner. I went quickly to the Lycée Bernard Dikoa Garandi de Doba and asked for my results. The secretary found my name, and he said my results were fine but my *bulletin* (or transcript) was not yet ready. I told him that I would come next time to take it. Nobody was at our house in Doba, so I quickly continued on my way to the village.

12

Spitting into the Wind

I T WAS A GREAT JOY TO MY FAMILY when I reached home. I went from house to house to greet my relatives. They said they had been expecting me to come back for many days, since Sanabé had left Doba to go to N'djaména. I agreed, Sanabé Abel had left Doba about two weeks before, but at that time, I had not yet finished my school term, and in addition I had wanted to get paid for my military service before coming back home.

I went to the home of my aunt Kôn Mara, who came out from her house and hugged me. She was so happy to see me back home and near to her. After we talked for a while, when I wanted to leave her, she asked me to wait a little bit. Quickly, my aunt prepared a special porridge for me. When I was eating the porridge, my aunt called me again and said, "Toïngar, when I see you I remember my father, Guétingar. When you finish your porridge, you may go and greet your aunt Kôn Moal." I left her and went to my aunt Kôn Moal's house, but she was away. It was later that I came to her house again and experienced a joyful reunion.

In our region people were unhappy that some CODOs had gone back to the *maquis*. Some people asked themselves why the CODOs had, after many months of fighting in the bush without proper weapons, as soon as they had received them from Libya, promptly responded to the call for "reconciliation" by handing over those weapons to Hissène Habré's fighters — and now they want to bring fire

93

and war to the region again? People lamented privately, among their families, but to avoid any betrayal, they did not criticize the CODOs in public.

During that period, we had also noticed the presence of some gunmen who terrorized shopkeepers in the villages. Villagers had been affected not only by the war and terror but also, of course, by famine. The food allowance sent by the United Nations (through the organization named PAM, to help people suffering from the war) arrived at the capital in sufficient quantity, but the distribution of this much-needed food was corrupt. By the time the allowance arrived in Doba, much had already been stolen by those responsible for its distribution, and the local authorities in Doba likewise took their share, for their families or for sale. Perhaps only one third of the original food allowance reached the people for whom it was intended. In the month of July, 1984, a few weeks after my return from Bébidja to the village, the local authorities of Doba grouped at least ten villages in different areas affected by the war to get the food allowance from the United Nations.

My village was among those grouped together with the village Takapti. Early in the morning on the appointed day, most of the residents of Béngamia walked to Takapti to get the allowance. Some refused to go, thinking that maybe it was the government's plan to gather them and kill them. When we arrived, some from our village had friends or relatives in Takapti with whom they could stay for a while, but most who had made the trip were assembled at one end of the market of Takapti, lounging under the mango trees and *caïcédra* trees, the bitter sap of which is the source of quinine. The distributors of the food had driven in by truck before we arrived, unloaded what they intended to distribute at this location onto the ground, and enlisted a couple of young village men to help hand out the grain. Whole or partial bags of wheat would be handed out, depending on family size. The distribution area was located on the veranda of a house facing the road.

About a dozen of Hissène Habré's fighters were there, too. Some were seated with the distributors, some were stationed around the market area, and others lounged under another *caïcédra* tree on the south edge of the market. Maybe the fighters were present for the protection of the distributors and to keep villagers from pushing ahead before they were called, or possibly they had arrived unbidden to get some benefit for themselves. The fighters were in the habit of taking whatever they wanted and killing whoever objected.

The distributors explained the procedure they would follow: when they called one village, the village chief should present himself, and then his people were to follow him to the pile of goods alongside the road and take their allowance. Women had brought their head baskets for carrying goods home. A chief who was not able to speak French or Arabic would need the secretary of the village to be with him to call the people of the village to take their ration.

After serving the villagers of Takapti, the distributors realized that there would not be enough food for all assembled there, so when they called the chiefs of Dôkapti and Maïnanga, and had them sign or mark the register with a thumbprint that they had received full allowance, they called the names of only some of the villagers and then skipped to the next village. People whose names had not been called complained because the distributors had not served all the people and then had moved on. The villages' chiefs and secretaries, who were supposed to defend the rights of their people, were not able to lay claim to their rights in the presence of Hissène Habré's fighters, men who used to terrorize those very people.

When it was our turn, because the chief of Béngamia had not made the trip himself, the man appointed by the chief to come in his place walked over to the distribution area. He had arranged for a man named Ézéchiel to be his secretary that day. Ézéchiel was a man who had been discharged from the military a few years before for a health condition and returned to Béngamia. He summoned the people of the village to line up and come forward to receive their share. The distributors had served only three of the five or six *quartiers* (administrative areas) of Béngamia and then, when they reached the *quartier* of Maïnan that I belonged to, they jumped to another village named Béndana. The representative of our chief did not speak French, so he could not communicate with the distributors, and Ézéchiel, who was supposed to defend the rights of our villagers, was afraid to object to the distributors that some people of our village remained without food. Masrabé, the elder brother of Sanabé Abel, who was the administrative head of our *quartier* of Maïnan, was likewise too timid to defend his people.

One of the starving women of Maïnan, who weak from hunger

and weariness was lying down under a tree very close to the area of ration distribution, called me and said, "My son Toïngar, you who speak the language of white men, go and talk about us to them, because your cousin Masrabé is too timid and will not take action. I do not know what will happen to us if we do not have that ration." I had not realized that people in our village were starving. Perhaps I did not know this because I had been away from the village for some time and because my family always seemed to have food and invite others to eat in our home, too. We were not wealthy, but our relatives were hard workers, good at managing their resources, and generous with each other during hard times. Moreover, they did not waste their money on alcohol. Therefore what this woman said affected me greatly and filled me with compassion for the suffering of our people.

I went to Ézéchiel, who stood very close to our village's representative, and said "Ézéchiel, we have *quartiers* that have not yet been served. You have a list of the *quartiers* in your hands, yet you did not tell the distributors that some people of our village still are empty handed?" Ézéchiel dismissed me as a child and also ordered me to get out of his sight. I quickly realized that though ashamed he was not going to demand rights for the people of Béngamia. The way that the woman was lying down, though, so dispirited and hungry, made me determined to help the remain *quatiers* of Béngamia to get their rightful food.

I walked out into the center of the yard to address the distibutors, who sat on the veranda to observe how the two local young men were doing their job of food distribution. When I addressed them in French and tried to explain the matter to them, Ézéchiel grabbed my arm and attempted to pull me back. When I tried to shake off his hand, one of Hissène Habré's fighters put the barrel of his rifle on my chest and pushed me back with it. I just pushed the rifle aside, knowing that it was not appropriate military behavior to put even an unloaded weapon against a civilian's chest, but he continued in my direction and pushed me in the chest again with his Belgian-made SIG. Again I pushed the barrel of his rifle away with my left hand. He poked his rifle into my chest again, and I pushed it off again. As I had spoken to Ézéchiel and then to the distributors in French, one of Hissène Habré's fighters (perhaps he had been in the regular military at one time) listened to me and understood what I said. Because he was standing not far from

Ézéchiel, he stepped between the other fighter and me and spoke to his colleague in Arabic, telling him to stop pushing me with the barrel of his gun.

Some of the women of my village signaled that I should move away to protect myself from danger. I just crossed the road and stood with my back to the wall of a family compound facing the distributors. One fighter was angry and agitated and asked the people in the square, "Who is that boy that was not afraid of us?" As Ézéchiel had served in the military in the North, he understood Arabic and answered him that I was the bodyguard of a high leader of the CODOs. Perhaps he thought he was doing me a favor. Because he did not specify that I was with the CODOs who had reconciled with the government, though, and also failed to mention that the man I body-guarded was at that time in the capital with Hissène Habré, their leader, the fighters apparently assumed I was an agent of the CODOs in the bush, sent to provoke them into a fight. Whatever the reason, the fighters used the message of Ézéchiel as an opportunity to end my life.

Massal, my cousin, was a wife of a military policeman and had traveled a lot with her husband in different areas of Chad, so she understood many languages spoken in the country. She heard one of the fighters tell the others in Arabic to surround me and make sure that I did not escape. When the fighters moved away to take positions to surround me, Massal started crying and called out in Gor to the villagers, "Who among you is man enough to save my brother? Nobody among you will save our brother?" I saw Massal crying and the other women shaking their hands, which usually symbolized helplessness in the face of some terrible tragedy or imminent death. I looked at them and thought maybe it was because the fighter had pushed me with the barrel of his rifle that they were crying.

Koïngar, one of my cousins, risked his life for mine. He put his hands in his pants pockets and walked casually along the road from east to west, past where I stood. When he passed very close to me, intentionally looking away from me, he spoke quietly out of the side of his mouth and said, "It is you that they are surrounding." When he said that, I looked around and saw myself already ringed with fighters.

I was standing with my back to the wall not far from the gate, so I slipped through the gate and then immediately ran to the far side of the compound and jumped over the wall on the other side. By the time the fighters had entered through the gate and searched through the yard all the way to the house, I was on the other side of the wall, creeping away through the tall grasses. While some were looking for me behind the house, others were searching inside the house. It apparently did not occur to them that I could have vaulted over so high a wall in so short a time. (It is still somewhat incredible to me that I was able to do so.) It was only later, after their search of the compound had turned up nothing, that one of them had the idea that I might have jumped over the wall. Even those who suspected that might have been my escape were not sure I could have gone over the wall, because it was perhaps six feet high. When they looked over the wall, they realized that the barbed and spiny grasses were very high and growing tightly together, so nobody wanted to take the risk of going very far into the overgrown area, prime habitat for snakes and hidden CODOs, to look for me.

When the fighters returned to the market without having found me, they arrested Koïngar, forced him to kneel, and asked him why he had told me to run away. Koïngar denied that he had tipped me off and said he had not told me anything. He spoke to them in Gor. One of the fighters kicked his back with his military boot and ordered him to speak Arabic. One of the distributors was nearby, someone from our region who spoke French, Sara and Arabic. He volunteered to translate for both Koïngar and the fighters. What saved Koïngar that day was that he said: "I do not know him, the guy you were talking about. I did not pay any attention to him when I passed. How did I know you were looking for him? I speak neither French nor Arabic, so how could I understand what you are saying to each other and then warn him to run away?" Confronted by the logic of his argument, the fighters released Koïngar.

Then the fighters asked the two young men of Takapti who had been hired to hand out the rations to go look for me. Perhaps the fighters feared that I had been sent by the CODOs to lead them into an ambush, or maybe they thought I would be less suspicious if these boys sought me than if they sent fighters. As the two young men knew all the villages around, they agreed to take the road to Dôkapti to see if they could find me. Samuel Adoumbaye, a cousin of my mother, was living in Takapti at that time and overheard the fighters' plans. He followed the young men and told them that if they captured me for those fighters, their family would have to fight his. The guys answered that they were not so stupid as to arrest me for the fighters. They were just pretending to follow the fighters' orders.

Meanwhile after I had crept through the grass for about thirty meters, I stopped moving for a few seconds. When I did not hear the noise of any movement close to me, I stood up partway and ran for a while bent forward. About two hundred meters from the wall, I figured I was out of range of the fighters' rifles, so I picked up speed and really ran. I continued running through the bush all the way to the river that separated Takapti and Dôkapti. I came very close to the road and hid myself, trying to catch my breath. As I waited there for a few minutes, I had time to think through what had happened and ponder the right action to take now. In the end, I decided to go back to Takapti. This was for two reasons. First, I did not see myself as guilty of anything but claiming rights for my people. If they wanted to kill me for that, I would give myself up to them. Second, I was worried that the fighters would torture or kill many people because of my actions. Therefore I preferred to go back and pay the price myself for my intervention.

As I boldly walked the road back to Takapti, I saw my cousin Ndouda. He had left Takapti for Béngamia to inform me that the fighters had sent people to come and arrest me. This was the cousin who was always serious and responsible and had been entrusted by the family to discipline the younger members. He was tall and strong, an elder of my family that I had to obey. When he saw me coming toward him, he ordered me to stop where I was, turn around in the other direction, and head for Béngamia. As our tradition required, I followed his instructions and did what he ordered me to do. I walked in front, and he walked behind me. When we had crossed the river on the road between Takapti and Dôkapti, Ndouda told me to emerge from the river walking backward, so that we would leave no footprints leading away from the river. Both of us walked backward for ten to twenty meters, and then we entered the bush. Ndouda cut some leaves of a tree and stepped away so I could not see what else he might be doing. Then while he held the leaves in his hand, we waited for ten or twenty minutes, and rain started pouring down, accompanied by a strong wind. I do not know how this happened, but we were not soaked by the rain. It rained just behind and in front of us until we crossed Dôkapti and Ndouda went to the bush to hide or throw away the leaves. A few minutes later, the rain stopped, and we continued on our way to Béngamia.

When we arrived home, I went to my aunt Kôn Mara's house to tell her what had happened to me in Takapti. I explained to her point by point the problem that I had with Ézéchiel and Hissène Habré's fighters. Then I explained to her how I had walked under the rain with Ndouda without getting wet. My aunt laughed at me and said, "You did not know that you are from the family of lion-men? During the time of your grandfather, he used the rain before, during, and after a fight. This power came from his great-great-grandparents and was transferred to him. From him we got it, and from us some of you younger people got it. The time will come when you will get this power, too, and you will give it to your children, and so on. All those things were supposed to come to your father, who was supposed to be in charge of our generation, but he rejected this power because he claimed that he was a Christian, a man of God."

My escape from that terrible arrest was explained by people in different ways. Kôn Mara clearly considered my escape to be a natural family occurrence. Animists and other non–Christians thought I had the power to disappear; some people who knew that I was from the family of lion-men said I used the darkness to escape; and Christians said that I had been saved by God. I personally think it was God who saved me that day.

The villagers meanwhile had strongly criticized Ézéchiel for telling the fighters that I was the bodyguard of a CODO leader and thereby endangering my life. Ézéchiel and the man who had repre-sented the village's chief were afraid for their safety. Even before they returned home to Béngamia, they presented their excuses to my rela-tives and the other villagers. Ézéchiel tried to calm tensions by claim-ing that the fighters had not understood what he had said. He was only trying to answer their question about why I was not afraid of their guns, by letting them know it was because I had formerly been with the CODOs, before the reconciliation.

To be prudent, after the problem at Takapti, I did not sleep in my house. Sometimes I stayed in the bush, and sometimes I spent the night with my aunt. By not staying in one place, I hoped to avoid being arrested. A nephew of mine named Dan-ngar, my cousin Michel, and I decided to leave Béngamia for Sarh. Michel and I had to ask permission of our Aunt Kôn Mara to allow us to travel to Sarh. Our aunt wanted to deny our request, but we argued our case. If we stayed in the village, not only would the fighters want to arrest us for our previous association with the CODOs — some of whom now had returned to the *maquis*— and for that problem at Takapti, but also we had deserted our units, co-led by CODO and fighter officers, after receiving our pay, as so many other CODOs had done. In our opinion, the safest course was to leave the Oriental Logon for a while and then return home later.

Our Aunt Kôn Mara wanted to know what exactly we were going to do or become in Sarh. I said I wanted to join my cousin Sublieutenant Tomal Alain in Sarh and attend the *lycée* in that town. (I did not mention the possibility of attending the military school at Sarh, although I considered that to be a good second option if it turned out to be safer to be in rather than out of the military.) I would be gone for only one year. If peace returned to our region, so could I.

Michel said he wanted to join some of our distant relatives that had fled the neighboring county of Bodo. They had run away more than twenty years before to escape the hardships of working under a traditional chief who was truly evil. These relatives now lived in the area around Dan-madja. He, too, said he would be back as soon as there was peace in our region. Our aunt considered our requests and our explanations and said that she would make a judgment later.

Two days later, when we had a family meeting, our relatives agreed that Michel and I could leave our region for our own safety, but they commanded us to be back as soon as there was peace. Our aunt was the last to give her final approval and asked me to be with her for two or three days before we left.

During my first night of this visit with my aunt, Kôn Mara, she shared with me a variety of stories regarding our family. She especially wanted me to know how my father's father, my grandfather Guétingar, successfully used his traditional powers to right the wrongs of his neighbors, even going to distant villages to defend their interest and to rectify matters. This meant that eventually he became known as the lionman who was defending his friends. Eventually, he was targeted for attack by the enemies of his friends.

It was rare for my grandfather to sleep inside a house. He usually slept outside on his traditional bed made of dry wood, positioned in the midst of the houses of his wives so as to protect with his vigilance the entire family compound. He had as his constant companion a big male dog, and always beside his bed was a supply of traditional tobacco for his pipe. During the rainy season, he and his dog did take shelter in the night. They slept in a special hut that was really only a roof, and of course he took his tobacco bag. He did those things for many reasons.

One of the reasons Guétingar slept in the open was that he did not want any of his enemies to sneak up on him and attack him in the night. Or perhaps an enemy might put his black magic in the area to kill him or a member of his family. Another reason was that most of his lionman friends visited him in their secret place in the area. So from time to time his friends came to his traditional place, his *nôn ndôʾt*, where he wore his lion skin. When his friends roared, he would take his tobacco and join them. There they smoked together and made their agreements on a variety of issues. After these parleys, the men would continue their trip to accomplish whatever mission they had undertaken, or they returned home. My grandfather was thus able to keep tabs on the whereabouts and activities of all the lionmen. On his way to the *nôn ndôʾt* or on his way back home, my aunt said, his big dog patrolled the path ahead of him.

According to my aunt, the big dog who accompanied my grandfather had a variety of ways to signal him. When some kind of danger was coming, the dog would warn his friend by continuously making noises. Guétingar would thus be able to prepare himself in advance for human or magical enemies. If the dog made noise and then stopped, that signified something else; the danger approaching Guétingar's territory had stopped, retreated, or passed by without success. (Kôn Mara implied that men of magic could sense my grandfather's power and of course could hear the dog and thus would know that he was well protected.) Then my grandfather would know it was safe to go back to his traditional bed.

My grandfather was sometimes ambushed on the road or near his millet fields by his enemies. He had, though, a special secret — a special power — to outwit them. Wherever he went, he always carried with him his bag of what the French call "armes blanches" — his blades — our traditional cutting tools shaped like arm-length scythes and forged from steel. My grandfather carried several in a bag, called *wam mieh*. When he was working in his field, he put his *wam mieh* on the earth ahead of him. As he worked down the row and reached the area where he had deposited the bag, he pushed it a little bit farther ahead and worked forward again until he finished his work. The reason he did that, instead of putting the bag in a nearby tree, was to be ready in case he was attacked. He wanted to be ever ready to react quickly. Guétingar's enemies were not able to outwit him through ambush his entire life. Men did attack him in his fields. They usually made the mistake of shouting, "We got you!" when they threw their spear at him or attacked him with their *mieh*.

My aunt said when someone attacked her father and said, "Jim in roï't nôn," meaning "My hand is on you," even when they were sure that their weapon would kill him, Guétingar would retort, "a ta rang el, na a le ngô, meaning, "Make sure before saying that. Your weapon may strike a tree and ricochet back to harm you." His attacker would be surprised to see his *mieh* or *ningeh* stuck on the dry wood somewhere. And then my grandfather would counterattack, Kôn Mara said.

My aunt ended our first night by telling me how my grandfather defeated his family-in-law. My grandpa wanted to marry a third wife. The woman lived far away from his area. The brothers of that woman were well known as a strong family in their region, and these men refused to let their sister marry a lionman. Guétingar, who felt disappointed at the reaction of his future brothers-in-law, asked why they had not told him from the beginning that they disapproved of the match.

During that time, fearing that my grandfather would steal her away, the woman's brothers put her in their midst before they slept, and even at night they were well armed. This was to protect their sister from my grandpa. Guétingar sent a message to them that he did not have any problem with them. He considered them his in-laws. He just wanted their sister to be his wife. The family of the woman said if he were a man he could have their daughter. This last sentence made my grandfather mad, and he replied to this family that he had come accompanied by other people when he had asked them to let their daughter be his wife, but now he would come alone to take her. He did not tell them when he should be expected.

While the woman's family were preparing and waiting for him and his band of lionmen, my grandpa went to his *nôn ndô't*, his secret place in the bush, and put on his lion skin. He traveled far away to the village of the woman he wanted for his wife. When he arrived at the family compound of the woman, all her protectors were sleeping. My grandpa took his wife to Béngamia without any resistance. The pretended protectors still slept—until Guétingar went to his secret place and removed his lion skin. Then the spell was broken, and the pretended protectors awakened, at around noon. Later Guétingar sent a message to his new in-laws that he was indeed a real man and that he had a real wife with him. A few months later, his new family-in-law still did not know what to do, so they finally asked for reconciliation.

The second night my aunt told the history of the conflicts and alliances that our family had in our region. And the third day she spoke of other traditions and some of the herbs and roots of trees that we could use for our protection and health. My aunt told me that many were the things that she could not share with me because I had refused to be a lion-man—and not only that but also the time was very short, so not all her knowledge could be shared with me. She promised to prepare me and show me many things when I should return from Sarh.

I thanked my aunt for all her teaching. The next morning Michel, Dan-ngar, and I left for Sarh.

13

Seeking Safety in Sarh

Early in the morning, Michel and I met Dan-ngar at his house, and then we walked together to the village of Kokat, which is situated on the main road from Doba to Sarh. We hoped to catch a ride on a vehicle heading for our destination. During that time there were uncontrollable CODOs in the region. Sometimes they stole money from shopkeepers or travelers. They were not like the fighters who terrorized our villages, burning and killing, but only took money and cigarettes. Dan-ngar had heard about those CODOs, but he had not told us. To keep his money safe in case we encountered any of these rogue CODOs, he hid all his money inside his underpants.

When we were about two miles (3 km) from Béngamia on our way to Kokat, Dan-ngar asked us to give him one thousand CFAs, and when we reached Kokat, he would return it to us. I wondered why Dan-ngar asked us to do this, since as a bachelor and shopkeeper he surely had enough money for the trip, and why would he return the money in Kokat? He would not tell us why he wanted a loan for only a few kilometers, and we hesitated to ask questions that might embarrass him. I agreed to lend him one thousand CFAs, and he put the bill in his pocket.

To avoid being interrogated and delayed by our relatives in Babo, when we arrived very close to the village, we took a path that bypassed Babo and led to Bégada, where we were careful also not to visit our uncle, the father of Sanabé Abel, who would try to detain us. From there we continued our trip. Arriving in Béangô late in the morning, we went to the home of another uncle to ask for water to drink. Unfortunately, nobody was at home, so we continued on our way to Kokat.

Kokat was deserted, and we realized that the villagers were hiding in the bush for their safety. This was because the village was only about 18 kilometers from Doba, where the fighters were headquartered. From Doba fighters could easily make quick raids on surrounding villages. A thought came to me, and I asked the others if we should leave Kokat and go instead to Bédôgô One, because we did not know precisely why the people of Kokat were not at home. Not only that, but also Kokat was part of Oriental Logon, where the fighters held power, and Bédôgô One was under control of Moyen Chari and therefore better protected from fighter raids. Without hesitating, Michel and Dan-ngar agreed with me to move forward to the village of Bédôgô One, where my cousin Michel's mother had come from, in Moyen Chari's area.

When we arrived in Bédôgô One, the three of us went to the house of Michel's uncle to greet him. He was not at home. He had gone to the fields with all of his family except one daughter, Madjidéné, who was at home preparing the meal for her family to eat when they returned from the fields. The girl was very beautiful, with long, gleaming black hair. Her skin was light brown, and her round face bore nine marks of initiation — three on her forehead and three on each cheek. When she smiled, her teeth were very white and her gums very black, a sign of great beauty.

When she went to fetch us water and groundnuts, I said to Michel that when our region got peace and we came back to the village, I would like to marry his cousin. Michel just smiled. To me it was not a joke. I told him that I was serious about what I said. Michel said there was no problem if I wanted to be his cousin and also his brother-in-law, but if we had a child, he wouldn't know what he should call that child.

Dan-ngar, in support of my position, said, "I don't see a problem. If the child is with his father, you call him or her *ngônoum* (my son or my daughter). If the child is with the mother, you call him or her *nanoum* (son or daughter of my sister). Now, in case you meet the child with both parents, call it *ngônoum-nanoum or nanoum-ngônoum*." We laughed at Dan-ngar's very diplomatic solution to this hypothetical problem.

We continued chatting and nibbling on groundnuts as we left the compound and returned to the road to wait and stop any civilian vehicle that came from Doba and was heading to Koumra or Sarh. We waited there for several hours, during which time Michel's cousin prepared porridge and brought it to us. I said to her, "You are a wonderful creature, and I have never seen anyone like you in my life. I would like to marry you and take you to live with me near your Aunt Marie, where you would not have to be alone in the world. You would be my first and last wife." She just smiled and went back home to cook for her family.

While we were finishing the porridge, we stopped a truck going directly to Sarh with a load of goods and about a dozen passengers already. When the driver asked us to pay before getting into the vehicle, Dan-ngar went behind a mango tree (as we found out later, it was to pull out the money hidden in his underpants) and when he came back, paid for his transportation and returned the one-thousand CFA bill that he had borrowed from me. We were just about to leave when the girl came and took back her empty porridge tureen and calabash spoon, and we climbed into the back of the open truck. I was sorry to note that she did not seem upset that we were leaving.

We had left Bédôgô One for Sarh. We were terrified that fighters along the way would ask us for our Ids. None of us had ID's. I had lost my student identification card and had failed to replace it. We had as identification only our birth certificates. When we arrived in Bédaya, it was late at night, and the military police would not allow us to continue our trip to Sarh. (This was their way not of maintaining security but of obtaining money from drivers willing to bribe them to travel on.) All of us passengers slept atop the truck, and early the next morning the military policeman processed our vehicle. He asked us all to show our national identity cards. Without identification, it was hard to cross the barrier at Bédaya, but we were lucky that that day the officer controlling the barrier was a regular military police officer from the South rather than a fighter from the North. The fighters tended to patrol in the evening and probably were still in bed so early in the morning. When he asked us for our ID, I told him that we had only our certificates of birth and were intending to get our Ids in Sarh once we arrived there. At that time Michel and I were under age 18, the age at which the national ID was required, but we were still expected to have a school or other form of identification. Luckily there were no fighters here to demand money to let us past without official Ids. This man accepted our explanation, did not demand a bribe, and let us cross the barrier.

The other checkpoints we came to in Guéré and Balimba would have been dangerous to cross during the previous months, because the fighters persecuted men and young women as CODOs and enemy sympathizers. However, because the CODO-Rouge (Red CODOs) had signed a ceasefire with the government, there was a temporary peace. In addition, the CODO-Rouge had their base in Sarh, not far from Guéré and Balimba, and therefore were in control of the entire area.

Our driver entered Sarh on the road that passed by the front of a government military base named G4, the headquarters for Military Zone Six. We were traveling slowly, partly because this was the rainy season and the roads were not good, and partly because fighters stationed at military bases often shot at vehicles that zoomed by too fast. As we rode past the main entrance of G4, we saw Djadngar, a young man from our village, on guard duty in front of the main entrance. We were very excited to see him. Dan-ngar called his name twice, and from atop the vehicle we waved our hands to hail him. Although he saw the three of us on the vehicle and was excited to see us, he just smiled. He could not wave, nor could he otherwise respond to our greetings, because he was on duty.

When we arrived in the central market of Sarh, which was the final destination for our vehicle, we got down, unloaded our bags, and quickly set off to the home of our aunt, Kôn Pierre Tokinôn, maybe two miles (3 km) away. Sarh is the second largest city in Chad, and Dan-ngar had to lead us, because he was most familiar with the city. We spent a short time at our aunt's home, where we left our bags, and then we went back to G4 to see Djadngar. When we arrived at G4, he had just finished his two hours of guard duty. Seeing us from twenty meters away, he ran to us and hugged each of us. He took us to his barracks and asked about his family and other relatives. We let him know that everything had been peaceful when we left. Of course, something good or bad might have happened after we had left. After spending about two hours with Djadngar, we left the base to head back to Kôn Pierre Tokinôn's house, and Djadngar, now off duty, accompanied us.

As we walked through the streets of the city, I asked Djadngar about Sublieutenant Tomal Alain and other friends that I suspected might be in Sarh. Djadngar said Tomal Alain had led his unit to the subprefecture of Maro about three weeks before. I was miserably unhappy when I heard that bad news, because I had been hoping he could get me into the *lycée* or possibly the military high school. I asked Djadngar how many units of CODOs were left in Sarh, and he said that two units, mixed with few fighters, remained — Unit Six led by Sublieutenant Ngarkada, and Unit Nine led by Sublieutenant Moueba.

As Tomal Alain was not in Sarh, it was hard for me to decide what to do. I did not think I should stay with Kôn Pierre Tokinôn. She was a widow, and her son, Pierre Tokinôn, was leader of the CODO-Rouge, stationed with his troops in the suburbs of Sarh. I did not want to impose on her. Dan-ngar asked us if it would be possible for us to continue to a village nearby where we had many relatives. I said, "Well, you and Michel could go to the village, but for me, I would like to find a way to salvage my year of school, even in Tomal Alain's absence."

Djadngar said it was time for him to go back to his base. We escorted him for a while and continued talking before we turned back for Kôn Pierre Tokinôn's house. During the night, we discussed whether it was better for us to go to the village or to join the army. Dan-ngar preferred that we either go to the village or join CODO-Rouge, led by Pierre Tokinôn.

I said to him that I did not wish to join these new CODOs, because they had signed a ceasefire with the government, and probably a few weeks later they would be sent to the North, just as our colleagues in Doba had been sent there. Or they might return to the *maquis*, in which case it would be hard for us to get food to eat. Dan-ngar said in reply that we had a lot of relatives in the Moyen Chari area that would feed us in case the CODO-Rouge went back to the *maquis*. I asked him, in case they wanted to take us to the North, what would happen to us then? We asked Michel for his opinion, and he said that whatever we decided, he would do.

We lay on our mats for a while without saying anything, thinking about what we should do, and then I gave them my last proposal, saying that Ngarkada and Moueba knew me, so they might let us join their units. In addition, their units were providing security for Sarh and therefore were not likely to be reassigned to the North. If we stayed in Sarh, I could try to continue my schooling. Therefore we should join their units. In case we did not feel comfortable with the kinds of orders we were given, we could always go to the village nearby where our relatives lived and wait until peace came to our region back home. Both Michel and Dan-ngar agreed with me, and we slept well that night, certain of the direction we would take in the morning.

The three of us went to Ngarkada's office the next day to let him know that we were former CODOs wanting to join his unit because our former units had been assigned elsewhere while we were gone from Doba. Because Ngarkada recognized me, he accepted me into his unit, but he refused to give Michel and Dan-ngar a chance to join his troops. Apparently he thought they should have stuck with their old unit when it was reassigned.

Michel and Dan-ngar then went to Moueba's office and pleaded their case to him, but Moueba likewise refused to admit them to his unit, saying that he had already submitted the list of his troops to the commander of Zone Six. Because our decision the previous night had been to join a unit together, it was hard for us to make a common decision now. Should Michel and Dan-ngar stay in Sarh with our aunt, join Pierre Tokinôn's CODO-Rouge forces, or go instead to the village nearby? Dan-ngar said that he wanted to go to the village. I asked the two of them to stay in town, though, and be patient and wait for me for two weeks, so that I could analyze my situation in Ngarkada's unit. I hoped that I could be considered a child-soldier (*enfant de troupes*), with an assignment to complete high school and then officer training, or at least that I could continue both with the army and school. If there were no way for me to continue with my schooling while in the military. If this didn't work out, though, I would continue with my cousins to the village. I did not want them to go on to the village without me, because I had no idea of how to get there.

My two companions took my requests into consideration. They continued to sleep in the house of Kôn Pierre Tokinôn for two weeks, and I stayed with my unit at G4's base. A week later, we got the news from Doba through some travelers. They said that the entire Oriental Logon was in serious upheaval, especially the areas of Bodo, Bébôtô, and Gôré. The travelers said that the CODOs who had returned to the *maquis,* the rebellion, controlled many parts of this area and were very close to Doba. They said that the CODOs might well be in full control of Doba by then, for all they knew.

14

He Was Called Ngarguerna

B Y THE END OF MAY AND BEGINNING of June, 1984, most of the CODOs clearly knew that they had been betrayed by their leaders. These CODOs were bitter about this betrayal and tried to find some possibility of returning to the *maquis*. I heard only part of the conversation when Ngarguerna discussed with Sanabé his intention to restart the rebellion. Sanabé, who analyzed the benefits and consequences of this potential action, encouraged Ngarguerna in his intention. Little by little Ngarguerna got in touch with other officers like Djobay, Adil, Daniel, Mbaïndag-djé, Guerngar, and others, including both sub-officers and troops. After a brief consultation with the people above, Ngarguerna left Doba for Bodo without the permission of his superior officers. This was the beginning of the new CODO.

Some officers followed Ngarguerna immediately, while others waited until they got paid before joining him. A few weeks later, after Ngarguerna knew he could trust his comrades, the neo–CODO added to its ranks and carried away some of the ammunition that had been hidden between Kou and Kan late in September of 1983. Before he could retrieve all of that ammunition, Koulangar, the former commander of the CODOs, took the fighters and the CODOs who had followed him and led them to the cache of hidden ammunition. They took away all that remained.

Ngarguerna, who was a very active man, fearless and highly motivated, had been appointed by the others as their leader. By the time he became leader of the neo–CODOs, he had made many travels around his zone. On these trips he gathered information and assured villagers of his intention to liberate them from oppression by the fighters.

One day Ngarguerna was on such a mission and stopped at his sister's house, saying that he wanted to take a bath before continuing on his travels. His sister took water at the bathing area and let him know that the water was ready for him. Ngarguerna left his secret *gris-gris* bag where he had been sitting and went to take his bath. His sister thought that he kept his money in his secret bag, so she was trying to open it and to take some of the money for herself while he was taking his bath. Even without being able to see what she was doing, Ngarguerna felt the intention of his sister and told her not to put her hand in his bag. When he said that, his sister already had her hand in his bag. Ngarguerna, who could foresee his own doom as a result of his sister's action, told his sister, "You have already killed me." Ngarguerna's bodyguards were there, but they had done nothing to stop her.

A few weeks later, Ngarguerna went for a meeting with fellow CODOs to the region of Moïssala. After their meeting, Ngarguerna and his followers left that region to return to the Bodo region. On their way back, he realized that his secret bag had disappeared. They turned back to where the meeting had taken place, but his comrades there said they had not seen his bag. The life of young Ngarguerna now spun out of control.

Ngarguerna went to the man who had prepared the *gris-gris* for him and confessed to him that he had lost what had been given to him. His talisman-maker reminded him that from the beginning he had told him to be very careful with what he was going to give him. The man said it took him about ten years to gather together what he had given him. He certainly did not have an extra *gris-gris* for him. This was a hard time for Ngarguerna, but there was nothing he could do to acquire the kind of protection he had received before.

When Ngarguerna arrived at his base after this bad trip to the region of Moïssala, together with his assistant officers he decided to attack the fighter bases in the canton of Bodo and the neighboring administrative post of Bébôtô. These bases had been well reinforced by fighters who had taken notice of the activity of neo–CODOs in the region. Bodo and Bébôtô were attacked by the neo–CODOs during the rainy season, perhaps September or October of 1984. The attack on Bodo was difficult to coordinate, but the CODOs were determined to take control of that county. Their victory over Bodo gave more ammunition and guns to the neo–CODO troops.

Immediately after CODOs took control of Bodo, sublieutenant Mbaïndag-djé asked his comrades to go liberate his own county of Bébôtô. Mbaïndag-djé was worried about the reinforcement of fighter contingents that would come from Doba to destroy that county and particularly his village of Dôh. The other officers wanted to wait a little bit before attacking Bébôtô, but Mbaïndag-djé did not give them time to plan. Angry at being pushed into another battle so quickly but finding it necessary to accommodate Mbaïndang-djé's urgent demands, Ngarguerna gave orders to attack Bébôtô.

Not only were the fighters of Bébôtô well prepared, but they had also welcomed reinforcements from Doba as soon as they knew that Bodo had fallen into the hands of their enemies. Ngarguerna and his men attacked Bébôtô. After many hours of fighting, the unit commanded by Ngarguerna was nearly out of ammunition. Luckily right then Ngarguerna's unit received reinforcements from another unit that heard the noise of their attack and quickly came to help. It was that new unit of men who gave victory that day to Ngarguerna's unit.

Almost all of the fighters in Bébôtô were killed in that attack by the neo–CODOs. After the victory of his neo–CODO troops, Ngarguerna with a few of his officers and bodyguards were counting the dead bodies of the fighters. One of the fighters, who had hidden himself on a branch in a mango tree in that area, shot Ngarguerna with his rifle. Ngarguerna fell down, shortly to die, and one of his bodyguards almost automatically raised his rifle and shot dead the fighter who had killed his boss. Before Nguarguerna breathed his last air, he clasped his two hands together and indicated that the neo–CODO should move quickly forward in the direction he was moving his hands. He could not speak.

Then it was the end of the life of the man who had brought the CODOs back to life. The neo–CODOs had counted on him for the final victory, but now they would have to continue without him. After Ngarguerna's death, the neo–CODOs almost lost their courage, but they still harassed greatly the fighters who now were allied with the old CODOs.

15

The Reconquest
of Bodo

AFTER THE VICTORY OF THE NEO–CODOs over the fighters stationed in Bodo and Bébôtô, Koulangar — the former commander of the old CODO who had now become the commander of government fighters in Zone Five (including the prefectures of Tandjilé, Oriental Logon, and Occidental Logon) went to Bodo to effect a reprisal against the neo–CODOs. On his way from Doba, he was ambushed by the troops of Jacques Tôlngar in Bérô. Koulangar fought hard to resist that ambush but lost some of his soldiers in the fighting. Among those whom he lost, the one man who figured most prominently was his well-loved bodyguard, Mbala, who was a cousin of Jacques Tôlngar.

Mbala was not lucky; it seems that he received the first bullet fired by the troops of his cousin in the attack on Koulangar's vehicles. The fighters loyal to Koulangar leaped out of the Land Rovers at the first volley and quickly assumed battle positions on the road and behind trees. They were desperately firing their weapons at the neo–CODO attackers and called to Mbala to get down and fight with them. They did not realize at first that he had received the first bullet and had died even before the others could respond to the attack. It was only after the neo–CODO troops had run out of ammunition and retreated from the area of ambush that Koulangar and his followers realized Mbala had perished.

After the attack, Jacques Tôlngar continued his way to Bédio and went to the hut of Mbala's mother. He said to her, "My aunt, my cousin Mbala and his boss ran across our line of troops today, and fighting broke out. I do not know what may have happened to him." Apparently at that time he did not realize that Mbala had been killed. It was not until a few days later that Mbala's mother heard about the death of her son in the battle with the neo–CODOs led by her nephew. Whether or not it was a bullet from Jacques' rifled that killed Mbala, I call this the killing of a cousin by a cousin.

Sublieutenant Koulangar and Sublieutenant Yaldé, who knew well the areas of Bodo and Bébôtô during their years in rebellion with the CODOs, asked for reinforcements from N'djaména to counter-attack these new CODOs with enough force to ensure success. Koulangar was in charge of the troops, and Yaldé led the special forces, having the power to arrest or have killed anyone who aroused his suspicions. After the merger of the old CODOs with government fighters, Yaldé became especially vicious toward anyone who had had sympathies for the earlier CODOs — and was especially hostile toward anyone with more wealth and goods than he. After getting enough people to feel confident that they could successfully counterattack their enemies, Koulangar and Yaldé came out with the new strategies that were destined to help them to defeat their enemies. Not only did they devise some new, more successful stealth strategies, but they also extracted information from traitors. Thus they were able to win their battles and eventually the war.

By threatening destruction on any who refused him information, Yaldé was able to turn men against their villagers and betray the movements of the neo–CODOs. No longer would the new CODOs be able to move in silence and secrecy through the bush. If anyone knew their whereabouts and activities, that person might well turn traitor and advise Yaldé of their movements.

One new stealth strategy the fighters now employed was to muffle the loud noise made by their *Véléras*, and they adopted a novel way to accomplish this goal. Koulangar and Yaldé ordered their fighters to use empty tomato boxes attached tightly to the tailpipes of their vehicles to reduce the noise of their exhaust. The troops made very small holes on each box and then covered the tailpipe of each vehicle with this muffler.

Another strategy arose from Koulangar and Yaldé's memory that as CODOs they had usually made their ambushes on the left side of the oncoming line of vehicles. This was an attempt to disable the driver as soon as possible so that the vehicle would no longer be maneuverable and could not avoid the ambush area. Since Koulangar and Yaldé were now fighting on the other side, the sublieutenants devised a plan to counter this CODO strategy.

Thus it was that on their way to Bodo with all the information that they had on the location and movements of the neo–CODOs, Koulangar and his forces sacrificed their drivers by ordering them to drive empty vehicles slowly, at the speed of cameleons, down the road. Meanwhile his forces walked parallel to the road, on the left side of the driver, but at a distance of at least one hundred meters from the road and about one hundred meters behind the vehicles.

When the drivers were ambushed, the neo–CODOs were so busy shooting at those vehicles that they were able to move forward only slowly and with difficulty. Koulangar's forces meanwhile quickly advanced behind their enemies and attacked them from behind. Koulangar's forces could theoretically have overcome the neo–CODOs, because they certainly outnumbered them. Most of Koulangar's forces were fighters, though, rather than former CODOs from the South, and these fighters were physically smaller and weaker than the neo–CODOs, who were tall and strong. The fighters were afraid and did not want to take the risk of attempting to shout out to the neo–CODOs that they had been ambushed from behind and should drop their weapons, raise their arms, and surrender. Instead of arresting the neo–CODOs, the fighters attacked, shooting at their enemies with rifle fire. At this, the neo–CODOs — who were greatly surprised by the bullets coming from behind them — did not wait for their commanders to give orders. All military discipline was forgotten. Luckily the neo–CODOs started running in all different directions — toward the vehicles, along the road ahead and behind, and even back through the enemy lines to reach the CODO base. This produced great confusion among the fighters of the two forces, and most of the neo–CODOs escaped with their lives. Because they had routed the ambushers, the numerous forces of Koulangar who had stayed behind the others and had thus seen no fighting at all in this battle, walked into Bodo with the victory.

Once again the fighters rebuilt their base in Bodo, but this time they did so with more troops and material support. Four to six weeks later, the reinforcements came from Moundou and Doba, led by the son of the area commander, Yaldé. Sublieutenant Yaldé now conceived a plan to attack his own village, Bémbaïtada, and then the rebel base of the neo–CODOs in Kou. They killed many people all along the way to Bémbaïtada and also in the village. (All the events here have been described to me by a villager who barely escaped death in Bémbaïtada and traveled from bush to bush to Sarh.) Between Bémbaïtada and Kou, there was a neo–CODO ambush, deadly on both sides, on December 14 or 15, 1984. Yaldé and Koulangar used nearly the same strategies that had proved so successful on their approach to Bodo. This time, the number of dead on the side of the fighters was greater than that on the neo–CODO side, but what seriously affected the neo–CODO troops was not the number of their dead but that death came to two of their officers in one ambush. Both Adil and Daniel were killed on that day. The latter had been the commandant of my CODO unit in Doba.

CODO officers Adil, Daniel, and Jacques could have saved their lives if they had pulled back immediately after the ambush, as soon as they realized that they were greatly outnumbered. In this battle, too, the fighters had many more heavy weapons than did the neo–CODOs. These officers, though, were not the kind to retreat. They were determined to face their enemies in battle despite the fact that their ammunition was insufficient for more than a few minutes of individual combat.

Daniel died first. To this date I do not know how he died. Some say that he was killed early in the fighting by Koulangar's fighters, while others have told me that he was shot by his own comrades because he tried to run away without signaling to his troops that they should escape and save themselves. He was the first officer to pass away. Then Adil was killed by the shell of a bazooka that landed on his assault rifle. Jacques (not Tôlngar but another Jacques) was wounded in both legs, but his comrades rescued him and hid him in the farm hut of a villager of Bémbaïtada. His comrades designated Ésaïe — commonly called Issaya, who is from Békolo, a village adjacent to Bémbaïtada — with the assistance of a group of neo–CODOs to protect Jacques in case the traitors betrayed his position to the fighters.

Just as suspected, the fighters were soon informed that Jacques was wounded and lay not far away. The fighters headed for the farm hut to attack Jacques and his protectors. When the battle began, some of Jacques' defenders faced the fighters and fought the enemies while the others carried Jacques into the bush and hid him. Then all the defenders ran away from the attack area. No one had been killed, at least on the neo–CODO side, until the fighters set fire to the fields and bush in the area. As usual, they wanted to destroy the villages and all the property of the villagers. Unfortunately, this fire reached the place where Jacques lay hidden. He felt the presence of the fire coming toward him and tried his best to remove all the flammable grass and stubble from the area where he had been hidden. The flames came closer and closer, though, and soon the smoke covered the entire area. He could not breathe, for the fire took all the life-giving oxygen from the air. It was not the fire itself but the smoke of the fire that took his life.

16

Hunting Logon Prey
During the Dry Season

K OULANGAR AND YALDÉ, NATIVES of the Oriental Logon prefecture, did not exterminate their neighbors alone. They were helped by brothers Idriss Déby and Ibrahim Itno from the North. At that time, Idriss Déby was commander-in-chief of the national army forces of Chad. That was their official name, but I refer to them as fighters, because they did not have the appropriate training to be considered an army, and a national army does not massacre its own people. Ibrahim Itno was internal minister in those days. These four men worked together to eliminate the people of the South.

The two former CODOs took the Itnos to their former area of rebellion in the South, determined to destroy anything that moved. Because they were having a hard time finding and fighting the neo–CODOs in the bush, the killers took advantage of the dry season to set fires in many different areas of the region. This went on for two years, and the population suffered greatly. Not only had the people lost their property at home and then their houses, which were burned, but also they lost all their fields of millet, which were damaged by fire. The people were starving and struggled to find safe shelter.

The population of the area, whose goods, homes, and fields had been totally destroyed, now was hunted like mice or rats during the dry season in Chad by the two Itno brothers. While these killers and thieves were laughing and enjoying the property of poor villagers, the people were crying to have lost all their belongings and grieving for beloved family and friends, innocent people who had been killed for no reason.

Some Christians whose belief in God was not very strong asked themselves if God really existed. If He was there, how could He turn his back on His children and let them be tortured and killed? How could He let their churches be burned to the ground like that?

Others, whose belief was stronger, including pastors who traveled through the bush to minister to their scattered flock, said they had read in the Bible that the situation in which we were living was a sign of the second coming of Christ. If this was so, then we needed to prepare ourselves to meet the son of God very soon. Other well-educated Christians asked themselves whether we Christians in Chad worshipped the same God as the majority of Americans and of French people did. If the answer was yes, then how could our brothers and sisters in Christ, living in the West, support Hissène Habré with war *matériel*, political support, and financial resources? How could Christians support a man who wanted to destroy us Christians?

17

Black September of Horrific Memory

E ARLY IN MY SECOND WEEK AT G4, the CODO-Rouge led by
Pierre Tokinôn intercepted an unclear radio message between the
fighters stationed at Sarh and fighters in N'djaména. I suspect that the
message was a plan to attack the CODO-Rouge. The CODO-Rouge
left Sarh and returned to the *maquis* in the middle of the night. The
following morning, when the fighters realized that the CODO-Rouge
were no longer in Doyaba, they alerted the commander of Zone Six,
Captain Bichir Agar, who then informed the different units in his zone
and the central command in N'djaména. Zone Six — and especially
Moyen Chari — were on high alert.

Sarh was now a hell for young men and even some women. Fighters patrolled everywhere, searching for CODOs and CODO sympathizers. They arrested many; some of those arrested never returned
home. Women known to have connections with CODO troops were
taken away to the fighters' houses and raped. Michel and Dan-ngar
realized what danger they were in if they stayed in the home of Pierre
Tokinôn's mother, so they decided to leave Sarh. They would try to
join Pierre Tokinôn and his CODO troops in the *maquis* because without the presence of the CODOs in the region of Sarh, the family village
and other villages in the region would be uninhabitable. Thousands of

people ran to the bush to escape the fighters, and Michel and Dan-ngar ran, too. It was hard for them to locate exactly where the CODO-Rouge might be. They took a chance that Dan-ngar knew the area of Moyen Chari well enough to find his way to the CODOs. He took Michel to the village named Saco and from there to the village where our relatives lived.

A curfew was immediately imposed from evening to morning in Moyen Chari. Since the CODOs had returned to the *maquis*, no fighters or regular military personnel were allowed to live off base. We troops were all stationed in the bases and camps or sent to other sectors to ambush CODOs in case they tried to attack Sarh. The fighters that went out a few kilometers from Sarh to attack CODOs were always defeated. To console themselves for these defeats, they killed as many unarmed and defenseless civilians as they could, on the assumption that all Southerners were CODOs, relatives of CODOs, supporters of CODOs, or spies. Even regular military troops from the South were murdered by the fighters. The region became a war theater of the kind people had not seen since the country achieved its independence from France. When fighters took the roads out of Sarh to seek out CODO units, they found themselves ambushed and bloodily slaughtered by CODO troops. As the situation of the fighters became more and more desperate, any men or women that they met would be killed and often tortured before being killed. Hundreds of people in and out of Sarh were deprived of their property and their lives. Any house where the fighters found boys, young men, adult men, even men in their 80's, was considered a house of CODO, and all within would be brutally murdered. My section of the unit was never sent outside Sarh but reserved for internal patrols. The fighters made sure our unit did not have many weapons or much ammunition, and a few Southern members of our unit — even officers who had served with the fighters before and after reconciliation with the CODOs — were arrested and killed.

A few days later, more than 150 presidential security fighters were sent to Sarh by Hissène Habré. Even before reaching Sarh, these security forces had killed many civilians between Moyen Chari and Tandjilé. When the unit arrived in Balimba, the fighters shot one of their heavy guns three times in the direction of Sarh. I suspect that they thought Sarh was under the control of CODO troops. Sublieutenant

Ngarkada, who was in the commander's office on the first floor of the building in G4 when he heard the guns, ran quickly down the stairs and ordered his troops who had guns to take position. As there was no hostile reaction from Sarh, twenty or thirty minutes later the presidential security unit entered peacefully into the city. I was on guard duty at the main entrance of G4 that day and saw a squadron of Sarh military police in armored all-terrain vehicles directing the presidential security unit to base G4.

After unloading their Toyota and Véléras, one of the bodyguards and drivers of the commander of the presidential security unit walked over to one of my fellow CODO soldiers named Jacob. The bodyguard asked Jacob in French if he would take him into town so that he could get something to drink. Jacob understood French but was not able to speak it fluently, so he called me to come over. He introduced me to the bodyguard, who asked me if I could take him to town. I said to him that I would be happy to take him to town, but we were not allowed to leave base, and I was also on guard duty. As he came from far away and was our guest at the base, he could ask my section chief to make an exception to the rules. I took him to my section chief, and the bodyguard talked to him for a short time. The chief gave me permission to go with the bodyguard at the end of guard duty at 6:30 p.m.

That evening we walked downtown and visited two or three bars. The commander's bodyguard was probably between eighteen and twenty years old at the time. We were in civilian dress, and the bodyguard kept his pistols in his right sock and left waistband. We could stay only a few hours, because at that time there was a curfew after 10:00 p.m. The bodyguard was from Ouaddaï, but he spoke Gourane, Arabic, and French. At the last bar we visited, we met a young woman who agreed to share a table with us. A few minutes later her friend joined her at our table. A group of young men from the North who were taking their beers to the other corner ordered the young women to join their table. My companion asked the young women in French not to join them, and he said that this kind of people, who ordered others around, made Hissène Habré look bad.

Two of the Northerners waited a moment to see if the young women would join them. Seeing that the women were not leaving our table, these two men came over to force the women to go with them. My companion started speaking angrily to them in Gourane, the language of the North and of the President, and the guys who had come over with the intention of threatening us instead left the bar. My companion ordered another drink for us, and one of the young women invited us to her house to eat the macaroni that she had prepared. After finishing our drinks, we went to her house.

Hissène Habré's fighters saw themselves as masters of the South. In typical fashion, one armed fighter had hidden himself behind the *caïcédra* tree not very far from the bar that we were leaving. As people left the bar to go to their houses, the fighter stopped them and "collected" their money. When we came close to his tree, we heard the clatter as he engaged his rifle, then saw him suddenly standing in our way. He ordered us to give him all the money we had or we would lose our lives. My companion spoke confidently to the fighter in Gourane, and to my surprise the gunman came to attention, answered respectfully, and then ran off. I suspect that the fighter realized he could be arrested by my companion.

When we arrived at the young woman's home, the bodyguard declined to eat any macaroni that the young woman presented to us. The other young woman and I ate it with good appetite while the cook took my companion to her bedroom.

The bodyguard and I made it back to base at about 10:00 p.m. My section chief was angry with me, because he had not expected us to spend so many hours off base. He must have informed Ngarkada (without telling him that in fact he had not ordered any specific time for me to return). The following morning, after morning assembly, Ngarkada ordered my section chief to put me in jail for my breach of discipline. It was my first and last time in the brig, but my penalty was for only an hour. It was that same morning when the presidential security unit joined some units stationed in Sarh and went to attack any CODOs they could find in the region of Ngalo, where fighters had often been ambushed by the CODO-Rouge.

During the evening, while those squadrons were still out on patrol, Ngarkada took his command troops, a few CODO troops, and a few fighters and went to the road beyond Balimba to ambush any CODO-Rouge who might attack Sarh from Balimba. When Ngarkada arrived with his troops between Balimba and Guéré, he placed his troops along the road. He placed the fighters along the first section of road, and then the CODOs along the next section. In the middle of night, Ngarkada apparently tapped his CODO troops to follow him. The fighters were not alerted, and it was only in the morning that they realized Ngarkada and the others were no longer among them. At that point, the fighters hastily left the ambush and returned to Sarh.

That evening, Nabia, who was the long-time bodyguard of Ngarkada, returned to Sarh. He had refused to follow his boss back into the bush. Ngarkada had not threatened him, but he had collected the Kalashnikov from Nabia before letting him return to Sarh. Apparently Nabia did not want to leave his family at the base, at the mercy of the fighters, and go back to the *maquis*. When he presented himself that evening to the guard on duty, he was arrested, interrogated, and put in the brig where I had been for one hour the previous day.

A few weeks before these events, Ali, one of the fighters in our unit, had been disciplined in the brig by Nabia for some offense, and when Ali had resisted arrest, Nabia had him beaten and forced into the brig. Ali, like the other fighters, saw himself as superior to Southerners and therefore deeply resented being disciplined by Nabia, whom he considered his inferior. Two nights after Nabia had returned to base and been locked up, Ali seized the opportunity to exact personal revenge on him. He asked Touka, the fighter who had co-commanded our unit with Ngarkada, to deal with Nabia for him. A few days later, Touka and Ali took Nabia in the middle of the night to Doyaba. They tortured him and then killed him.

When we heard that Nabia was no longer in the brig, we thought that he had been transferred from G4 to the military police. A few days later the paymasters came from N'djaména to dole out our salaries. When they arrived at our unit, they called Nabia to take his salary. Touka said he was in the brig. The paymasters asked Touka to bring Nabia to get his money before returning to the brig. Then Touka asked them to cross his name off the pay list. It was then that we realized that Nabia was dead. A few weeks later Ali boasted about the way that he, Touka's bodyguard, and Touka himself had tortured and killed Nabia. Nabia's family, when they had been given no official information about Nabia and had not received his pay, left the base for their own village. We CODOs in both units, Six and Nine, felt bad about the behavior of our new leader, Touka, but there was nothing we could do about it at that time.

Captain Bichir Agar was the one who had led the presidential security unit and some units of Moyen Chari to attack the CODO-Rouge in the Ngalo region. As the CODO-Rouge troops were divided into many guerilla units and dispersed to many different locations, Bichir chose to focus on one target. With his fighters he went to the region of Ngalo and surprised Colonel Kotiga with his CODO troops at the mobile headquarters. After a wild and frenzied combat, the CODO troops folded, and Bichir's units reached the place where the CODO troops kept their packs of belongings. To show off the victory of his fighters over Kotiga's unit of CODOs, Bichir sent word that we should assemble at the base in Sarh named *Sécurité Présidentielle* (SP), downtown about a mile (1.5 km) from our base. Though most of us in Units Six and Nine thought that Bichir was gathering us into the SP camp to kill us, we followed orders and marched there, singing as usual.

When Bichir, his bodyguards, and some of his command troops drove into the SP base, we were lined up at attention on the assembly grounds. He strode from the car to greet his officers stationed at the base, and we were ordered to salute him and present arms. Then he addressed us, briefly saying that his fighters had completely destroyed the CODOs. Only a few of them, like Kotiga, had escaped by chance, but their capture and death were also imminent. Then Bichir asked one of his bodyguards to show us the underpants of Kotiga that had been left behind. He said some adventurers, like Ngarkada and others, would be arrested or destroyed by his fighters during the coming days. Bichir finally said that we former CODOs who were with the government were lucky and nothing would happen to us. Before Captain Bichir left SP, we saluted him again. Then he said we were under the command of his co-commander, Yangar. Yangar ordered the unit commanders to march us back to G4. I suspect that Bichir had other plans in mind at that time, but perhaps at the last minute he received instructions from N'djaména not to kill us.

This Captain Bichir who had gathered us at SP and said he and his fighters had destroyed CODO troops had not boasted of all his accomplishments. It was not only CODOs that they had fought. While they were in the *canton* of Ngalo and spread out through other villages in neighboring *cantons,* they had destroyed all the houses, granaries of food, and any living creature in that region. Hundreds of innocent people had been slaughtered during that month of black September.

In Sarh, the capital of the *prefecture* of Moyen Chari, thousands of Southern officers, engineers, doctors, teachers, traditional authorities, businessmen, men of all trades, and even very young men and women would now be tortured and killed. The reason for this slaughter was, ironically, an opportunity presented by a particular compassionate cultural tradition. In Chad, and especially southern Chad, when someone had lost a relative, the other relatives, friends, associates, and compassionate people would contribute food, money, and other assistance to the grieving family. A trusted friend or two of the grieving survivor would keep a list of the gifts brought or sent by others so that the survivors could later send words of thanks for their generosity in a time of sorrow. This was the case when CODO Colonel Kotiga lost his mother after the ceasefire between the CODO-Rouge and the government in N'djaména. At that time the CODOs had their headquarters in Doyaba, and Kotiga was stationed there. As he was a popular man in Moyen Chari, many different people in Sarh brought food, drink, and money for the funeral of his mother. Kotiga had a list of the people that assisted him during that sorrowful time. Bichir apparently got that list during his September attack against CODO headquarters, when he found some of Kotiga's belongings there, and he seems to have used that list to arrest anyone who had contributed any kindness when Kotiga's mother died. The excuse Bichir gave for this slaughter was that anyone making gifts to Kotiga was indirectly contributing to the CODO-Rouge. Had he restrained his fighters and killed only those whose names were on the list, Bichir might have been believed. In fact, though, Bichir and his colleagues from DDS arrested not only those on the list found in Kotiga's bag but all of the co-workers and relatives of those on the list.

The slaughter was not restricted to Sarh and Ngalo. The massacre expanded all over the Moyen Chari and its neighboring prefectures. As an example, the populations of three of the subprefectures — Koumra, Moïssala, and Béjondô — and their *cantons* had been destroyed. The fighters seemed to hate all in the South: even some administrators of the South who had been sent there by the central government were not spared. And the fighters tortured and killed some of the best medical staff in many of the private medical centers created by an American named Seymour, known in Chad as a great missionary and physician. Seymour himself had left Chad because of Black September, but his staff, who had nothing to do with politics, were brutally butchered anyway. This left the southern regions with no medical care. The entire region of the South, and particularly Moyen Chari and Oriental Logon, experienced then the worst time that the country had never known since its independence. The fighters and their bosses had an unreasoning and unjustified hatred for people of the South. The very people who had tried to educate, heal, and lead the backward people of the North became their victims.

Corporal Chief Yondo, a former Codo-Rouge soldier who a few months before the ceasefire had separated himself from the rebel movement for some reason, had gone back to his home region in Moyen Chari and recruited about one hundred young men and women. Yondo named his rebels the CODO-Bleu and then signed a separate ceasefire with the fighters in Moyen Chari. Now in Black September he became very useful for the fighters against the CODO-Rouge. He and his unit had been rewarded by Bichir. One of his two co-commanders named Ganda had been sent to our unit to share command with Touka, who had been confirmed as the commander of Unit Six in place of the deserter, Ngarkada. Another one of Yondo's co-commanders named Kahlil had been promoted to the position of co-commander with Sublieutenant Moueba, commander of Unit Nine. We had always laughed at the troups of Yondo, who until then had not even the very basic military training the fighters had received. When Yondo's troops joined ours, they were always confused because they did not know anything about the military rules — not even how to "right face" or "present arms" on the assembly ground. They were supposed to seek our help to get used to military orders, but they refused to care about such things.

A few days after the CODO-Bleu had joined us, we had one soldier from that group who was promoted to the grade of *assimilé* (acting) officer and was co-leader of my section with our section chief. When my chief was sent on patrol with other fighters, he was killed by the CODOs, and his new colleague became the titular section chief. As mentioned previously, the CODO-Bleu had little familiarity with military tradition. My new section chief was not able to make a half turn at assembly. Always after assembly, the men of my unit laughed about the way he tried to make half turns or quarter turns to report our number every morning and evening to the adjutant of the company.

This man was only one example of the general state of things. It was amazing that *assimilé*-officers in Chad during the time of Hissène Habré and Déby did not know the elementary rules of the army. It shamed Chad, which had always had an educated and disciplined army in the French tradition, now to see the situation of the military turned from excellent to good, from good to bad, and now from bad to worse. Foreign diplomats coming through Chad with important documents to be signed might meet with illiterate, ill-trained officers. Hissène Habré, in elevating his uneducated fighters to positions of authority in the military, gave them power over the regular officers, who had national and international training, and put these educated officers into positions of subjection to fighters who hated, scorned, and sometimes beat them. Sublieutenant Daniel's prophecy had come true. The army of Chad, which had been ranked twenty-sixth in the world for its skill and strategy, now no longer would be sought out by African countries to train their troops. And what would be the state of Chad's military tomorrow, when officers could not read and write nor reason clearly through perplexing events?

The fighters who spoke Gourane or understood Gourane, the language of Hissène Habré, became the lords of the South. Paymasters who would come from N'djaména to pay us in the region of Moyen Chari on an irregular and inscrutable schedule went from one place to another to pay the fighters rather than entrust the soldiers' pay to undisciplined officers. It was not the responsibility of Touka, a commander, to serve as bodyguard to the paymasters, but because Touka and his bodyguards spoke Gourane (and most were of the Gourane ethnic group), they appointed themselves to escort the paymasters and get thereby a daily indemnity. After a few stops in Moyen Chari, they left Koumra for Moïssala to pay the fighters there. On their way, Touka's team was ambushed by a group of CODOs. Some of the fighters were killed, and Touka and his bodyguard were seriously wounded. They were transferred to N'djaména for appropriate medical care.

When Touka had sufficiently recuperated to return to Sarh, he transferred his frustration to us (Units Six and Nine), assumed that all of us were CODOs. A few days after his return to Sarh, he arrested two former CODOs from our Sixth Unit and also Sergeant Madjadoum, one of our section chiefs. Why would Touka's suspicion fall on him? Adoum, one of Touka's bodyguards, wanted Sergeant Mad-jadoum arrested because his girlfriend, Claudine, was one of the young CODO women. Adoum had become infatuated with Claudine despite her great love for Madjadoum. Adoum decided to kill Madjadoum so that he could have Claudine. The three CODOs under suspicion had been put in the brig for a while. Then one night Touka brought some fighters and a Toyota from the military police and took the three CODOs away. We who had lain down under the mango tree close to our unit's jail realized that there was something wrong, because the fighters came with rope and tied the hands of each of the three CODOs behind them before putting them in the Toyota. Allahdoum, the adjutant of our unit, was present when this happened. I suspect that he was the one who informed Sublieutenant Moueba what was going on.

At any rate, someone informed Moueba, commander of the Ninth Unit. That night he left the house with some of his bodyguards and headed to the military police brig but did not find the prisoners there. Moueba and his men then continued to the military prison, but the three prisoners had not been transferred there. They tried the *commisseriat central* but did not see them there. Finally they came back home. During that long night Moueba knew the three prisoners might already be dead, because he had been informed that as they were taken from their cells their elbows had been bound tightly behind them. The fighters generally bind prisoners this way not when transferring prison-ers from one location to another but rather when they plan to torture and kill them. The following day, Moueba wanted to find out from Touka what had happened to the prisoners but did not have the authority to investigate directly. Instead he told Touka that he had given money to Sergeant Madjadoum for safekeeping, and he wanted Madjadoum to give him back his money. If Touka would tell him where Madjadoum had been taken.... Touka replied only that Mad-jadoum and the others had been transferred to N'djaména. A few days later, however, the bodies of Madjadoum and many other men were discovered not far away from Doyaba.

Touka decided to finish us off, but indirectly, by staging a mock CODO ambush. He planned with other fighters from the military police to ambush us between Manda and Guéré. Touka could give the MP unit the approximate time that we would arrive on that stretch of road. The fighters were stationed there and waited for us. After our morning assembly, Touka ordered our section to go to Guéré to buy firewood for our kitchen. He had arranged for an enclosed truck to be brought to G4. I suspect this was so that we would be not able to react when the fighters attacked us, nor would any wounded survivors be able to identify the attackers as military police rather than CODOs. Already we knew that there was something wrong, though, because we usually bought firewood in Sarh and did not need our entire section — except the fighters — to do the job. In addition, only a few of us had weapons, and there was not enough ammunition to provide protection on our trip. Some questioned using an enclosed truck and not the usual *Véléra*. When we had filled the truck, where would we ride on the way back?

Unfortunately for Touka and his criminals, the truck — which had been working fine until that morning — broke down not long after we left the G4 base, and the driver spent some time poking around to see if he could solve the problem. Then he sent a few of the men of our unit to walk back to base to get some mechanics. When they were not able to fix the problem, they had us push the truck back to camp. The mechanics asked Touka if he wanted to send the *Véléra* for our use instead, but Touka refused to have us travel in it. As the mechanics were from the South, I suspect that they had figured out Touka's plan and created the truck problem themselves. The fighters probably waited for us along the road until evening and did not see us. When they returned to Sarh that evening, some of the men in our unit deduced the plot against us. Luckily for us, they had failed in their plot against us.

During that period, Kahlil, who had dropped out of high school for some reason to join the CODO-Bleu and was then Moueba's co-commander of Unit Nine, was ambitious and wanted the position held by Moueba, who was a regular military officer and one of the best paratroopers in the army. Kahlil got the support of some fighters to kill Moueba when there was an opportunity. Moueba received a call from headquarters to find out whether Kahlil, who had been missing on patrol for a couple of days, was in trouble. Moueba must have suspected an ambush on the way, so he took a large contingent of men with him and detoured around the direct route to arrive at Kahlil's position. There he surprised Kahlil, whose co-conspirators were outnumbered by Moueba's forces, and Moueba and his troops brought Kahlil back with them. Thus was another plot against former CODOs foiled.

A few days later I was sick and in bed for a week at the military clinic off base. The fighters who had been wounded worst by the CODOs in the recent fighting were transferred to the municipal hospital of Sarh, and the others were in the military clinic. Because the usual military rules seem not to have been in effect during Habré's rule, the wounded were allowed to keep their guns at both hospital and clinic. Those that were only lightly wounded carried their guns to the clinic in the morning, spent the day there, and then left for their evening and nightly rounds terrorizing citizens and extorting money at gunpoint. On their way back to the clinic, they were always drunk, and many smoked drugged cigarettes. This put me in an uncomfortable situation, being the only Southerner in the clinic.

I remember one of the fighters, a man in the next bed, who used to call me François Mittérand and was the only one who could speak a little bit of French. It was because I was able to communicate with them neither in Arabic nor in Gourane that he gave me the name of the President of France. We were able to talk together in the evening when the others left on "private patrol," and his presence comforted me greatly. I do not know what would have happened had the others challenged me in their language, since I could not communicate with them.

I could not speak Arabic, but I could understand the local Chadian dialect of Arabic. One night, the lightly wounded fighters had come back to the clinic from money-making ventures and were drinking the beer that they had brought with them and complaining. They said that during the time of President Goukouni, they received a regular salary and bonuses, but under Hissène Habré, they had neither bonuses nor salary. Another one said that their bonuses and salary had turned to wounds and death. It was then that I realized not all the fighters liked Hissène Habré. Not all of them came with him from the *maquis,* but some of them were the soldiers of Goukouni that had joined Hissène Habré because they saw no alternative. I now realized that if they had received a regular salary and bonuses, they would not be killing and stealing the property of civilians as they were doing then.

18

Going to War
as a Fighter

D URING MY WEEK-LONG STAY AT THE military clinic, there were
    some CODO girls that visited the military clinic for consul-
tation and medicine. Three of the four regular-military medical
staffers who were ordinarily stationed there had been sent on a military
mission. Only Daouda, a soldier from the North, was on staff while
the girls were at the clinic. Daouda was very good in French and spoke
a little bit of a Southern dialect called Mbaï. He had a problem,
though, trying to communicate with the CODO girls because none of
them spoke French. Since I was hospitalized at the clinic and therefore
available, one of the girls named Lucienne called me to come and help
them communicate with Daouda. I interpreted from Gor to French
then French to Gor. The nurse Daouda and the CODO girls were all
satisfied with my translation service.

Before the CODO girls returned home, they came and stayed for
an hour with me at my sickbed. A few days later they returned to the
military clinic and asked me for help again. I was very happy to help
them. My mother had hoped that I would learn French and use it
whenever necessary away from home, and once again those French lessons were of use. The following day Daouda called me to his office
and asked me which area of Chad I came from. I replied that I was

from Oriental Logon. He asked me from which part exactly of Oriental Logon. I replied only that I was a Gor. I wanted to tell him neither my village nor my county. I was afraid, thinking that he wanted to take fighters into my region.

I suspected from Daouda's slim, light build that he might be from the northeast, perhaps the prefecture of Batha or Biltine. He was about forty-five or fifty years old at that time and was very kind to me. Nevertheless I was cautious.

Daouda said that he had joined others from the North in rebellion against Tombalbaye more than ten years before and followed them without thinking. Now he saw that the rebellion had not reformed Chad but destroyed it. He himself had been ordered to turn his gun against relatives, friends, and neighbors, and many that he loved had died in the fighting. He would never permit his sons to go to the *maquis*. He told me "You are very young, intelligent, and educated. I wonder, why are you in the army during these days of fear and bloodshed?"

I answered him that I had no intention of a military career. If today he saw me in the army, it was because I had no choice.

He wondered how that could be. I replied that our region had been the theater of civil war for two years, since 1982. It was dangerous to stay in the villages because fighters made constant killing raids. It was for this reason that I joined the CODOs, to be protected, and then after "reconciliation" I found myself among the fighters.

After Daouda knew about my reason for being in the army, which was dominated by fighters from the North, Daouda had great compassion for me. He said that he wanted me to go back to my village. I said to him that I should agree, but that I preferred to stay in the army because if he sent me to the village, I might be killed on the road. In addition, I had heard the day before that our region had been burned again.

As Daouda had been determined to help me to go back to school, he proposed to send me to his parents or relatives in N'djaména so that I could attend a good school in safety. I could have agreed to go to his parents or relatives in N'djaména, but I refused for many reasons. I was not sure of his motives and suspected that Daouda might be ferreting out my opinion in order to take action against me later. Also, we had different cultures and religions. How might Daouda's relatives feel if I wanted to go to church or if they asked me to go to the mosque with them? I could imagine only trouble in a future with his family. I told Daouda that I really appreciated his kindness and interest in my future. Nevertheless I would like to wait until the dry season for word from my relatives before I would go to N'djaména. He said that any time I would like to join his relatives, I could let him know.

A few days after our conversation, I was released from the military clinic and rejoined my unit at camp G4. I was very happy to leave the wounded and drunken fighters that frightened me so much at the military clinic. The only benefit that I received during the period that I spent with them was the opportunity to hear more Arabic of the kind spoken in Chad. It was a joy for me to leave the hospital to rejoin my friends at camp G4, and play card-games like *albatacha* (three- or four-deck rummy), *kos* (perhaps a kind of poker) and *jeu de chance* (solitaire) and tell stories during the night.

About two weeks after I was released from military clinic, a part of the armored squadron of Sarh that was stationed in Dan-madja, the neighboring county to the south, headed to Sarh for their monthly allowance and were ambushed by the CODO-Rouge between Dan-madja and a village on the property of a nationalized sugar refinery known as SONASUT *(Société National Sucrière du Tchad)*. A few of the fighters escaped this ambush thanks to the skill of the driver of the *Véléra*. The driver himself was not wounded, though the vehicle was pierced by many bullets, and some of the tires were also hit. Driving on the rims, he managed to reach SONASUT, and then, after time for repairs, to Sarh.

The squadron of government fighters in Dan-madja had thus lost many men and needed reinforcements to face anticipated attacks from CODOs. Our armored squadron in Sarh was gone on patrol. The headquarters of the sixth zone, which was at camp G4, asked our second commander of the Sixth Unit to select a dozen troops from our unit for a mission.

It was about 2:00 p.m, just after our dinnertime, and most of the fighters and regular military and CODOs were off base. Just a few in our unit remained in camp. At that time, I was relaxing under one of the mango trees on the base and singing a Protestant hymn to myself in Gor.

One of our section chiefs gathered about a dozen of us who were in the area and ordered us to prepare our mats to leave base for a mission. We had not expected this, and we dreaded being sent off base, but we had to follow orders because it was the basic rule of the army. We gathered under one of the mango trees near the main entrance of G4 to wait for a vehicle.

Corporal Laoukoura, one of the regular military who was in our unit, had great affection for me. He came near, about three meters from us, and called me to come to him. I left our small line of troops, and he told me that we were going to face a bitter fight. He advised me not to take anything from the battlefield and nothing would happen to me. I would return safely if I did not loot anything from the people. I agreed with him that it would be wrong to take anything that was not mine; there always seem to be consequences for sin. I thanked Laoukoura for his concern. He patted my back encouragingly and said I should rejoin my colleagues.

I returned to my place, and a few minutes later our two lines filed in to receive some ammunition and weapons from the armory. But we did not know where we were headed until the military police vehicle arrived from the armored squadron's base. It was riddled with bullet holes, and the fighters who rode on the vehicle let us know that we were going to Dan-madja. We knew then that we were traveling in the vehicle that had just escaped ambush on the road.

I was sad when I heard that we were going to Dan-madja. I started thinking: I had been in the *maquis* to protect our people, and now I was turning the gun against my people. When I had arrived in Sarh, I stayed in the house of my aunt Kôn Pierre Tokinôn, and now I was taking up arms against her son. I had grown up, left the village, and suffered on the road together with my cousin Michel and nephew Dan-ngar, and now I was turning a rifle against them. Was it a moral thing to do? My prayer was to reach Dan-madja safely and find a way to join my relatives and friends rather than to kill them or destroy the property of innocents.

We arrived in Dan-madja safely, but all the villages along the road to Dan-madja and the homes in that village itself had been burned to the ground by the fighters. We rode into Dan-madja probably after 5:00 p.m. When we arrived, we realized that the fighters had divided into two groups for their safety and protection. One group had stationed itself at a primary school on the south side of town, and

another, I believe, at the compound of the *canton* chief on the north
side, which faced the market. The vehicle we rode in stopped under a
mango tree just behind the compound that I assume belonged to the
canton chief. We hopped out of the vehicle and were lined up by one
of the fighters who had accompanied us and then joined by other
fighters. A few minutes later, Faki Saboun, the commander of that station in Dan-madja, came out from the compound to us, and we were
ordered to salute him.

He started his speech to us in Arabic. He said, "You are now part
of my unit in Dan-madja here. It is an area of war. You have to be
ready at all times. Do not leave your weapon out of your reach. We do
not have a prison here. Therefore, if you make a mistake, we will whip
you with at least 50 strokes and will release you. But if it is your guard
duty, and you are sleeping, and my second commander or I surprise
you, he or I will kill you because your dereliction of duty would kill
us. And anything that you take when you are on patrol will belong to
you because you have bought it with your blood." When he finished
his speech, we saluted him again. He ordered one of his fighters to
divide us between the two groups.

Some of my colleagues and I were in the compound of the *canton*
chief with Faki Saboun, and others were sent to the primary school.
That school was approximately two hundred meters from our compound. At night, Faki Saboun showed us the different holes that they
had dug to hide in and face the enemies in case of any attack. He said
we could also hide ourselves behind the mango and *karité* trees to fight
if it were necessary.

The following morning, the second group went on patrol, and
some of my fellow CODOs were among them. One of them was
named Radjim. He, like me, was from Béngamia, but his *quartier* was
about two miles (3 km) from Béngamia. During their patrol far away
from Dan-madja, they saw some civilians who had left their villages
and lived in the bush for their safety. The troops of Faki Saboun
started shooting at the villagers. Radjim, inexperienced and naïve, had
advanced ahead of his colleagues. When they started shooting, they
were shooting at him.

When Radjim realized that his platoon was trying to shoot him,
he dropped down, turned around, and opened fire on them in return.
Faki Saboun started shouting, "*Anina, anina, anina!*" (It is we, it is

we, it is we!) Radjim stopped firing on them. A few minutes later, they also stopped shooting, and immediately all of them left the area to run back to Dan-madja, in case the sound of their shooting had invited a CODO attack. When they arrived close to the base, they stopped under the mango trees to catch their breath and relax a little bit before entering camp. It was there that Faki Saboun told Radjim in Chadian Arabic, "*Allah antook afé*," meaning, "May God give you peace."

When I heard that Radjim was in the platoon on patrol and that they had returned, I took my Kalashnikov and went to their base to make sure nothing had happened to him. I ate rice and drank tea with his platoon. On my way back to our place, Radjim accompanied me. When he told me about the events of the day, it seemed obvious to me that his platoon had intended to kill him and that Faki Saboun's bless-ing — a kind of apology for their "misapprehension" — was intended to allay Radjim's suspicions. This incident strengthened my earlier resolve not to kill CODOs and innocent people, and I seized the opportunity to urge Radjim to abandon the fighters and go with me back to the village or join the CODO-Rouge.

Radjim rejected my suggestion. He said it would not be possible for us to get back to our village, nor could we join the CODO-Rouge from Dan-madja. In response to my urging that we at least try to reach our village, Radjim said that when they had been on patrol, he had realized that the fighters were everywhere. He mentioned this to me so that in case I intended to leave, I would be careful, especially when I reached bridges or rivers. He now knew from his experience on patrol that the fighters liked to lie in ambush under the bridges and in the vegetation along the rivers.

As Radjim had refused my plea to escape with me, I was a little bit afraid that he might tell our friends, and little by little the entire unit might hear. I told Radjim that I appreciated his frank opinion and agreed with him that we would not leave Dan-madja. But it was important not to tell anybody about our discussion. He asked me to have confidence in him. I said, "I trust you, my brother." Then he returned to his section, and I continued on my way back.

A few days later, I was selected for a group that would go on patrol. I was sad to go and fight against the innocents who were hiding in the bush to protect themselves or had concealed themselves as CODOs fighting for a just cause. For the sake of our innocent people who were being killed, I had asked God not to allow me to kill. I remembered that during our time with the Green-CODOs in the *maquis*, we had learned an important military rule: the authority that gives soldiers the order to kill someone or to do something is responsible for the consequences of the soldiers' actions. If I killed someone, therefore, it was not really I but the officer who gave the order who did the killing. On the other hand, my religious conviction did not allow me to kill someone, because it was said in the commandments of Moses, "you shall not kill." So I could not rely on the military rule for spiritual justification.

We left Dan-madja early that morning heading to the southwest on patrol. We drove very far from our base — 40 to 50 kilometers away. Luckily we met no CODOs, so my ethics were not put to the test on the way there. We did find many huts of villagers out in the bush. I assume that when their houses in the village had been burned by fighters, they ran away from their village and built huts in the bush. Fortunately for them, they had heard the noise of our Toyota and *Véléra* and were able to run away before we arrived.

One of the regular military policemen was with us. He was originally from Tandjilé and had been with the fighters since Hissène Habré had taken control of the country. He was one of the first to spot a hut, dash out of the *Véléra*, steal what he wanted, and then set fire to the huts. I was completely disillusioned. It was unbelievable for me that a Southerner and an educated person would do something like that against his own people. I had gotten down from the *Véléra* with the others but was just walking around in confusion and sorrow. I refused to set fire to any huts of these innocent people. What should I do?

My first thought was to find a way to run away. If I did that, though, I would face three groups of people who would want to kill me. If I happened to escape the group of fighters on this mission, I could still be arrested and killed by angry villagers who knew I had been in a unit of fighters. In case I escaped the fighters and the villagers and made it to the CODOs, I would surely face death. The CODOs — and I knew their rules — were going to kill me or at least torture me horribly. What were my chances of reaching my village so someone could send for Pierre Tokinôn? Escape did not seem likely.

My second thought was to be ready. If the fighters tried to shoot

me and did not succeed on their first volley, I had to be ready to counterattack. In horror I remembered again, "You shall not kill," which
meant to me that I was forbidden to take the life of even one of these
fighters.

I was left with only one option, and it was one I could not
accept. If the fighters ordered me to steal or burn the huts, would I
have to execute that order because military discipline says that the
authority who orders you to do something bears responsibility? Perhaps the officer is responsible for my actions, but he could not be
responsible for my soul.

As I was thinking these things, Faki Saboun's bodyguard noticed
that I had done nothing since we had arrived. He spoke to me in
Chadian-Arabic, saying "Iti da nassara wala, mala mat so kidmé ma
anana? Are you a white man, that you don't want to work with us?"
(In other words, was I like some of the Frenchmen in Chad, who put
their hands in their pockets when work was to be done, and supervised
the efforts of others.) I had already figured out that this might be my
last day alive. I had to do something to look as though I was helping,
so I decided to gather the dry grass that was around the area, set it on
fire, and burn the grass along the road. Faki Saboun suddenly ordered
us to leave. I suspected that he wanted us to go back quickly before
smoke from the huts attracted the CODOs, who could ambush us on
our long way back to Dan-madja. Because of the reaction of Faki
Saboun's bodyguard, I suspect that if we had met CODOs, the fighters
would have seized the opportunity to end my life that day.

Returning from patrol, we came close to Dan-madja, and then
Faki Saboun ordered us to take the road that went south to Maro from
Dan-madja. We went perhaps 30 to 40 kilometers. We stopped in one
village that had been burned by these fighters before my fellow
CODOs and I had been sent to Dan-madja, and the village was now
deserted, but our patrol took anything it could find. We then took the
road west from that village and went about two or three kilometers,
looting villages on the way. We saw a big granary filled with groundnuts and well hidden by millet plants all around, but from our perch
on the *Véléra* we were able to spot its round top. One of the fighters
went over to investigate.

As the fighters knew that the groundnuts could be sold for
money, they brought the *Véléra* near to the granary, dropped the side

of the vehicle, and sliced open the woven-grass wall of the granary with their bayonets. Thus they filled the *Véléra* while the rest of us took up positions for their protection. They filled the bed of the Toyota, too. When both vehicles were full of nuts, one of the fighters set fire to the granary to burn the remainder of the groundnuts. The fighters wanted to return quickly to Dan-madja before they could be ambushed by CODOs drawn to the area by the smoke of the fire, but they also wanted to loot the village located about three kilometers from the granary, so we headed off on foot ahead of the vehicles.

Before we reached that village — probably the village of the people who had worked so hard to gather and store the groundnuts — a swarm of bees swarmed out of a *karité* tree and attacked us. The first fighter to be stung cried out and swatted at the bee on his back. All of us scattered. Most were stung by the bees. For some reason, I was lucky enough not to be stung. As soon as we could, we gathered under one of the mango trees in the village. Even the bees could not deter these fighters from stealing what goods remained in that poor village. The men loaded bicycles onto one vehicle, though their tires were melted from an earlier raid on the village, and also three plows and other goods that the villagers had left behind. Since the bees continued to exact revenge on some of the thieving fighters, we got quickly into the *Véléra* and Toyota, then we continued to another village near Dan-madja.

Once we arrived in that village, some of my fellow CODOs and the fighters hopped off to loot the property of the villagers. To avoid attracting attention from the fighters again, I entered the burned and deserted village with them. A few minutes later, I saw even my fellow CODOs coming back with plows and bicycles. The villagers must not have realized that the fighters would return one day to pick these goods out of the rubble of their devastated village. One of my fellow CODOs told me to try to get something for myself. I just told him that I was not in need of these materials. He said that I could take them to Dan-madja and sell them one day. I replied that maybe I would take something next time.

My friend did not know how sad I had been since morning, sad about the innocent people whose property was stolen or burned by our group. I might have carried off their goods along with the other men, except that my parents had taught me from childhood about the

Christian God and how the child of God should control his behavior with respect to material things. I had realized also that God might not get down from heaven to talk to us in person, but He uses other people to talk to us. And if Laoukoura back in Sarh had called me out from among the others to advise me not to take anything that did not belong to me, I had to be careful in every respect. In brief, I could not steal because of my conscience and my religious convictions.

We left that village and headed back to Dan-madja with all the things that our patrol had looted. When we arrived, the groundnuts were loaded into one of the huts in our compound for Faki Saboun. The other goods belonged to those that had looted them. I was angry and thoroughly unhappy. I felt unwell. The food served by my friends who had not gone on patrol tasted bitter to me. I should have been hungry, but anger curbed my appetite. My fellow CODOs, men with whom I had made common cause in the *maquis,* had acted like the fighters. I loved them but hated their actions. I was with them, but I saw myself as alone. I walked with them, but I saw myself far from them. Though we shared the same room, I felt that a vast sea separated me from them. When they were laughing, I was crying. When they were acting against our people, I was weeping for them and praying for the innocents from whom they had stolen.

The following Saturday, the presidential security unit arrived from Sarh to Dan-madja in the evening to join us for a special patrol. The unit passed the night with us. On Sunday morning, a few women took the risk of coming to the weekly market in Dan-madja to look for salt to buy. During that period, it was hard to get salt in the areas where there were troubles. As we were not allowed to move around without our rifles, I took my Kalashnikov and entered the market.

I saw two women who were relatives of my mother. One was about thirty years old and the other about fifty-five. Both of them were very afraid when they saw me coming toward them. I said, "*Kaka* (grandmother) Kôn Touba and *Kôm* (my maternal aunt) Claudine, I am from your blood. Do not be afraid of me." I knew that Kôn Touba's son was the bodyguard of one of the leaders of the CODO-Rouge.

After the brief formalities of greeting, I asked the women to inform the CODOs that the fighters might attack them early that same week. The CODOs should prepare for attack. In response, Claudine showed fear and started trembling. She said that she and her relatives did not know any CODOs and did not know where they were.

I was sorry to have caused her distress. Quickly I reassured her, saying that I had given her this information so that she and others could take precautions to protect themselves. I was trying to help them, and not to betray them. Then I quickly left them to avoid any consequences to them or myself.

I had not realized before that Claudine and Kôn Touba might be afraid thinking that I wanted to spy on them. On the one hand, I also started to be afraid for myself because through the women's display of fear the fighters might suspect that I was plotting something with them. On the other hand, I felt bad because when I wanted to help my relatives, instead they were afraid of me, thinking that I was trying to betray them. I felt very much alone in the world. Only my God and I knew that I was not a fighter.

I had a hard time getting to sleep that night. I said to myself that I was totally against people who kill. People of Chad and especially the relatives of my parents — people for whom I felt a great love — might reasonably assume today that I was a spy for the fighters. I asked myself a question: what were those two women going to tell the CODOs and all my relatives near and far?

The following day, Lotongar, one of my relatives from Babo that came with me from Sarh to Dan-madja, was among the troops chosen to go on special patrol. When they had driven far away from Dan-madja, they sensed in the bush the presence of the villagers who were living in that area because their village had been burned. The fighters wanted to surround all the people in the area, arrest them, and kill them. In an attempt to save the people, Lotongar fired his rifle to alert them. He wanted it to look to the fighters as though he were aiming into the bush, but in fact he was shooting off to the side. Other fighters thought the order had been given to shoot, and they shot on the direction of the vil-lagers. Lotongar's strategy had worked; none of the innocent villagers was killed. The villagers successfully escaped. After the patrol, the fighters wanted to punish Lotongar for discharging his weapon too early, but he told them that he had seen a few people in the bush and thought they might be CODOs who were preparing to fire on the fighters. It was for this reason, he said, he had shot his weapon before the order to fire. He was told not to make that mistake next time.

19

Malingering My
Way to Sarh

AWEEK LATER THE ADJUTANT CHIEF BARDABA, the new commander
of Zone Six who had replaced Captain Bichir, went for an official
visit to the subprefecture of Maro. Daouda, the fighter I had met in the
clinic during my recent illness, was among the troops that escorted the
new commander of Zone Six to Maro. On their return to Sarh, they
stopped in Dan-madja. Daouda was surprised to see me there. He
called me aside from among the others to come to talk with him. He
asked me how I happened to be in this unit in Dan-madja. I told him
that about a month before, my friends and I had been ordered suddenly
on this mission. Once we arrived in Dan-madja, Faki Saboun had told
us that we were effectively assigned to his unit. I saw on Daouda's face
great distress to see me in a danger zone. He told me directly that the
fighters were most likely to put us CODOs in the front line of action.

Of the three classes of fighters, the Gourane were definitely the
upper class because of their presumed connections to Hissène Habré;
the Zakhawa and Kanembou from the North formed the middle class;
regular military troops, Southerners, and all the rest formed the lowest
and most expendable class of fighters. As former CODOs, my friends
and I had the least prestige within the ranks of fighters and were in the
greatest danger.

146

Daouda said he was going to talk to Faki Saboun about me. He would tell him that I was an unhealthy person and that I should still be under treatment for my earlier illness. I agreed to his proposal. He took Faki Saboun aside and talked to him in Gourane. I did not understand that dialect, but I believe that Daouda let Faki Saboun know that I was not a healthy enough soldier to be in Dan-madja. Faki Saboun knew and trusted Daouda, apparently. When Daouda was ready to leave Dan-madja for Sarh, he told me that he had already informed my unit commander. Daouda asked me to find a way to join him when I arrived back in Sarh, and he would get me out of the military.

One night a few weeks later, a group of CODOs attacked us with mortar fire. They fired shells three times into our compound. They had made a little mistake calculating the distance. Instead of falling on our compound, the shells fell into the market of Dan-madja. We quickly took our defensive position and waited for the attackers until the next morning. We did not know if the CODOs would move forward or pull back during the night. In the middle of the morning, one of our groups went for a patrol — but not far from Dan-madja — and then came back.

One Friday night, I decided to return to Sarh and look for a way to leave the military as Daouda had hoped for me. Faki Saboun had promised us from the beginning that if his co-commander or he himself surprised someone sleeping on guard duty, he would shoot him with his pistol. I had prepared myself to be either shot dead or sent back to Sarh. I was on guard duty in the middle of the night. I saw Faki Saboun coming in my direction. I fell down and started crying. To avoid being shot by him, I cried somewhat loudly. Faki Saboun asked me, "Shunum indak? What happened to you?"

I said to him, "Ana mardan, I am sick."

As Faki Saboun knew that I did not speak Arabic fluently, he probably thought I had been shot by the enemy. Faki Saboun quickly returned to headquarters, ordering the fighters to be on alert. I was taken to our medical station. Salomon, a former CODO who had been sent to Dan-madja before my unit, started examining me. I told Salomon that the problem was in the lower abdomen. Salomon was looking for a hernia in my groin, but he could not find anything. He said to Faki Saboun that he would like to send me to Sarh for an exam. As Daouda had already spoken about me to Faki Saboun, he gave his approval and said that on the following day I could go to Sarh with the weekly market's vehicles. I suspect that Daouda's word counted for something with Faki Saboun because Daouda spoke Gourane and was from the North.

The following day, late in the morning, I prepared my bundle for Sarh. I tied my mat and put it beside my bag inside the room. While I was outside with my former CODO colleagues, one of them named "Nassekingar"went inside the house and stole antibiotic drugs from "Charles," a former member of the regular army. To create confusion, Nassekingar took a shirt from Charles' things and put it inside my mat. When it was about thirty minutes before the vehicles would leave for Sarh, Charles realized that his shirt was missing. Perhaps he had been prompted by Nassekingar to make sure I was leaving with only my own goods. I suppose that he told his colleagues he was missing a shirt, and Nassekingar told him to look inside my bag and mat to see if I had stolen them. Charles called me to come and open my bag so that he could verify that I had not put his clothes among mine by mistake. I told him that I did not have any of his clothes, but he insisted that I open my bundle. When I did so, there was Charles' tee-shirt in my mat. I was thoroughly surprised and completely wet with shame. I knew that someone must have put Charles' shirt in my mat, but I did not have the courage to say that, because I was so ashamed to be in that situation. I told Charles that I remembered tying my mat and was sure that I had not put his shirt there. But I could not understand how his clothes were in my mat.

I asked him to forgive me. He could have accused me of theft to Faki Saboun and caused me that day to receive fifty strokes of the cane, *coups de chicotte,* but Charles was kind enough not to put me in so great a jeopardy.

It was after I had left for Sarh that Charles realized that he had also lost his drugs. When he was asking others if they had seen his antibiotics, Nassekingar said it might have been I who had taken them, because apparently I had taken Charles' shirt.

A week after I left Dan-madja, my friends said, Charles retrieved his drugs from Nassekingar. Then Charles and the other colleagues realized that Nassekingar had not only stolen Charles' drugs but also hidden Charles' shirt in my mat to cover his theft. Nassekingar was apparently taken to Faki Saboun for discipline and was beaten. My honor was therefore restored. And Charles sent an apology to me through my friends who came to Sarh to get rations for the unit at Dan-madja.

20

A Miraculous Escape
from the Ranks

FORTUNATELY MY TRIP FROM DAN-MADJA to Sarh was successful. I thought we would be ambushed by CODOs, but we reached Sarh without any problem on the road. The day following my arrival in Sarh, I entered the hospital there. A French physician named Leclerc received me and tried to diagnose my health problem. After several tests, Leclerc realized that I was in good health. He gave me one week to remain in Sarh so that he could do another check up, but he expected me then to return to Dan-madja. I agreed to do as Leclerc told me, but my intention was to leave the army as soon as possible. In the meantime I visited my cousin and childhood advisor, Maïna Domtiné, who worked in his elder brother's bookstore. Fearing he would never see me again, he had our photograph taken together. He kept the picture as a souvenir for my relatives should I be killed in action.

During that time, Sublieutenant Moueba's suspicion of his co-commander Kahlil was growing. Kahlil and his men already had tried to kill Moueba to remove him from his position. Kahlil had indirect support from many of the fighters, partly because he shared their religion. For this reason, Sublieutenant Moueba had finally decided to go back to the *maquis*. Because it was the troops of Unit Nine — Moueba's troops — that assured airport security and also guarded food provisions for headquarters at Sarh, Moueba seized the opportunity to send extra ammunition to the CODOs whom he trusted so that he and his followers could use it later.

One evening, I was visiting Moueba's house with a friend of mine. His wife was preparing a lot of cakes, but we did not suspect that Moueba was planning to leave Sarh. Two days later in midafternoon Moueba apparently met with his bodyguards to determine the place where they would meet in the bush, and then he sent each of his bodyguards to a different security location

Maïna Domtiné (left) and me in Sarh, late 1984.

to take those troops immediately to the rendezvous. Some of my former fellow CODOs of Units Six and Nine were informed suddenly that they should leave their post and join Moueba in a particular cassava field. Unfortunately, I was not there at base G4 when the word came to escape. I was with my friend Moussa at his uncle's house. About fifty-four lucky CODOs who were at G4, guarding the airport, or providing security for provisions left Sarh with Moueba.

A few moments later, Bardaba, the commander of Zone Six, was informed — probably by an agent at the airport — that the soldiers on airport patrol duty had abandoned their posts. When Bardaba arrived at the airport, he noted the absence of troops. Because Bardaba knew that it was the troops of Unit Nine that had been assigned to airport

security, Bardaba looked for Moueba to figure out what the problem
might be. When Bardaba arrived at Moueba's house, there was nobody
at home. Some minutes later, Bardaba also noticed that the other
CODOs, those responsible for guarding the stock of provisions, had
also left their post. He finally realized that Moueba had chosen the
camp of Habré's enemies and had taken with him some of his troops.

Bardaba quickly ordered the fighters assigned to the military
police station to join him and help pursue the deserters. Bardaba knew
at that time that the only direction Moueba and his fellows could go
was northwest, because on all other sides there were fighters. Northwest and north of Sarh, there was a river. Bardaba guessed correctly
what direction Moueba and his troops would go. Unfortunately for
Bardaba and his fighters, they could not intercept Moueba and his fellows. The fighters followed a farm path, moving quickly in their Toyotas, but they did not find any trace of the deserters.

It was three years later that I met Élizabeth, one of the deserters
who left Sarh with Moueba. She joined Koulangar in Moundou a few
days after leaving Sarh, not being able to keep up with Moueba's fellows because of a leg problem. During our friendly conversation, Élizabeth told me that Moueba had left Sarh even before his bodyguards
privately informed the troops at base G4, the airport, and the provisions warehouse that he would be leaving. According to what she told
me, none of them had been informed before his departure except
Moueba's bodyguards, who may have been informed only a few minutes before Moueba left his house.

Élizabeth said that when they joined Moueba just behind the
quartier named Kamkian on the periphery of Sarh, he ordered them to
sit down in the field of cassava. Some minutes later, the fighters bar-
relled down the farm path on the edge of Kamkian, and Moueba and
his fellows lay down under the cassava plants, which by this time of
the year were about five feet tall. When the fighters were not able to
find the deserters, they returned to their base, and the CODOs waited
until the middle of the night before continuing on their way to the
maquis.

Meanwhile, as I was returning to camp from my visit with
Moussa that evening, I met Allah-adoum's wife. She told me,
"Moueba has run away with some of our colleagues." She was afraid of
what would happen to those of us former CODOs who remained in

Sarh. I had no other option but to return to camp. The fighters were sure to be suspicious of any CODO found outside the camp, and it was too late for me to try to follow Moueba. Far from family and abandoned now by friends, I did not know where else to go but back to camp.

During that night, there was a curfew in the town. The troops of the two units, Units Six and Nine, were not allowed to leave base G4. The fighters were lying in ambush in the *quartiers* adjacent to Sarh in case any of us tried to leave.

The following morning, Bardaba ordered tractors to clear off all the fields of sorghum, millet, and grasses that surrounded base G4 and the airport. The entire area between the base and airport, which had been packed densely with sorghum and millet plants, after the plowing looked like the desert of northern Chad. From the CottonChad factory about half a kilometer west of the base and from the Hôtel de la Chasse about a kilometer east of the base, people could see the walls of base G4 clearly, with no living thing between except some big mango and *caïcédra* trees. Now no one could hope to escape to the bush.

Those of us at the base, however, knew nothing of these events. At the same time that tractors were plowing and clearing all around the base, the men of Units Six and Nine and I were kept inside the barracks and surrounded by fighters all around base G4. (I was no longer a member of Unit Six since my transfer to Dan-madja, but I was kept with these men.) After the areas around the base had been successfully cleared off, Bardaba ordered his co-commander to gather us at headquarters.

Both units assembled and stood at attention before the headquarters building. A few minutes later the fighters drove into headquarters. One of the regular soldiers in Unit Six who had been with the fighters for many years realized that something unpleasant was planned for us. He had the courage to step aside from his unit, salute Bardaba, and tell him and his co-commander that he and other regular soldiers had served loyally with the fighters for many years before the CODOs came to Sarh. Then after reconciliation, he said, headquarters had distributed the regular soldiers into the CODO units. What, he wondered, would be their situation now?

The regular soldiers, of whom there were about five in Unit Six, were lucky that day. Bardaba asked them to step out from our ranks and come forward to him. Then Bardaba ordered one of his body-guards to escort them to his secretary. Whatever our fate was to be, these men would not share it.

At that moment we CODOs knew that something serious was going to happen to us. Everybody was extremely anxious now. The fighters who surrounded us at headquarters and those that surrounded the base were well armed. There was at least one heavy automatic weapon positioned at each entrance of base G4.

I was terrified. I stepped out of line, left my rank, and headed to the main entrance of base G4 about 100 meters away. For some reason, Bardaba and his fighters surrounding our troops neither spoke to me nor arrested me. My fellows and their section chiefs whom I left on the parade ground did not move, and none of them asked me why I had left the ranks. As I walked from headquarters to the main entrance, none of fighters bothered me or talked to me. I ignored them, too.

At the entrance gate, I saw two heavy, automatic anti-aircraft weapons and one 14-millimeter *Butive* artillery gun mounted on a Toyota with at least six fighters in the vehicle. None of the men guarding the gate talked to me or disturbed me in any way. I just went out.

To this day I cannot explain why this happened. It seems to me that God must have protected me.

When I left base G4, I saw that the peripheral area had been totally changed. The fields of sorghum and millet that had covered the area had been cleared off. It was impossible for me to hide myself. I kept walking, therefore, all the way to the house of Moueba, the deserter. When I heard the noise of vehicles behind me, trucks that were taking my fellows away, not knowing what else to do I stopped walking and faced the road. As the vehicles went by, there were some stupid fellows among the CODOs that called to me and asked me why I was not going with them. Luckily, though, because they called to me in the Gor dialect, the fighters were not able to understand what they were saying. I waited until all of the vehicles took the troops to the airport, and then Bardaba rode by in his own vehicle. I continued my way downtown.

I was the only of us who escaped from that terrible situation. I assume that Bardaba had wanted to kill us all but that Hissène Habré said to send us to the North instead to fight against the rebels. My escape from certain destruction was incredible to my fellow soldiers and to me, as well.

From downtown Sarh, I continued to Bolngar Domtiné's house, where I passed the entire evening with my close childhood friend and relative, Maïna Domtiné. Not wanting to endanger him by my presence, during the night I walked to Colonel Ndoubatôg's house to sleep with his children, who were friends of mine. The situation in Sarh turned desperate. The fighters thought Moueba might come back with other CODO-Rouge troops to attack Sarh. Patrols were everywhere in town. To avoid being tortured or killed, the young people did not show themselves outside early in the morning or late in the evening. Some young people refused to be seen outside at all because of the fighters that could arrest them at any time.

A few days later, the paymasters started paying fighters and CODO-Bleu soldiers at headquarters. I presented myself for my salary. Touka ordered his bodyguards to arrest me and accused me of having been sent back by Moueba to spy on them. Fortunately Touka's co-commander remembered that I had been sent to Faki Saboun's unit in Dan-madja for a while. He knew also that I had been sent back to Sarh from Dan-madja for a health condition. I had visited with him twice since my return to Sarh, so he was familiar with my situation. Because Touka's co-commander stood up for me and objected to my arrest, and because this was a public discussion before the paymasters, Touka could not at this time put me in jail and then finish me off later.

As I had now one more reason not to trust Touka, I kept in my mind that he could arrest me at any time, so when I got my pay that day, I started distributing some to my friends and the remainder to Madjadoum Nassôdam, the husband of Salomé, my mother's cousin. I told Madjadoum to give two thousand FCFAs to his wife and please send the rest to my mother. I kept only a little bit of money in my pocket.

21

Trying for a Ride to the Capital

I EXPLAINED TO MADJADOUM NASSÔDAM and his wife about Touka's hostility to me. Madjadoum had been a military police officer in pre-war Chad. From his years in the North he had acquired many languages and dialects, including Gourane. When the civil war began, he joined the CODO forces in the South. Then, after reconciliation, he had been assigned to the military police station in Sarh. No one there knew of his CODO connections, because he was conversant in all the dialects of the fighters. I expressed to Madjadoum's family my intention to leave Sarh to go to N'djaména. Madjadoum Nassôdam told me that he had a friend in the military police that was a guard at the gate of Balimba. Madjadoum Nassôdam said he could take me to that man, who would get a vehicle that would take me to N'djaména.

During that period, it was impossible to travel in Chad without the new national identification card or student identification card. Because I was very young at that time, I went to the office of the director of a primary school and told him a story, giving as my name a combination of my middle name and the name of my grandfather. I said that I was from Koumra and had come to Sarh for a visit, but I had lost my scholar identification card. I pleaded with him to provide me with a replacement card. The man asked me to give him 500 CFA before he would deliver the identification card to me. I agreed to pay him this nominal fee, and he asked me to meet him in his office the following day. That same day, I went to a photo studio in the central market of Sarh and had my picture taken. The next day I went back to the school, and the director handed over a scholar identification card, just as he had promised.

After receiving my identification, I immediately went to Madjadoum Nassôdam's house to inform him that I had an identification card and planned to leave Sarh the following day. Madjadoum gave me his congratulations and promised to take me to the barrier gate the next day.

The following morning, I walked with Madjadoum Nassôdam to the barrier gate between Sarh and Balimba. He had me wait in Sarh while he negotiated our departure from the city, because troops were still on guard all around the city, prepared for an imminent CODO attack. When we had traversed the bush between Sarh and Balimba, he presented me to his friend and asked him to help me get to N'djaména to join my parents. When his request was granted, Madjadoum Nassôdam said farewell, wished me luck, and headed back to Sarh. The barrier guard asked me to wait there, and when there was an opportunity to catch a vehicle headed for N'djaména, he would get it for me.

I stayed at the control post of Balimba for an hour or so before I heard the voice of a man from Sarh continuously crying in the backyard of the control post office, behind a wall. I was curious, so I entered the yard and saw an unfortunate man trussed up with his elbows and hands tied behind his back and his legs bound. His entire body was badly swollen because he had been beaten and then tied in this torturous position. I did not recognize the man. A few hours later, the military policemen came with their Toyota from Sarh and took the man to Sarh. According to what I heard about that man, he had a field of millet some distance from Sarh, and he had left Sarh early that morning to harvest his crop. Unfortunately for him, the fighters who were at the control post of Balimba assumed he was a CODO. They arrested and tortured him, then tied him up and left him at the gatehouse all day.

That day I was not able to get a vehicle for N'djaména. Because of the curfew there would be no more traffic in or out of Sarh after

6:00 p.m., so I decided to go back to Sarh and return to the barrier the following day. That night in Sarh I slept with Ndoubatôg's children.

The second day, I came early in the morning to the barrier to try my chances again. Around noon there was a vehicle headed for N'djaména that arrived at the barrier gate. Nassôdam's colleague was looking for me to go with that vehicle, but I hid myself among the mango trees and would not come out. I did that because from far away I had seen the Toyota of Faki Saboun, the commander of my unit in Danmadja, coming from Sarh to Balimba behind that vehicle. I waited until the vehicle for N'djaména had left and Faki Saboun had turned back to Sarh before I came back to my place at the gate. One of the guards asked me where I had been. I told him that I was hungry and had been looking for some mangos to eat. He said I had missed an opportunity to get to N'djaména because I was not around. He said, too, that he did not know when he was going to get another opportunity for me. Sure enough, I did not travel that day and instead went back to Sarh again after 6:00 p.m.

Why had Faki Saboun showed up at the barrier gate? I suspect that someone had informed him that I was trying to leave Sarh, when he came to Sarh for the ration of his unit. Therefore on the evening of this second day I was careful not to draw attention to myself going back to Sarh. Instead of taking either of the two roads that led to Sarh after the bridge of Bar Kôh, I followed a small path that led to a suburb, Bégou, and from there I entered Sarh.

The following day I returned to Balimba and waited again for a vehicle heading to N'djaména. About noon, again there was a vehicle that left Sarh for N'djaména. A few minutes after the vehicle arrived at the barrier, I saw the Toyota of Faki Saboun coming again. I crossed the small road that went to the Protestant Clinic of Seymour and continued to the border of the river Bar Kôh. I stayed there and waited until I saw Faki Saboun returning to Sarh before I came back to the control post. Nassôdam's colleague at the gate was little bit angry with me. He asked me why I always waited around until there was a vehicle for N'djaména and then disappeared. I told him that I had gone to relieve myself in the bush. The guard seemed suspicious and asked to see my scholar identification card. I presented it to him. He took it and looked at my name. Then he returned it back to me. He told me not to move any more.

A few hours later, I saw a trailer carrying cotton bales coming from Sarh to N'djaména. There was only a driver in the cab, and his apprentice supervising the load up above, so there would have been room for me either in the cab or above. I thought the guard would ask the driver to take me to N'djaména, but he did not say anything about me to the driver.

It was at that point that I began to suspect that Faki Saboun, who had come to the barrier two days in succession, had given the guard instructions about me. Especially since the military policeman had asked for my scholar identification later, and then had said to stay in one place, I feared he would know, despite the false information on my ID, that I was the one Faki Saboun sought. I just waited while the driver completed the required formalities with (and paid the expected cash to) the customs official, police officer, and forestry agent. When the guard's attention was on a conversation with his companions, I left my position and escaped up the road. I ran about one hundred meters ahead of the cotton truck and hid myself behind a mango tree at a curve in the road. When the trailer left Balimba, it had to go very slowly on the rough road around the curve, so there I hopped up onto the trailer behind the bales and rode the trailer until we arrived at Guéré.

At Guéré, when the trailer stopped at the control post, the driver immediately went to conduct his formalities once again. But before the driver got down from his cabin, I jumped quickly down from the back of his trailer. All my body — and particularly my face — was covered with the red dust of the road. The fighters at Guéré took me for a young trucking apprentice. The guards neither approached me nor asked me questions.

The driver's apprentice, who had come down from the top of the cabin, was walking around the trailer, checking to see if the load were well tied. He greeted me and asked me where my vehicle was. I told him that I had ridden on their trailer. He was surprised but kept quiet, and finally the driver returned from the office area. When his apprentice started to tell him that I had ridden behind their trailer from Balimba to Guéré, before he finished what he was trying to tell his boss, I immediately started explaining to him my situation as Nassôdam had coached me to do. I told the driver that my parents had been posted to N'djaména. I was supposed to have gone with them, but I had been absent from home when the administrative vehicle picked them up.

The driver, who was very kind, asked why I did not ask to come with them, and instead hung on behind the trailer. I presented to him my excuses, as Nassôdam had advised me: I said I was afraid to ask him for that assistance, thinking that in case he refused to take me, it would be a hard life for me in Sarh. He said now if he refused to take me, what was I going to do? I said I apologized about what I had done, but at Guéré here my life depended on his wisdom. Finally, the driver took pity on me and allowed me to travel with them to N'djaména.

22

N'djaména

BEFORE WE LEFT GUÉRÉ, THE DRIVER ordered his apprentice to let me ride atop the cabin with him. We probably left Guéré at 5:00 that evening. As the condition of the road was not very good, we traveled at a chameleon's pace and arrived at Kanu, an administrative post on the way, late in the evening. We could have continued our trip, but the driver was tired because he had drunk a lot of beer before he left Sarh, so he told his apprentice to arrange his bed under the vehicle for him.

I was not able to sleep that night at Kanu for several reasons. First, I was hungry because I had not eaten anything that day. The guard at the Balimba gate had told me to stay still and not move any more. Second, I was afraid, fearing that Faki Saboun might pursue me or send a message to fighters at Kanu to arrest me on the road. Third and last, it was very cold at Kanu, and my one and only shirt that I was wearing was too light to protect me from the cold.

While the driver and his apprentice were sleeping, I gathered dry stalks of millet and sorghum and then got permission from the control station staff who were brewing tea to get a spark from their fire. Thus I made a fire to sleep beside for the rest of the night. The problem of my hunger was solved early in the morning when the apprentice made coffee for his boss. The men shared their coffee and doughnuts with me for breakfast. The problem of my lack of sleep was solved when we were on our way to Guélinding. I slept atop the cabin in the warm sunshine and the gentle wind of Chad all the way until we reached Kômogo.

I slept well despite the fact that in my pockets from Sarh to Kômogo, I had only 75 FCFA, approximately seven cents. At the market of Kômogo, the driver agreed with the local agent to take about 20 full 40–50-pound bags of millet seed to N'djaména for pay. Men started loading the bags of millet onto the cotton bales of our trailer. I joined the laborers and helped them to load the bags. When we had done the job, the owner of the millet paid the laborers. One of them said to the other workers to give something to me, too, because I had helped them. Unanimously, they agreed on 100 FCFA ($.10 USD) as my share. I was so happy to receive that unexpected money. I had not helped the laborers for the purpose of being paid but rather because I appreciated the help I was receiving from the driver of the trailer. Before leaving that village, the driver gave money to his apprentice and ordered us to go and eat at the restaurant.

After our noon meal at the restaurant in Kômogo, we drove on toward N'djaména. When we arrived at a checkpoint between Guélinding and N'djaména, it was very late at night. The driver ordered us to sleep there. In that area, it was even colder than the night before. I was not able to sleep. I felt warmer atop the cabin than on the ground, because above the cabin I could cover myself with the rain tarp. Under the trailer, I had no cover at all. The place where we stopped had no millet or dry wood with which to make a fire for warmth. Early in the morning, the apprentice saw me shivering and trembling, and he took two logs of the dry wood that he had bought for his own use, doused them with gasoline, and lit a fire for me. I kept myself very close to the fire to recover from the cold. A short time later, we left that place for N'djaména.

We entered N'djaména at midmorning across Chagoua Bridge, located on the south side of N'djaména. Because the driver had believed my story about searching for my parents and knew that most Southerners lived in southwest N'djaména, he had me get down at the entrance of N'djaména to start looking there. I thanked the driver and his apprentice for their great help and many kindnesses. They replied by saying that thanks were due to God.

I walked into town from Chagoua Bridge and headed downtown. I crossed the *quartier* Nônsané and reached the primary school of the *quartier* Paris Congo. As I was crossing the schoolyard, I asked another pedestrian if he knew the house of Mbaïlem-mou, the younger brother of my grandfather Mbaïlemdana. The man did not know where Mbaïlem-mou lived, but he knew where his workshop was located, and he very kindly took me there.

When we arrived at the workshop, the man told Mbaïlem-mou that he had brought him a guest. My granduncle was unable to recognize me because he had not seen me for perhaps seven years. He just greeted me politely and waited until the man left before he asked me, "My son, where did you come from?" I suspect that my granduncle was afraid of asking me where I had come from in front of a stranger. During that period our region was once more under great suspicion, and the spies and agents of the DDS (Direction de la Documentation de Sécurité) were everywhere. In addition, it is always hard to talk in the presence of anybody with whom you do not have a strong relationship, and he graciously allowed us a private conversation.

I responded, "Granduncle Mbaïlem-mou, I came from Sarh, and I am the son of your niece Ngambaye."

My granduncle stood up from his chair, hurried to where I stood, and hugged me warmly. He took me home with him to bathe and eat after my long journey. When we arrived in front of the house, he had water brought for me to drink, asked for a basin of water for my bath, and ordered tea. Even while I took my standing bath behind the wall and as he drank tea, he was so excited to see me that he continued to ask questions about what was going on in the South. I explained to him the terrible situation in Moyen Chari, but I could not say much about the situation in Oriental Logon, because I had no real idea about what was going on there.

My granduncle said Bérangar had arrived from the village in Oriental Logon about two days before. Bérangar had reported that most of the villages in that region had been burned to the ground by fighters. The people were hunted like deer in the bush. Bérangar himself had needed to travel through the bush to reach Moundou in Occidental Logon because Hissène Habré's fighters were so likely to ambush travelers on the road. Then he got a ride with someone to come to N'djaména. I was sad to hear what my granduncle was telling me, because I knew the mentality of the fighters and had experienced first-hand the cruelty of these men.

After my bath, very distressed by the news he had told me, I hoped to get away for a while to calm myself. I told Mbaïlem-mou that I would like to join my cousin Sanabé Abel. He asked me to wait until one of my uncles came back from school to take me to Sanabé's house. It was finally about 6:00 p.m. that my uncle Mbaïtidjé Richard took me to Sanabé's house. Unfortunately, when we arrived, he was not at home. Instead, it was a cousin, Djimtengar, that met us. He was surprised and happy to see me. I myself was surprised to see him, too, because from Doba we CODOs had scattered to different regions of the country.

Djimtengar was lucky. He had been sent to the North through N'djaména a few months before, and when he was stationed nearby, word reached Sanabé, who asked him to abandon the army. We talked for a while, and since Sanabé did not return home right away, my uncle left me with my cousin Djimtengar and went back home.

When Sanabé came home that evening, he was as surprised and happy to see me as Djimtengar had been. He said "Ngôwn njé gom, oyo le Allah ke ré seï adoum." This means, "My junior brother, thanks to God who has brought you to me." Sanabé sent Djimtengar to Ndongar's house for *argué*. Djimtengar brought the jug of *argué*, and Sanabé — along with Rayam, Adjutant Moré, and Djimtengar, all sharing the same house — drank to celebrate my presence among them. We were talking about general things, but before they finished their *argué*, sleep had captured me.

23

Earning Money
to Attend School

A FEW DAYS LATER, I ASKED SANABÉ ABEL to help me get enrolled in high school. He wanted me to wait for the next year because school had started in October, and now we were in the middle of January. I felt sick at the thought of having to wait until the next October. It was hard for me to stay home alone while others were busy all day. For the short time that Djimtengar was in town, I had a companion at home when the others went to their jobs. Unfortunately, Djimtengar returned to our village only a week after my arrival in town, and our nephew Béoungar, who shared the house with our other cousins, had a job at a refreshment bar near the district government office until late every night.

I was often alone at home. Out of boredom I walked every day around the area of Nônsané where we lived. Every day I increased my familiarity with the neighborhood, playing soccer with neighborhood boys or watching the local men play a card game. One day I went a little bit farther than usual and discovered a junior high school, the Collège d'Enseignement Général, Numero 2 (CEG II), very close to the senior high school, the Lycée Félix Éboué. I went to the office of the director of the CEG II. His secretary allowed me to see him. I informed him that I had formerly been a student of the Lycée Bernard

Dikoa Garandi de Doba. I had lost all my papers that would show him that I had studied at that Lycée, but I requested his help to enroll at his school. The director told me that without any paperwork attesting to my level, he could not know if I qualified for admission to that level of schooling.

I told him that I had successfully finished my third year in high school *(classe de quatrième)* and had passed for the fourth year *(classe de troisième)*. I explained to him that it was because of the war in my region that I could not bring him all my papers. I assured him that I was a good student. I asked him, if he did not trust me, to allow me to take classes for two weeks and then ask my instructors to assess my level. Then he could make his final decision in my case. Finally the director agreed to admit me to CEG II. Unfortunately, despite this opportunity, I failed in my attempt to enroll because the fee would be 5,000 FCFA per year, and when I asked Sanabé Abel to get me that money, he told me that he did not have any money.

I was so disappointed to miss the opportunity that the director of CEG II had offered me that I did not know what to do. To avoid having to be alone at home or walking around the *quartiers* without purpose, I preferred to hang out with my nephew Béoungar David in his temporary job at the refreshment bar. One noon, a diplomat named Pagnamé, Chad's representative for cultural and educational affairs at the embassy in Cameroon, came to N'djaména to get the money for his budget. During that period, Hissène Habré required diplomats to report to him in Chad and take the money in person for their respective services. Mr. Pagnamé, who had come to N'djaména for that reason, happened to come to the refreshment bar where Béoungar David was working. I sat on one of the benches in front of the cashier's desk. After drinking one bottle of Gala beer, Mr. Pagnamé asked Béoungar to bring him another glass. When Béoungar complied, Mr. Pagnamé asked me to come and share the bottle of Gala with him. I said, "No, thank you, sir."

He said, "My boy, when your elder speaks to you, you must honor him." I immediately got up and took a chair at the table with Mr. Pagnamé.

When the first bottle was empty, Mr. Pagnamé ordered two more bottles of Gala for us. Because I had grown up in Protestant, non-drinking areas, I had only just started drinking beer, and then only occasionally. With my second or third bottle of Gala, I started talking more than Mr. Pagnamé himself.

Mr. Pagnamé talked about his years as a primary school teacher before becoming a diplomat when Hissène Habré came to power. Now he introduced himself as a man of Mayo-Kebbi. I presented myself to him as a young man of Oriental Logon and, more precisely, a youth of Bodo, the granary of Chad.

Mr. Pagnamé said, "I did not serve in Oriental Logon, but I heard about the people of Bodo, who are said to be skilled in agriculture. Produce from your area stocks even the markets of Camaroon."

"Yes sir," I replied. "I appreciate my people of Bodo and respect their skills in agriculture. Sir, you said you are from Mayo-Kebbi."

Mr. Pagnamé responded in the affirmative.

I went on: "When I was in my last year of primary school, my instructor told us that Mayo-Kebbi is the largest prefecture in southern Chad. But which area are you from, I wonder?"

Mr. Pagnamé replied, "Yes, your instructor is right. Mayo-Kebbi is very large, and I am from Léré. My boy, you are very intelligent."

I replied modestly, "No, I am not. I am just managing."

Mr. Pagnamé repeated his praise for my intelligence and then asked me what else my instructor had taught me about Mayo-Kebbi.

I told him that an important thing I had learned about his region was the rearing of stock. The people of Mayo-Kebbi were said to have a lot of goats and oxen. Their cattle and goats were more highly valued than those of the North.

Mr. Pagnamé asked me why this would be.

I replied, "According to what my instructor said, and what I read in a book of Chad's geography, the center of Chad is dominated by the savanna, the North is a desert, and the South is the zone of agriculture and forest. In my estimation, the goats and oxen in the central and northern areas of Chad do not have as much grass to eat as ours do in the South. It may be the rainfall that explains the difference between the failure of animal husbandry of the North and its success in the South."

Mr. Pagnamé replied to this, "Now instead of referring to you as merely an intelligent fellow, I prefer to call you Mr. Geographer because you know well the geography of our country. When did you learn so much about Chad?"

I said that about four years before I had learned the geography of our country at my last year in primary school.

To Mr. Pagnamé's question about my current level of schooling, I responded, "I have completed the program of *quatrième* [ninth grade in high school] and passed for the program of *troisième* [10th grade]. I am planning to return to school next year, God willing."

Mr. Pagnamé said then, "Because I have been an instructor, when I talk to a student for a while, I can quickly tell if he is clever or not. I know already that you are intelligent. I advise you to go back to school. I am sure that you will be somebody one day in the future."

I thanked him, and we continued our conversation, talking about diverse cultures and traditions in Chad as we drank. Mr. Pagnamé, who disapproved of some traditional ways of our old people in Chad, told me his story. His father had disliked him and loved only his elder brother. Mr. Pagnamé said when he was teenager his father had considered him to be a recalcitrant child. Though his father trained the elder brother to take his place and property someday, he sent the younger to school to be punished by the instructors.

Here I said, "Sir, if I were in your place, I would say, 'Thank you, my father,' if he sent me to school, whether for my benefit or my punishment."

Mr. Pagnamé asked why I would do such a thing, and I replied, "Because your father wanted to punish you, but the punishment turned into a blessing. Today you are able to write and speak French. You have friends all over Chad and around the world. What you have is more than what your brother has. And another thing, you are drinking the white man's beer — something that a villager cannot easily get."

Mr. Pagnamé smiled and admitted that I was right about that. Then he put his hand in his shirt pocket and brought out a 5,000-FCFA bill for me. My words had apparently pleased him greatly.

That day, because it was noon, Béoungar did not yet have many customers. Mr. Pagnamé asked him to bring three bottles of Gala and one more glass. When Béoungar brought them, Mr. Pagnamé asked him join us at the table. He explained to Béoungar the reason that he blamed his father and also said that I was trying to convince him that his father in fact had helped him to get a better life.

I said to Mr. Pagnamé, "Sir, what I told you is true. If today, sir, you go back to Léré and tell people of your area that your father punished you by sending you to school to be maltreated by instructors, people will tell you the same thing that I am telling you." Mr. Pagnamé seemed to appreciate this opinion, which he had me repeat once again in the presence of Béoungar and himself. I imagine that he was now pretty happy about his life, because he brought out another bill — this time a 10,000-FCFA bill — and gave it to me. Mr. Pagnamé realized that Béoungar's face betrayed some unhappiness, so he brought out from his pocket two 10,000-FCFA bills, giving one to Béoungar and the other to me.

Mr. Pagnamé continued buying Gala for us. He gave another 10,000 FCFA to Béoungar to bring us a case of Gala, and then he gave me 10,000 FCFA again. When Béoungar brought the case of beer, Mr. Pagnamé asked us to excuse him because he needed to go home and lie down. He asked us to continue to drink the rest of the beer. He promised to return that evening.

When Mr. Pagnamé had left, I quickly emptied my glass. I told Béoungar that I would go home. He told me to give him the money for safekeeping, because all that beer had made me "tired," he said. I said at first that I would be okay. Béoungar said the house was far away (about 3 kilometers), and in a bad area. He advised me to give him that money to keep it for me. Naïvely, I gave him my money (35,000 FCFA) and headed home.

On my way home, I was very happy. Not only had I enjoyed quite a quantity of beer, but also I had "earned" more than enough money for an entire year's education. I jogged, walked unsteadily, talked and laughed to myself on the road from Paris Congo II to Nonsané. When I reached home, Sanabé Abel, Rayam, and Adjutant Moré, who were sitting and talking together in the front yard, were surprised at the way I was walking. When I came close to them, I fell down near them and said I was dead. My cousins thought something horrible had happened to me. None of them suspected I was drunk, because it was not my habit to drink. Sanabé Abel, who thought someone had poisoned me, asked me to tell him where I had been and what I had taken. When I tried to talk to them, they all smelled Gala on my breath.

I told Sanabé Abel and the others that I had been with Béoungar, that there was someone who bought us some drink and gave me about 35,000 FCFA. Sanabé asked me if I knew the person. I said no, but the person said he had been a teacher who then was posted to Yaoundé as a diplomat. When Sanabé asked me where the money was, I told him that Béoungar was keeping it for me.

Sanabé Abel asked Adjutant Moré to go and collect that money from Béoungar and bring it to him. When Moré met with Béoungar at the bar and asked him for the money, Béoungar just laughed and told his uncle Moré that I had told them a strange story because I was drunk. He said someone had come into the bar and asked for Gala. He served him, and the man allowed us to drink with him. Later he paid for the beer, and apparently I was so drunk that I thought the money was for me. Moré was confused and returned to the house, where he told Sanabé what Béoungar had said. Because Sanabé Abel knew me well, and knew me to be an honest person, he waited until I awoke some hours later from my stupor before asking me to relate to him the events as I recalled them.

24

Recouping My Wealth

I SLEPT FOR A WHILE, AND ABOUT THE TIME Béoungar came back from his workplace, I awoke. In the presence of my other cousins and Béoungar, Sanabé asked us to relate to them the wonderful evening that we had passed at Béoungar's bar. As Béoungar was my senior in age, I waited for him to take the floor before me. He kept quiet, though, so I chose to speak and reported briefly about our evening by saying that someone had bought us a drink, and then had given about 35,000 FCFA to me, and 15,000 FCFA to Béoungar.

Sanabé asked me to show him that money, and I told him that Béoungar had told me to give it to him for safekeeping when I left the bar. Béoungar replied calmly, "Nobody gave us any money. Someone came to the bar and bought some bottles of Gala and shared them with us. When he was leaving, he gave to Ésaïe 5,000 FCFA for the Gala that we had drunk, and Ésaïe thought that the man gave him the money as a gift. I think it was because Ésaïe was 'tired' that he gave you some wrong information."

I replied to Béoungar that I had indeed been tired, but I was the one who took Gala in the glass and drank it. "I was aware of everything that happened," I said. "I came back home alone on the road without mishap and found the right house without trouble. I remember what I told Sanabé, how Sanabé sent Adjutant Moré to you. And I heard Adjutant Moré when he reported to Sanabé what you had told him."

171

I explained point by point all that had transpired during the time that we spent in the bar with the diplomat. Then I explained point by point how Béoungar had asked me to give him my 35,000 FCFA so that he could keep it in a safe place for me and bring it to me when he would join me at home. When Béoungar rejected all my explanations and said he owed me nothing, I told him, "You say with your mouth that you owe me nothing, but in your conscience you stole my 35,000 FCFA that the diplomat gave me."

Sanabé told Béoungar that the way I explained the events, it seemed to him that someone gave us some money. Sanabé asked us to come to agreement among ourselves so as not to lose that money. He said that when we get drunk, we become more generous because we are out of our normal thinking, but when we come to our senses, we regret our acts. Sanabé warned us, "If Béoungar does not find an appropriate solution, and I go to the diplomat to help us solve this problem and let him know how much money he gave us yesterday, he will take back his money from us, and this would not be to our advantage."

Sanabé's words broke Béoungar down, and he finally acknowledged that the man had given us some money, but he still contended that my money was not nearly as much as 35,000 FCFA. He went to the bathroom and came back with 10,000 FCFA for me. I insisted that the diplomat had given me 35,000 FCFA and not 10,000 FCFA, so I could not take it. After a brief argument between us, Béoungar added 5,000 FCFA. I said there was no way I would accept so small a sum. I needed all my 35,000 FCFA.

Sanabé asked me to take the 15,000 FCFA and leave the rest for Béoungar. I refused angrily. Sanabé told me again to let Béoungar have the rest. Because he told me twice and was my elder, I collected 15,000 FCFA from Béoungar and left him the remaining 20,000. I gave the 15,000 FCFA to Sanabé and asked him to pay for my admission at the College d'Eseignement General II. I also reminded him that I had met the director of the school, and he had asked me for the amount of 5,000 FCFA for my admission.

While I was giving Sanabé the money, one of our cousins named Matthieu Kôdingar came to visit us. Sanabé asked him to take me to CEG II the following day to see if I really qualified for admission. He was concerned that I might not be admitted to the school because the term had already begun and I had no documentation of prior schooling.

25

Back to School

MATTHIEU KÔDINGAR TOOK ME THE NEXT morning to CEG II. He asked to speak with a member of the faculty, Mr. Ndira, the former director of the CEG of Béndjôndô. Matthieu knew Mr. Ndira, who had escaped from the Black September. He was lucky to have reached safety in N'djaména and become an English teacher at CEG II. When Mr. Ndira entered the reception area, Matthieu Kôdingar greeted him, walked him outside with me, and explained my situation to him. Mr. Ndira agreed to speak on my behalf to the Director of Studies, so the two of us met with the director in his office. Mr. Ndira told the director that I was lucky to have reached N'djaména alive. This was a great truth.

The Director of Studies reminded us that all the classes were full. Not only that, but we had come in February, and the first semester was already finished. In mathematics, the teachers had finished with algebra and were into geometry already. But the Director of Studies apparently felt obligated to Mr. Ndira and did not want to disappoint his colleague. He looked at me from the feet to the hair and he said to Mr. Ndira that the first semester was over, and he was not supposed to admit any students in mid-year. Also the classes were full and there was really no room for me. Nevertheless, he was going to admit me. Because of the way I dressed, he knew I was no hooligan, he said. Mr. Ndira gave thanks to his colleague, and I did, too. Then the Director of Studies asked me to come back the following day to pick up my schedule and class list. I thanked him most sincerely once again.

Mr. Ndira took me back to Matthieu, who was waiting for us outside under a *nimier* tree. He took me back home on his moped, but first we stopped to see Béoungar, where we met Sanabé. Matthieu let Sanabé know about my admission to class. I received words of congratulation from Sanabé. The two men were drinking their Gala — apparently at Béoungar's expense, perhaps to utilize some of the funds he had received from the diplomat the previous day through me — and told me to go home to prepare myself for classes on the following day.

The next morning, I went early to CEG II and to the office of the secretary and informed her that I was there to see the Director of Studies. She asked why I wanted to see him. I told her that he had admitted me yesterday and asked me to come for my schedule in the morning. The woman asked for my name, and when I told her, she said my schedule was already set. She gave it to me and asked me to go to the first floor of the building that faced the office building, so I crossed the courtyard and looked for the class of *troisième* F.

I located my classroom and knocked on the door. When the mathematics teacher, named Mr. Obain, came out, I greeted him and presented my class schedule. Obain informed the class that they had one more student. Most of the students shouted that the class was full, and indeed there were somewhere between 80 and 100 students in the room, five to a bench. The elected representative of the class, named Youssouf, stood up and said, "This class is full, and we are not sardines that the administration should pack us together like this." The class applauded him.

The negotiation between Obain and the class took a few minutes, but the students refused to let me join them. When I tried to open my mouth, saying that I was as much in need of this class as they, most of the students taunted me, calling, "CODO, CODO!" They recognized from my face that I was a Southerner. As Obain was from the South, he now closed his mouth because the students were trying to politicize the situation by using the term CODO.

I plucked up my courage and said to them, "First of all, the CODOs are Chadians just like you. Hissène Habré seeks peace in this country and is asking CODOs to come out and work with him to rebuild the country. It is people like you who have spoiled the politics of Hissène Habré. Yes, I am CODO. If you want to, go ahead and inform Hissène Habré that you have a CODO in your class. He will be pleased to hear it."

I realized that some students had closed their mouths when they heard these words confirming that I was CODO. One of the students, nicknamed *Explosif,* was one that continued to argue against my admission. I entered the class without their permission and sat on the same bench where *Explosif* sat. (I thought if we were going to fight each other, this would prevent his spending the day urging everyone else to attack me.) They still talked, but in quieter tones, and I did not answer because I already had taken my place. Obain, who had kept quiet during the argument, recommenced the lesson in geometry.

The following day when I came to class, nobody said anything bad to me. A few of them even greeted me. Day by day, I became friends with many students in my class. A few days later, some of the students from the South said they admired my approach on that first day. I asked why they had not spoken out in my support then, but nevertheless I thanked them for their present kindness.

Ndira, who had helped to get me admitted to CEG II, was my English teacher that term. To demonstrate to him that his faith in me was not misplaced — and thereby to encourage him to help future students in the same situation as I — I worked hard in his class. My first test at CEG II was in his English class. I got a score of seventeen out of twenty on that first test. That made me one of the best students on that test. After class, he praised me and said only two students had earned a score that high. He encouraged me to work hard and said that if I did so, everything would be fine for me.

In other classes, my tests were not so good — especially in mathematics, where I got eight out of twenty correct on the first test. The mathematics studied in this course was probably the equivalent of Algebra II and Trigonometry in a U.S. high school, and I had not yet studied Algebra I. I was not discouraged, though, and I continued studying hard.

I put myself into a study group made up of Alexandre, Miskine, and others who were from the Lycée Félix Éboué. It was their second year at this level, and I had entered the class after algebra had already been covered, and so their knowledge of mathematics was much higher than mine. I could not understand the way they solved the mathematics problems of the type we needed to know to earn the *Brévet d'Études du Premier Cycle au* Tchad (B.E.P.C.T.), the diploma toward which we were all working hard. I took them for super-intelligent beings because I was not able to solve factoring and development (polynomial) problems that these five young men could solve.

I decided I needed more intense work to catch up in math class, so I joined another study group, as well. The other was a group led by Marguéritte Laoungou. I took advantage of the fact that the two groups had different days of training. A month later, I was able to factor and develop most of the equations. In the second month of my training with these two groups, I was able to discuss alternate solutions with them when we had some especially hard problems. Before the end of the semester, I knew how to apply the theorems of algebra and geometry. My friends whom I had earlier feared in mathematics now had great respect for me at the end of semester.

My teacher in mathematics had noticed my considerable progress in his class and advised me to take a test for admission to an industrial-technical high school. Unfortunately, I was not able to take that test for several reasons. First, the Industrial Technical High School — the only one in Chad — was located in Sarh, and if I returned there I would be arrested and probably killed by Touka or Faki Saboun. Second, the deadline for applying to take the test had passed. Not only that, but according to policies of the technical high school, first-semester scores at the *troisième* level were required to be at least twelve out of twenty. I was disqualified because I had missed the entire first semester and had no scores. Also I doubted that I would attain so high a score in the second semester.

June arrived, the main month for exams in Chad. We were informed that we must go and take our B.E.P.C.T. exam at a different school, CEG I. I was determined to do well. Some of my relatives, friends, and neighbors thought me overly ambitious to attempt the B.E.P.C.T. exam after only three months of study. They did not think I was likely to succeed. As for me, though, I was confident because I had studied my lessons diligently. When the day arrived, I went to CEG I and took my exam.

In about one month, the names of those who had passed the exam were posted at every high school and in every school office in Chad. My name was on the list! Because my scores put me among those conditionally admitted to technical school rather than among those definitely admitted, I elected to undergo the oral exams that would, I hoped, place me in the higher category. A month later I learned that I had been successful and had raised my score on the B.E.P.C.T. to the highest category.

When the new list was posted, I received words of congratulation from all my friends and relatives and even those who were not my friends. Some of them confessed that they had thought I would fail the exam, because they had known many students who had attended *troisième* from the beginning to the end of the year who had failed. I was one of the first they knew who had passed the test. Sanabé was so proud of the effort I had made that he talked quite positively about me to many of our relatives and his friends, though never in my hearing. Some of my cousins, whose misbehavior, drinking, or laziness Sanabé wanted to correct, found themselves compared unfavorably with me. This did not make me popular with my cousins.

From time to time Sanabé when he was drinking would have an idea and propose it to me. After I had succeeded on the exam, one day when he was drinking *argué* at home, Sanabé suggested that I take the class of *troisième* again, but this time the entire year. He wanted me to have a strong foundation of knowledge so that I would not have problems in *terminal* (the final year of high school) for my *bacalaureat* diploma. At first I did not think much of this idea. I had noticed, though, that many students reached *terminal* and then stayed there several years without earning the degree. After a few weeks I agreed that it would be an excellent plan for me to repeat the *troisième* year.

A few weeks after my success on achieving the B.E.P.C.T., I heard that my cousin Ngarnadji was arrested by the fighters in Doba for some reason. I was demoralized to hear that news. It was hard for me to sleep because I was worried about Ngarnadji's family, his wife and three children. I was plagued by questions. Who would take care of Ngarnadji's family, since our people from the villages were living in the bush? Who in Doba could assist them?

During that period, the government sent Sanabé to Belgium for a conference. Without Sanabé, I did not know to what relative I could plead help for Ngarnadji's family. I decided to take responsibility myself and raise some money. One morning I looked for a job all over the city. I was lucky to get a job in a refreshment bar in the *quartier* called Ridina. I was hired as manager of the bar, with a monthly salary of 4,000 FCFA (about $6 to $8 USA).

I saved my tips plus my monthly salary, and by the end of the month I found myself with 10,000 FCFA. Going to the headquarters of CotonTchad (Cotton Manufacturing of Chad), I sent that money to Issac Doumalta, who was an employee of CotonTchad of Doba and a deacon of our church there. I hoped he would be an honest man and get the money to those who needed it. I learned later that Ngarnadji's wife indeed received that money through Issac at the moment that she had nothing at home to feed her children and her husband was still in prison.

I continued working until classes restarted in the month of October. The small amount of money that I had saved allowed me to buy my school supplies at the central market of N'djaména. That day, I saw a notice about two action films that would be showing at a cinema by the market. That same evening, I returned to watch the movies. I was sitting on the first row near the main door of the theater, close to the screen. When the first movie was nearly over and the action at its highest, the film stopped suddenly, and the door was opened from outside. Armed fighters pulled open all the doors and stepped inside. One of the fighters ordered us to come out one by one. There was suddenly

Two weeks after I (left) was hired as manager in a refreshment bar in N'djaména, 1985. Laoukoura (right) was my assistant and young Tibo, our friend.

panic throughout the cinema. I quickly put my coins in my mouth not to allow the fighters to take them away from me. Because I was so close to the door, I was among the first people to come out. They were asking for our identification, and while we retrieved it, they frisked us for money, took everything they wanted, and loaded people onto *Véléras*. As my mouth contained the coins, I was not able to talk, and immediately the idea of playing deaf came to me. I made myself seem deaf and used the signs of deaf people to respond to their words. Not to waste their time, the fighters released me and looked for other people. I ran off, and soon the trucks pulled away with many men on them.

On the following day, people realized that the men arrested were taken to the North to fight for Hissène Habré. Habré's army was threatened by the forces of Goukouni, who was supplied with weapons and troops by Moammar Kaddafi of Libya. Since that evening, I have not attended the movies.

I went back to class at the *troisième* level at the beginning of the term. The physics teacher who had given me the oral examination in mathematics during my B.E.P.C.T. was surprised to see me back in the *troisième* class, and he asked why I was retaking the same course. I told him that the previous year I had been in class for only three months. I preferred to take the entire year again so that I would not have any problems in *terminal* three years hence. My teacher — whom I had apparently impressed during my oral examination — said I might be fine if I just moved on to *seconde* class. He added that there were many students without my skill in mathematics in *seconde*, but if I wanted to be in *troisième* again, it was fine with him.

The next day, the young girls Achta Yalngar and Fatimé, who on the first day of class sat one row ahead of me, decided to join me on my bench. I figured out later that they wanted me to help them in mathematics and physics, perhaps having overheard our physics teacher's praise of my skill in mathematics. The two girls arrived before any of us boys and took over my bench but invited me to sit between them. The girls then discouraged any of my former bench-mates from sharing the desk with us.

These two girls were very nice to me. Every day they brought me something to eat in class or during the break. Sometimes I received lunch money from them. As they became my good friends, I helped them with homework, and during the tests I did not hide my exam sheet from them — until one day our teacher realized that the grades of us benchmates were very similar. Our teacher thereafter moved us to separate benches for the next exam. Fortunately for Fatimé, who was much less successful on the test without my assistance, she married a few weeks afterwards and could leave math classes behind her. Achta became pregnant at the end of our school year and did not attend regularly thereafter.

The *troisième* class was one of the best classes in my life. Not only was I befriended by Fatimé and Achta at school, but also other women that were in our class invited me to their houses to help them in mathematics and physics. I received several gifts from them and their husbands. A few weeks before the B.E.P.C.T., I was requested by many colleagues to help them in mathematics for their exams. *Troisième* was a class that I really enjoyed — except the horrendous day when Masdé betrayed me to the militia of the Fifth District of N'djaména.

26

Betrayed

EARLY IN OUR SECOND SEMESTER IN *troisième,* a portion of the bathroom wall at home collapsed. Because Sanabé wanted to be able to take his bath early in the morning before going to work, he asked Masdé, the son of our cousin Tinguengar who was with us, to help me fix the wall so that the following day we would not have any problem taking our morning bath. I took the day off from school to work on the wall. Masdé refused to help me that day. In my anger, I cut a small branch of the *caïcédra* tree with a few leaves on it and beat Masdé twice with it. This was to show him that it was not good to be lazy, and he had to respect the orders of Sanabé, our elder.

After this bit of discipline, Masdé moved toward the wall, as though to help me, but when he came near to the wall, he ran away. Apparently he went to the Fifth District and informed the militia that there was a CODO in the house where he was staying. About a quarter of an hour later, while I was working alone, Masdé came back with six militiamen well armed with Kalashnikovs and semi-automatic rifles to arrest me. The six men ordered me to go with them to the Fifth District. I had been mixing clay with water to construct the wall and was filthy, so I asked them to allow me to wash my dirty hands and legs before going with them. I was not allowed to wash, and the leader of the group took offense at my having requested this dispensation. I was tightly surrounded by the six militiamen. One was before me, another behind me, and two were on each side. When we entered the yard of the Fifth District, the other troops that were standing around outside the office asked the six guards surrounding me if I were the CODO. Some of the militiamen that had "captured" me answered yes, apparently proud to have accomplished their mission. It took only a few minutes for us to enter the office, which was attached to the jail. I knew that the door of the jail was a "one-way" door; that is, once I went in, I could not expect to come out alive. Very quickly the office was invaded by the militia. All the men were well armed with clubs and fan belts to beat me as soon as I could be put in jail. The men seemed eager to have at it.

In our area, I was well known and loved by children because I liked to jog with them. Five-year-old Florence and her younger brother Caleb, who were children of our neighbor Samuel Kétté across the street, started crying when they saw me framed by well-armed militiamen and heading for the Fifth District station. Samuel Kétté, who was returning from his workplace for breakfast, saw his children on the street and asked them why they were crying. His children told him that I had just been arrested by the armed militia.

Samuel Kétté had compassion for his children who were crying for me, so he asked his children not to cry and to go inside. He said he would bring me back. Quickly Samuel followed me to the Fifth District. He was well respected in this district because of his dynamic activities on behalf of the political party of Hissène Habré named UNIR (National Union for Independence and Revolution). (Habré considered any who did not belong to his party to be his enemy.) Samuel was also well favored because his elder brother, Moïse Kétté, was at that time the director of DDS, the organization responsible for torture of prisoners and enemies. Samuel Kétté entered the office of the militia boss without knocking. I was lucky he arrived when he did: already one soldier had opened the jail door, and the boss had just ordered me taken inside, so I had taken only one step into the jail. Samuel Kétté grabbed the back of my shirt. He shouted loudly, "Do not enter!"

Samuel Kétté knew in advance that if I entered that jail, it would be hard for me to return once again to life. He asked the chief of militia what evil thing I had done to them that they wanted to put me in the jail.

The man told him that I was a CODO.

Samuel Kétté said that I had been in N'djaména for many years, and he doubted I could be a CODO without his knowledge. He asked who had told them that I was a CODO.

The militia chief let Samuel know that it had been Masdé, a member of my household, who had informed them about me.

Samuel Kétté said next time there was this kind of situation, he would appreciate their letting him know. He said I was not a CODO. Masdé, on the other hand, had only just arrived from the village, so he might be a CODO.

God set me free through Samuel Kétté. Before Samuel took me out of the office, the chief asked me if Masdé were a CODO. I said I was not sure. I did not want to make Samuel angry, but on the other hand, I did not want to incriminate my nephew, who was sitting outside the office. Then the chief asked me what I wanted them to do to Masdé on my behalf. I said to do nothing. He offered at least to beat Masdé for me because of what he had wanted to do to me, but I told him that Masdé was my nephew, and I would like for them to leave him unharmed. The chief said they would decide what to do to him. He was kept there for about half a day before he was released. Denied the opportunity to torture me, the militia took out a few of their frustrations on my nephew before sending him home.

When Sanabé returned home early the following morning and heard from his wife and daughters what had happened, he talked with Masdé. He told him to leave the house and to get out of N'djaména. The boy was still at the house that evening, so Sanabé repeated his message. Sometime the following day while Sanabé was at work and I was at school, Masdé left us. The bathroom wall was completed eventually but without his help.

27

Djiguingar, the Lucky Prisoner

THIS IS AN EVENT THAT A COUSIN, Djiguingar, told me had happened to him. Early in 1985, fighters had been burning huts and killing many villagers from Béti county to Bodo county. Djiguingar and his one hundred neighbors who had fled Takapti II in fear were suffering from lack of drinking water and pondered whether to return to the village to dig deeper an old well that had gone dry some time before. There were two groups of villagers in the bush debating the issue, with opposing ideas. The first group did not want to take the chance of coming back to the village and digging the old well, fearing that they might be surprised by fighters still in the area. A second group preferred to take the risk because children were suffering from thirst. Djiguingar, who supported the idea of trying to redig the well spoke persuasively, saying that he had been in many big towns in Chad and he knew the Muslims. Djiguingar said that usually Muslims set aside Friday as a holy day of the week and avoided killing or stealing people's property on that day as a sign of respect for Allah. He said he believed the next day would be Friday and doubted that any fighters would come. He urged his neighbors to join him the next day to get the water for their children.

There were still a few people who did not trust what Djiguingar said, but "when the mass applauds, reason keeps quiet," so those few people kept quiet and joined the others the following day to dig the well.

Early that Friday morning, the men took the cords of their wives' well buckets and plied them together to make strong rope. One piece of rope they tied to a bucket for drawing up the earth from the bottom of the well. Then they cut some tree branches and knotted them onto the sturdy rope at regular intervals to make a traditional-style ladder long enough to climb down into the well. When they arrived at the village, since the diameter of the well was not large enough for two people to work in it at the same time, someone entered the well and dug for at least one hour and then was replaced by the next person. The digging went on all morning.

It was about noon when the fighters attacked Takapti II. Djiguingar was the unfortunate villager who had entered the well last, just a few minutes before. The fighters surprised the men of Takapti II and started firing their rifles. Villagers who were working with Djiguingar did not forget him; however, afraid for their lives, they did not have time to send down the ladder so he could escape. A few of the villagers were killed in the sudden attack, but the others were able to save their lives on that horrible Friday.

Djiguingar was left alone, the only man of the village, in the well. He tried to hide himself in the well, but there was nothing to hide under. Both the bucket and the ladder had been taken up to give him room to work in the well. As it was noon, the sun was in the middle of the sky, so there was no darkness in the bottom of the well. When some of the fighters came near the well and looked into it, they clearly saw Djiguingar crying in fear and trying to hide himself. When one of the fighters aimed the barrel of his rifle into the well, Djiguingar covered his head with his hand and cried more. Djiguingar's action made the fighter laugh. He called his comrades to come and watch the actions of the little man in the well. When others came, that fighter aimed his rifle into the well, and Djiguingar did the same thing. All of fighters who were present laughed at Djiguingar and sent down the ladder to come up out of the well.

When Djiguingar got up, the fighters made a circle around him. They looked at him and laughed again. One of the fighters hit Djiguingar's head and asked him if he thought that his puny hands could protect his head from bullets. (Djiguingar was a short man with small hands.) From there, they took Djiguingar to the Toyota where their chief was standing.

One of the fighters explained to their chief the way Djiguingar had tried to protect his head from the rifle bullets, and their chief just smiled. The chief accused Djiguingar of being a CODO.

Djiguingar responded in Arabic that he was not a CODO and would never in his life be a CODO. He said he favored peace. (In point of fact, despite his numerous positive qualities, Djiguingar was a bit of a troublemaker, but he could hardly tell these fighters the truth about himself.) He could not carry a gun against people from the North because all his friends were from the North, he claimed. Nor could he carry a gun against people from the South, who were of his blood. Djiguingar said his only wish was that God would bring them together with those that were against them to make peace so that we could be one loving nation.

The chief said he did not trust what Djiguingar said because he had been making a well for the CODO to get water to drink. Therefore Djiguingar himself was a CODO and the enemy of the chief and his men.

Djiguingar said he could not be a CODO and that he and his fellow villagers were digging the well near the road for government people like themselves who were traveling, so they could have water to drink or to make the necessary ablutions before praying. Probably because he spoke their language and used honeyed words, the fighters spared his life.

After the fighters had left, Djiguingar and the other villagers tried to bury their dead at night. Then he left Takapti II forever and went back to Béngamia. Djiguingar then passed away about ten years after his short imprisonment in the well and this incident with the fighters.

28

The Value of Diplomacy

I N MAY OF 1985, FIGHTERS WERE HUNTING people in most of the areas of Oriental Logon from bush to bush. Bodo was one of the areas most targeted. One of my uncles, Mbaïngomal, lived in that area. People in the county of Bodo used to call him "the strong man." This was because he was one of the tallest, a giant in that county at well over six feet in height. Not only was he tall, but also he was very active in providing people with health care, so he was "strong" in more than one sense.

Mbaïngomal was at least three times surrounded by fighters, but he was always lucky to escape and save his life. A fourth attack pushed Mbaïngomal to leave Békôdô 1. Even after destroying the village, the fighters followed the villagers into the bush to attack them. Mbaïngomal was nearly killed by the fighters; the fighters had chased after him, trying to shoot him. A courageous man, he took the time to pick up his bicycle that he kept beside a tree. Under the bullets of Kalashnikovs and SIGs, the man was helped by his bicycle to speed away from danger. He continued down the footpath to the area of Bégada. Unfortunately the area of Bégada itself had been attacked, and people from those villages were running away through the bush, going the opposite direction of my uncle.

After one day and a half, my uncle was back to where he and his family had been attacked. His wife and children returned to that place also. Together with other relatives, they changed their initial hiding place and decided to build a new place to conceal themselves. My uncle quickly made a new hut for his family, and then he informed his father and mother and his wife that he would go to Fianga and then to N'djaména to recuperate before coming back. My grandfather prayed with him before he left for Fianga.

It was a great joy for me to see my uncle in N'djaména — though I did not know then that it would be the last time I ever saw him. My uncle gave me information about what was going on in the village. Because he had been a nurse and then a mechanic for Conoco and then Esso in Chad, I asked my uncle if he would wait in town for a job with Esso, which was trying to restart its operations in Chad. My uncle had chosen another option, instead, which was to try to open his own clinic in Békôdô 1. He wanted to help people in that region when the war would finally be over.

He had left N'djaména and returned to Fianga where he got financial assistance from one of my great-uncles, Bétoubam Mbaïoreta. With that money he bought some clothes for his wife and children to replace the clothing that had been burned by the fighters with all their belongings in the huts. On his way back to Békôdô 1, he was arrested on the bridge of Moundou that separates the two Logons (Oriental and Occidental). Under an instruction given by the former CODO, Sublieutenant Yaldé, who later became a very powerful danger for his own people, Mbaïngomal was accused of buying the clothes to give to the CODOs. He was taken to the central commissariat of Moundou for few days.

My uncle's cousin, Adoumbaye Tolmbaye, visited him at least twice and also washed his clothes for him before he was transferred to the *maison d'arrêt*, the jailhouse. There he was tortured and killed, cruelly and inhumanly.

Mbaïngomal's wife, named Dénéasbé, traveled from the village to Moundou to see if she could visit her beloved husband. Hoping to see him, she presented herself at the *maison d'arrêt* with food and fruits. The fighters took her food and fruit and told her that they would be sure to give them to her husband later. Every day they did that to her, but the truth was that her husband had been tortured and killed already. When the fighters had thus eaten all the money of Dénéasbé, one of them — who had taken Mbaïngomal's watch — took pity on her, so he handed her her husband's clothing and told her that her husband wanted her to go back home. (Because he was so tall, Mbaïngomal's clothing would not fit any of these fighters from the North, so this jail guard knew that he could hand them over without arousing the suspicion of his comrades.) From this Dénéasbé knew that she belonged to the circle of widows.

When Dénéasbé went back to the village, Békôdô 1 and other villages in the county of Bodo were sad not only about the death of Haroun Mbaïngomal but also the death of his cousin, Jacob Mbaïnadjibé, the chief of Bodo county. The grandsons of Mbaïnaïkou had both been tortured and killed on the same day. Worse yet, nobody was able to locate their corpses.

As a result of the death of my uncle and his cousin, my grandfather refused to run away from fighters any more. When all the population of Békôdô 1 ran away from the village to live in the bush, my grandfather and his wife Ranguel were the only two persons we could find in the village. Sometimes we could also meet the youngest brother of my grandfather, Jean Tôlmbaye, with him.

From time to time the fighters came on patrol to Békôdô 1 and 2. They always assumed that these were the villages of CODOs because of the homonym of the village name. When they arrived, the only couple that they would meet were my grandfather and his wife Ranguel. The fighters, who did not really know the reason that couple had refused to run away from them any more, tried to get to know my grandfather. Little by little, the fighters came to realize that he was filled with wisdom, and they asked him to summon his people to come back to the village. A few weeks later, some villagers who realized that the fighters came sometimes to the village but were no longer aggressive as they had been before, started returning to the village in the evening and then leaving for the bush early in the morning. Some of them that visited my grandfather asked him what the fighters had done while they were in the bush, and whether he had been tortured. My grandfather always told the villagers quite honestly everything the fighters had told him. He told them that the fighters wanted the villagers to return, but that he could not urge them to come back to the village, because he could not take responsibility for what the fighters might do.

A month later, people needed to come to the weekly market of Békôdô 1 because they had used up all their supplies of salt, soap, medicine, or food. Some turned back to their hiding places when they met with bad omens: stubbing a left toe, biting their tongue, meeting an unlucky person on the road. Others encountered only good omens and therefore traveled along the treacherous paths hoping to avoid the fighters. Unfortunately the market was suddenly surrounded by fighters. No one could escape, except one woman who hid herself somewhere and avoided detection. The fighters had been able to ambush the villagers because the fighters kept their cars far away and walked stealthily into the village to surround it. That day most of the men had judged it not safe to come to the market, so it was mostly women there except for a few men. Among the men was one of my cousins named Dingam-madji. As my grandfather had felt the presence of the fighters who surrounded the area, he had come quickly to the market. By that time Dingam-madji and other men were already arrested. Fighters asked them if they were CODOs, but none of them declared himself as CODO.

When the fighters saw my grandfather, they said he was only the person in the village that they could trust, so they asked him about the men they had arrested. My grandfather claimed loudly and firmly that none of them was CODO (though of course Dingam-madji had just arrived from the *maquis* to visit his newborn baby).

In Africa and particularly in Chad, most of the fighters and CODOs used *gris-gris* (traditional magic) to protect themselves. The fighters knew where the CODOs used to hide those magical objects. They ordered each of their prisoners to move their pants and underpants down so they could find out if they were CODOs or not, despite what my grandfather had told them.

Dingam-madji, who had tied his *gris-gris* between his pants and underpants, was very lucky. He was able to move his pants, *gris-gris,* and underpants, down and back up all together. Finally the fighters believed what my grandfather had said and let the men go. Later the fighters continued their patrol to the next villages. My grandfather, who was a strong believer in Christianity, had been tempted by Satan and had lied to the fighters. Under these circumstances, should we say that my grandfather sinned because he lied to save the life of his great-nephew?

29

The Death of
Dingam-madji

SOME MONTHS AFTER HIS ARREST IN the market of his home village
and then the grace of release by the intervention of his great-uncle
Mbaïlemdana, Dingam-madji found himself in the same situation in
Dan-madja. This time, though, his life would end.

It was one morning that Dingam-madji and a few CODO comrades came to the market of Dan-madja, probably to buy food. Unfortunately, they were surprised by fighters in that market. That day,
there was one former CODO among the fighters who had brought his
new comrades to Dan-madja to attack the village that used to supply
him and other CODOs with food.

During that attack on Dan-madja, the former CODO — who had
now become the CODOs' enemy — recognized his former companions
in suffering, and he asked the driver to pursue them in the Toyota.
Dingam-madji tried his best to reach the bush and then hide himself
to catch his breath. As the former CODO knew the CODOs' method
of operating, he asked his new companions to go farther into the bush
with him to see if they could capture Dingam-madji. They saw my
cousin hiding himself among the trees.

Pitilessly the former CODO told his former friend Dingam-
madji that he had asked him to join the fighters with him but that he

had refused, so today he would pay him for this act. The fighter murdered his former friend there, and then he and the other fighters proudly returned to the village.

That day, many men, women, and children lost their lives. It was very hard for people that escaped from that attack to come back to the village to bury the bodies of their loved ones. Some brave women in Dan-madja risked their lives to come back and bury their family members. Even so, though, not all bodies were buried because, after another attack in Bémbaïtada, a village next to Dan-madja, the fighters returned to attack Dan-madja again.

It then became very hard to find anyone in the area of Dan-madja. And during that time the fighters went from bush to bush to attack people. It was as though they were hunters of harmless and defenseless people.

Gôïmbaye Mbaïnanbé, one of my aunts, heard about the death of Dingam-madji. She took her hoe and a piece of her cloth and traveled during the night through the bush to Dan-madja to find and bury the body of her nephew. At last Gôïmbaye found him, and she dug the whole night. At last early in the morning she buried her nephew. When she was ready to leave, the fighters arrived once again in Dan-madja. The courageous woman ran away just before the fighters arrived where she was.

This sad news I received from one of my cousins when we met five years after the events. My informant, Dimanche Djimtôloum, is Dingam-madji Djimtôloum's youngest brother.

30

A Christian Woman Accused by a Man of Traditional Belief

BOÏKETÉ, A VILLAGER OF BÉKÔDÔ 1 KNOWN for his skill in traditional fetish making, gathered different "traditional power" items to protect his village while the area was under pitiless attack by the fighters. His magic had apparently been quite successful, since the fighters had left his village unharmed while pillaging other villages nearby. Early one morning, Boïketé buried his usual fetishes in the earth of each of the five roads that led to his village. It was on the road that led to Békôdô 1 from Bédouada that Boïketé finished his magic making and returned home with great hope that his village was now protected from the evil men of Hissène Habré.

Mrs. Gay, usually called kôn Ézéchiel (meaning "Ézéchiel's mother") was following her husband to their millet field. She took a small path that crossed that road. When she arrived at the junction and noticed the place where the old man had buried his ritual objects, Mrs. Gay used her hoe to remove what Boïketé had buried, and then she continued on her way behind her husband.

Boïketé somehow found out what Mrs. Gay had done and apparently decided she was acting from Christian motivation to eliminate traditional beliefs in the village, for he went to pastor Diara's house and confronted him. "You Christians, has it come to the point that you teach each other to get involved in things that do not concern you?"

Pastor Diara gently asked Boïketé if one of his flock had done a bad thing to him or to others. Boïketé said, "Yes, that 'thing' (Ézéchiel's mother) unburied what I had buried to protect our villagers from the danger of fighters. Since the fighters started destroying our region, our people have not been killed as in other villages of the Oriental Logon region. What that lady has done is the equivalent of setting fire to our village. Békôdô 1 is no longer protected as before. I have not slept to protect our people since our region has been in trouble, but now there is nothing I can do to shield this people from now on. The wretched woman has already killed us."

Pastor Diara knew that the enraged villager could punish Mrs. Gay, her husband, and her family for her actions. He was known to be able to sicken and kill others as well as heal people. To cool him down, Pastor Diara said if Mrs. Gay had really unburied his fetishes, he could not approve of that. He congratulated Mr. Boïketé for all he had done for his village and asked him for forgiveness. The pastor said he was going to investigate this matter and would also let his people know not to do these kinds of things in the future.

Diara sent one of his children to inform Mr. and Mrs. Gay to come and meet him at his house. Mr. Boïketé, whose anger did not go away despite the words of forgiveness that Diara presented him, went from one place to another to inform the other elders of village that Békôdô 1 was no longer protected by his ancestral objects, so the population needed to be more careful. The village had been already killed by Mrs. Gay. Not all the population of the village took seriously what Boïketé said, but some did.

When the Gays arrived and Boïketé had returned, Diara exposed the matter to the couple, and Mrs. Gay remembered unburying something that Boïketé had buried in the road. Diara said to the couple that in this world we had two categories of people. One group believed in God and another held the traditional beliefs. "We Christians," he said, "have our trust in God and follow His words, but others have their own beliefs and follow different ways. We are not supposed to counter-attack their actions physically, but we have to show them the good way spiritually, morally, and through love."

Boïketé seemed pleased with this outcome and welcomed Mrs. Gay's apology. Pastor Diara asked Mr. Gay to take his wife to Boïketé's house and tell her to present her apologies again to him there.

Boïketé was sufficiently appeased not to take reprisals on the couple, but he continued to believe that his magic could no longer protect the village. It was only when there was soon a deadly attack on that village that people started lamenting the foolish and inappropriate action of Mrs. Gay. From bush to bush, when you visited people who had lost their homes, their fields, and all their belongings, they said, "Kôn Ézéchiel has killed us."

31

Békôdô 1 Cries
Over Its Dead

Békôdô 1 BECAME A REGULAR TARGET of fighters who had their base in Bodo, which was less than five miles (8 km) away. Under consecutive attacks, that village had fewer than four hundred people remaining alive. Villagers no more, the people were obliged to live in the bush like wild monkeys to wait for the next attack. They had little hope of escaping the fighters in this life, and they buried their dead in the bush, as did people of other former villages, because it was not safe to bring the corpses home for burial. Békôdô 1 was in the region where Idriss and Ibrahim Itno started their hunting of people in the bush. Within just a few weeks, Békôdô 1 lost most of its great figures. Among all these dead were two brothers worthy of special mention. The murderous circumstances of the time took their lives just a few weeks apart.

Bangounda was Mao's youngest son, the Benjamin of the family, and Mbaïnayal was his next older brother, son of the same mother. These two youngest brothers in their 40's still had a great love for each other. This affection was one of the reasons that during the civil war in N'djaména on February 12, 1979, Bangounda ran away from N'djaména with his family and joined Mbaïnayal in Békôdô 1 instead of seeking safety in Takapti, where the elder brothers of the family had settled and were farming with relatives.

During one of the deadly attacks on the village of Békôdô 1, Mbaïnayal was shot and killed by the fighters. Bangounda, who searched desperately for his brother after the attack, finally discovered his body. The man cried for his brother and asked his murdered corpse why he had left him alone in this life. Bangounda wept that it would have been far better that he be in his place and that Mbaïnayal be returned to life. He said he had run from death in the capital city and had joined him in their native land — and now Mbaïnayal had run away and left him alone. Where could he go now? It was tragic and painful to see Bangounda sobbing over the body of his brother and crying for so long. But there was nothing he could do at that time. His brother was dead.

Some days later during another attack in the Békôdô 1 area, it was the turn of Bangounda and his fellow villagers. The fighters, who had followed the villagers into the bush, circled behind the people to attack them again and eventually reached the area where Bangounda's family and other villagers had hidden themselves. Although they had tried to approach silently, when the fighters started shooting people as they found them in the bush, the sound of their guns betrayed their location. Bangounda quickly hopped onto his bicycle and carried off the bag containing his family's food, hiding it a little bit away from the settlement. He then returned for his elder daughter, Aphénique, whose leg had been paralyzed by a childhood inoculation and who therefore could not run. On his way back for Aphénique, Bangounda encountered other villagers, who urged him not to go back again, because the enemies were dangerously near to their location. Bangounda, though, took the risk to save the life of his daughter. Within moments, he was shot and lay dead on the ground.

Bangounda, well known in N'djaména as one of the best tailors in the country, had built a new life in his home village, and later he expanded his business between Sarh and Bodo. Bangounda was not a CODO, had never harmed anyone, and was killed for nothing. His death, the death of Mbaïngomal, and the death of Mbaïnadjibé had a profound effect on the young people of the county of Bodo, because all three of these men had supported the local soccer team, Jas-Ra ("We can do it"), and made it unbeatable in the prefectures of Oriental Logon and Moyen Chari.

32

Application of Folk Tales to Real Life

I N AFRICA, AND PARTICULARLY IN CHAD, our parents teach us many
important things through tales. Tales are generally told in the
evening when we gather around the fire during cool weather, or in the
hot season when an elder calls for a child to help husk manioc or
groundnuts, for instance. Other children gather, and the elder recites a
tale and then asks, "Now, who can repeat this tale for us?" One child
might volunteer to tell the story again from the beginning, and the
other children will be quick to point out lapses or mistakes. Then
another child attempts the tale. The next evening, it may be another
elder with a story to share. On visits with their parents to other villages, children hear new tales and expand not only their repertoire of
stories but also their stock of cultural wisdom. It is also through these
stories that we know who has the ability to memorize things quickly.

Usually, children who memorize a lot of tales and know how to use
them in real life become wiser and smarter than others who do not. This
was the case in a story of one father and his son who saved their lives
during the murderous events of the South of Chad. Before explaining to
you how they escaped from death, let me tell you one of the tales that
they knew and probably used to outwit danger on that day.

The tale teller begins by calling, "Sou, sou, sou." This signifies

198

that a story is coming. The listeners respond, "Gre, gre, gre," the meaning of which is lost in obscurity for me.

One day, the tale goes, a father and two of his sons went to one of their fields far away from the village to cultivate the crops. When it started raining, they ran to hide themselves in their *keïlo* (a small hut in the corner of the field) to wait until the rain stopped before they continued their work. It was a little bit cold, so they started a fire to warm the little *keïlo*.

The story goes on to say that certain lion men came by. I no longer recall whether they were expressly looking for the man and his son or whether they were on a trip somewhere and sought shelter from the storm. At any rate, they joined the father and his sons in their hut to smoke their traditional cigarettes and wait until the rain abated before continuing their trip.

The father, who realized that his sons and he himself were in danger from these lion men, used body language to signify his meaning to the children before he spoke. One of the two sons was stupid and stubborn, but luckily the other was intelligent and wise. The father used both body language and words to order his stupid son to go and uproot some fresh groundnuts and bring them to the hut for the strangers to eat. The stubborn young man said it was too cold to go out, and besides, it was raining, and he did not want to go digging around for groundnuts in the rain for some lion men.

The father then tried to get his wise son to go. This young man understood what his father intended and agreed to go. Once he was out in the rain, instead of digging groundnuts he ran to the village. When he did not return quickly, the father said to his stupid son that he must follow his brother and urge him to be faster in his task. He told him to get the other son to bring those groundnuts for their "grandfathers." The stubborn son said, "Daddy, I told you, it is too cold, and it is raining. I do not want to go out in the rain."

The father then made excuses to get after his wise son to bring the groundnuts for the lion men. As he made his way to the field, he pretended to keep looking for the son who was supposedly digging the groundnuts. As soon as he was concealed from view by the millet plants of his field, he ran to the village.

The lion men waited for the father and his smart son to come back. In the story, they planned to kill them. Fortunately for the father and son, though, they reached the village safely. Unfortunately for the stubborn and stupid son, he was killed and his body put on the fire. When the rain stopped, the villagers — hearing from the father what had transpired — went to the *keïlo* to see what had happened to the poor young man. They found his body.

The moral of this story is that stupid and stubborn children always pay the price of their stubbornness. Wise, respectful, and intelligent children will always overcome danger and succeed in their lives.

This was precisely what happened to a villager and his son in Bodo. The fighters who surprised Bodo had not found anybody in the village except one man with his son. To find more people, the fighters decided to question these two, before killing them. The man agreed to answer their questions. He was very smart and asked his son to go and quickly find a sheep for the "commanders." The title of commander brings particular pride to any fighter in Chad, whether he has earned the title or not.

The son was quick to understand both the words and the secret signals of his father. He deceived the fighters just like the boy in the story: he went out ostensibly to bring them the sheep for a fine feast and instead ran to the bush. Soon the father started lamenting that his son was so slow about bringing back the sheep. He asked permission to go and help his son more quickly get the animal and bring it to the house. He got approval from one of the "commanders" — a young man who apparently had not listened to the stories of his elder — and headed off in the direction that his son had taken earlier. As soon as he could seize the opportunity of concealing his flight in the long grasses, the father ran away.

The fighters were probably hungry and weary from their day's manhunt through the bush. As Muslims, they needed to kill the sheep themselves, ritually, and then would have wanted the man and his son to butcher the animal and barbecue the meat. They would keep the two villagers alive only long enough to cook them dinner. They probably had plans to take them into the bush and force them by torture to reveal the whereabouts of their friends and relatives before killing them. Fortunately for these two villagers, the "commanders" failed in their mission.

The man and his son met up in the bush and then crossed the border between Chad and the Central African Republic. Twenty years later, the father still lives in that neighboring country.

33

My Comrade
of the Gun

S ARIA HAD BEEN A COUSIN OF MINE, then my comrade ever since we had met in the *maquis*. I met him once again in Unit Six of Ngarkada in Sarh. We used to share our tales and talk about our relatives in the villages from time to time. One day I was sent to Dan-madja to face the enemies. (The fighters called them our enemies. I would call them the liberators of our people.) When I was sent back to the hospital of Sarh from Dan-madja for a sickness the cause of which I alone could know, I met Saria again, because he was still posted to that camp.

The last time I saw him was several years later in N'djaména, when he was sent there after having been wounded in battle. We talked together and worried about what was going on in our home region.

We complained that our leaders Ngarkada and Moueba had led us into trouble and then run away. For the second time, the military authorities had no confidence in us CODOs, and tried to get hold of all of us and send us to north to face the new GUNT and Libyans. I had been incredibly lucky to have escaped from the line and run away, as described in an earlier chapter. Saria, who was not able to escape as I did, was sent to the North with the others of our company in 1984.

When I met him five years later in N'djaména, he started questioning me and telling me what opinion our other comrades had about me. "Toïngar, my cousin, could you explain to me how you disappeared from the line when we were surrounded to be taken to Abéché?" he asked.

I replied that I had not "disappeared" from the line.

Saria responded, "Oh, cousin, my grandmother used to talk to us about how powerful your grandfather was. She said sometimes your grandfather could use darkness, rain, or wind to go and fight, or to liberate someone from his region who had been taken away by others."

I replied, "Your grandmother may well be right, but I can neither confirm nor deny it by my own knowledge, because my grandfather passed away before I was born, and no one told me all the things that you are telling me."

Saria acknowledged, "You do not know, but let me tell you that you belong to a strong family in our region and probably my uncles protected you without letting you know."

I responded that it might be possible, but that I did not believe it. Because my parents had been good Christians, their wedding had been celebrated at church and I grew up as a Christian. I thought I was protected by God, not by my uncles and their traditional powers.

Saria agreed with me that God had surely protected me, but then went on to say, "I could not believe the way you escaped from the line and disappeared, despite all the precautions that the fighters had taken."

I assured him, "You could not believe it though you witnessed it, but nothing is impossible to God. My escape was just the will of God."

Saria then explained to me every episode of their trip to Abéché. "First," he said, "our friends and I were surrounded and separated from G4 camp. Then we were taken in the *Véléra* vehicles to the airport of Sarh and were well surrounded by fighters who were very well armed. We had no chance to escape. At the airport each of us was called to get his 15,000 FCFA in pay and then entered the airplane with no idea as to where we might eventually land."

When everybody got his money, the airplane took them to Abéché. Before the airplane touched down at last, it circled the town at least three times. The men started applauding the two pilots for having gotten them safely to their destination, still without knowing where they were.

Before Saria and his comrades exited the plane at Abéché, Abdoulaye Fall, the second in command of the old CODOs who had been sent to Abéché as commander of the zone of Ouaddaï, came on board with his guards and many other former CODOs to welcome the newcomers. At their descent from the airplane, there was a great joy, because the old comrades had a chance once again to meet — now on the opposite side of Chad from their home region. The newcomers gave more information about what was going on in the South to the others, those who had been taken to Abéché earlier.

Saria said that the first two weeks most of our comrades did not stop talking about the darkness I had used to disappear from the line and escape from the entire surrounding area. I told him that I had not used darkness, nor had I made myself disappear. Instead, I had just walked away from the ranks and then left the area. I told Saria that if I had disappeared or used darkness to cover myself, they could not have seen me when they were taken to the airport, but in fact some of them had seen me near the villa where Moueba used to live and had called to me from the truck.

Saria said he remembered what other friends had said. They suspected I had some kind of black magic that protected me that day. Otherwise, when they called to me from the truck and asked me why I did not come with them, the fighters would have stopped the vehicle and taken me with them to the airport.

Saria said another point he had almost forgotten in proof of my mysterious powers was that the man who had stood just behind me in formation at G4 said he was seeing me right there as usual and then I disappeared. I said, "If this was the case, why didn't that guy grab onto my back and disappear with me?"

Later, I asked Saria to tell me about his life in the North and how his accident had happened. Saria said that he and some of the men had been sent to Zaïre for six weeks of intensive military training. They became commandos. After their first month in Abéché, they were divided up among various units located in the North. Saria's group then was sent farther north. Then they started to re-conquer the north prefecture of Chad, which was under Libyan control. He said they had lost many, many lives, but they persisted until they took control of

Ouadidoum, Fada, and Faya. Their offensive continued until they reached the Aouzou band, the territory bordering Libya that had been controlled by that country for a decade.

Saria said that, after some hard-fought battles, they controlled Aouzou for a few days, but then the Libyans counterattacked them with air fighters. He said it was hard for the Chadian fighters to defend themselves because the airplanes attacked them with bombs and hot water. When Saria was explaining that situation to me, he stopped talking for a while. After a few moments he resumed telling me his adventure in the North.

Saria said after losing control of the Aouzou band, he and his comrades had been forced to retreat. A few months later, the Commander in Chief of the national army, Assan Djamous, and Commander Djimtôloum came and met them again in Faya with orders to go and attack the Libyan army. These commanders brought their guards and bands of fighters to join Saria's commando unit. This time, it was not their intention to attack the Libyans in Chad but rather to attack them in their homeland — at Majan as Sàrah, a military base in Libya itself. Saria said they were guided by a native of Borkou Ennedi Tibesti, a nomad who knew the area between Libya and Chad. He was able to find his way by feeling and smelling the sand in that desert region.

Saria, who was not well educated and could not read well, was not able to explain to me what route they had traveled to avoid detection by Libyan radar. They had access to US military information about the location of Libyan forces and bases. They might have traveled through the Sudan or possibly through Niger, or even been allowed to enter Egypt so as to approach Majan as Sàrah by an indirect route. Our fighters were on a suicide mission to destroy that important military base; Majan as Sàrah was where Khaddafi had most of his military supplies of all kinds, as well as soldiers. Reports on Chadian radio indicated that some of the pilots stationed at Majan as Sàrah were from eastern Europe. Libya was well fortified to destroy our country, Chad.

From Majan as Sàrah, the Libyans used their radar to control a part of north Chad. Because our brave soldiers came from the middle of Libya to their position farther south, the Libyan radar was not able to detect them.

Even though the Libyan soldiers, who might have numbered more than five thousand in that town, were well armed and could have defeated the four hundred Chadian commandos, they mistook the Chadians for friends and comrades who wanted to join them. When they detected forces moving from the north toward their base, they assumed these were friendly forces, so they did not take their defensive positions. When some of them stood up to welcome the newcomers, instead of receiving greetings in return, they were mowed down by our Chadian commandos.

This caused total panic among the Libyan soldiers. They were surprised and disheartened, because they knew that these attackers must have made it safely through many barriers to reach Majan as Sàrah. Only men on a suicide mission could have made it past their sophisticated radar and through the landmine fields and military forces protecting them on the north. While some of our troops were attacking the Libyan soldiers, others who had bazookas destroyed the Soviet Tipolov fighter jets, helicopters, radar installments, and other kinds of equipment.

As a result of their skill and stealth, our four hundred commandos killed nearly three thousand enemies, and in addition destroying more than a hundred vehicles of different kinds and more than twenty-three airplanes. This may well have been one of the greatest losses that Libya had experienced since her independence.

Saria said that action took less than one hour, and then they ran back to Chad. Although their movement into Libya had been carefully coordinated, to avoid military reprisal on the way back into Chad, the fighters scattered. Many of the soldiers who knew how to drive hopped into captured Libyan vehicles and drove to Chad. Because they had gotten so many vehicles from their enemies, in each vehicle there were only a few soldiers, and they all took different routes to reach their home base. They drove across the roadless desert any way they could, hoping to reach a town from which they could navigate their way back to Faya Largeau, or to encounter nomads who could tell them the way they should take.

Saria said his comrades and he who shared one vehicle were not lucky. They had made it back to Chadian territory, but then their vehicle ran across a bomb on the road. After all he had been through, it was there that he lost his leg and forearm. At that point my cousin started weeping and could not speak further.

34

Back to Sarh

A FEW WEEKS LATER, I HEARD THAT the charmed Faki Saboun had been killed by CODO-Rouge fighters in the region of Moyen Chari. Many people and I myself could not believe that this man had been killed by a gun. Faki Saboun had often claimed himself to be an "armored" fighter, specially charmed so that he could not be killed by a bullet, but that day he was killed by the CODO during an ambush. Faki Saboun could have saved his life by running away, as some of his fighters had done when they were nearly out of ammunition. Instead he not only stayed to fight but walked toward his enemies, firing his weapon until it was fully discharged, and then continued marching forward. Finally he was brought down by a CODO bullet.

The death of Faki Saboun shook Hissène Habré by the throat, and news of his death weakened his fighters in the South of Chad. A few months later, Hissène Habré undertook to renegotiate with all the different groups of CODOs in the South. Because the CODOs then agreed on a general cease-fire in the South, in late June I found the courage to take the test for admission to the Industrial Technical High School of Sarh. On the basis of my test score, I was admitted to the "second class" or junior year at the school.

On my way from N'djaména to Sarh in September, I traveled through Cameroon, which had a faster road, at least during the rainy season. I was lucky to meet Ngarnadji in Doba. I had not seen him since he had been arrested and then had escaped from prison to join

Farewell visit from relatives before returning to Sarh in 1986. In front, Dandé (Sanabé's wife) with daughter Neloum and son Dingamadji. In back, left to right, cousin Béngar, friend Djangmbaye, and me.

the CODOs. During the period that Ngarnadji was in prison, people from our church and other churches in Doba prayed a lot for him. Ngarnadji himself spent his time in prison praying and preaching the gospel of God to other prisoners. Almost all of those prisoners gave their lives to God before they escaped from prison or were killed.

Ngarnadji was well protected by God when he was in prison. One

Farewell visitors at Sanabé's house in 1986. In front, maternal aunt Omyal Thamar and friend Djangmbaye. In back, three daughters of Sanabé (Neloum, Hortance, Rémadji), cousin Béngar, me, and maternal uncle Adoumbaye.

of fighters, a prison guard who was a devout Muslim and feared God, discovered Ngarnadji to be a strong believer and protected him from death on several occasions. Each time when fighters planned to take some prisoners during the night to kill them, that good fighter who was in charge of the prisoners took Ngarnadji away before the goon squad arrived to choose the unlucky prisoners.

One day, the CODOs around Doba had defeated fighters on

their patrol rounds, and in frustration and retribution the commander of fighters ordered all prisoners in the *maison d'arrêt* of Doba to be killed. The virtuous fighter guarding prisoners there let Ngarnadji know that there was no way to help him this time. He said everybody was going to be killed in the middle of the night. That night, Ngarnadji shared the word of God with his fellow prisoners. Some prisoners gave their lives to God, and others confessed their sins to Him. Then, shortly before midnight, all the prisoners pushed at the same time on the prison door. The door fell, and the prisoners ran away. I do not know how many of them were arrested or killed later that night.

Ngarnadji arrived in our home village the following night. He had decided to join the CODOs in the *maquis* not only for his own safety but also for the safety of his relatives and the neighboring villages. He was with CODOs in the bush for about a year.

After the CODO officers had signed a cease-fire with Hissène Habré in 1986, a CODO headquarters was installed in Doba. All CODOs were gathered in Doba for a possible merger with the fighters. The fighters were astounded and furious to see Ngarnadji alive and among the CODOs. When CODOs were mixed with fighters and sent to different regions in Chad, Ngarnadji decided to re-enter civilian life in Doba rather than serve in the military surrounded by his former torturers and guards.

In the fall, though, before the CODOs were rallied to the government of Hissène Habré, I traveled to the Industrial Technical High School of Sarh. Crossing Cameroon on the way there, I was lucky to meet Ngarnadji in Doba. During that period, our cousin Simon Bémbaye, who was a pastor in Bébôtô, was visiting Ngarnadji at his house. Both of them were very happy to see me. Ngarnadji blessed me for thinking of his family when he was in prison. Simon Bémbaye said what I did had been remarkable and that few were the young boys or girls from my generation who would do that. He said God must have his own purpose for me in the future, perhaps to help them in some other way. Both cousins spent all their time that day giving me advice, and then they asked God to bless me for them. When I announced my departure to Sarh, there was a long silence in the house. Pastor Simon Bémbaye prayed over me. Once again I was blessed in their prayers before I left.

The agreement between the government of Hissène Habré and the CODOs was supposed to allow the civilians who had joined the CODOs in the *maquis* for their safety now to return to their civilian lives and be protected by that agreement. About nine months after the CODOs had been mixed with fighters in different regions of Chad, the fighters in Doba tried again to arrest Ngarnadji. Fortunately for him, he was not at home when the murderers came to his house. Once again, Ngarnadji ran to the village to preserve his life.

Ngarnadji had decided to restart his new life in the village. There he would stay, he thought, until the country could retrieve its soul and he could come back to Doba to continue with his carpenter's job. Unfortunately, fighters always liked to create hostile situations and to steal the property of Southerners. They went to our village and neighboring villages to look for Ngarnadji, though he had nothing to do with politics or the army. With the help of village leaders, Ngarnadji escaped the fighters and left the village. He lived from bush to bush for some weeks before he finally decided to leave Chad. Before he left for the Central African Republic (this was in 1987), he sent me a letter through his younger sister, named Massal. So that the fighters could not identify and arrest or kill me, Ngarnadji put in place of his own name the former name of his father given by the committee of lion-men, and he addressed the letter to me in the former name of my father (Mbaï-inwôl) given by that committee. He gave the letter to Massal and asked her to try her best to take it to me in Sarh.

I received Ngarnadji's letter a few months later when he had already left the country for the Central African Republic. For reasons of security, Massal, the bearer of the letter, attached the letter to her loincloth to bring it to me at my school in Sarh. Before handing the letter to me, Massal warned me to open it only when I was alone. She spent about one hour with me at my campus. The groundnuts that she brought to me I shared with most of my colleagues that came to meet her. It was only when I escorted Massal back to where she was staying in Sarh that she explained to me the situation in our region and particularly in our village.

When I returned to campus, I lay on the bed and opened the letter at last. The contents of Ngarnadji's letter disheartened and discouraged me. This was the content of the letter:

My dear younger brother Mbaï-inwôl Guétingar,

Good morning or good afternoon, according to the circumstance in which you read this unexpected letter.

Mbaï-inwôl, my little brother, circumstances force me to leave the country. I do not know if I will see you one day again in this life, but I am confident that I will see you in the house of our eternal Father. To that end, I recommend that you not go out with drunkards, and avoid any friendship with people who have no close relationship with almighty God. Let the Holy Spirit guide your steps and shine in your life.

I give you all my three children (Judith, La Foi, and Grace). My concession in Doba is yours, and all my property in Béngamia belong to you from the date that I write to you this letter. Do not worry about me, but worry about the children that I give you. They are your children, and you are like their father and mother. Work hard every day at school, and let the Holy Spirit guide you and your children.

I love you. May God protect you.

Gotdjim Guétingar

I spent all night on the bed without sleeping. Ngarnadji had been my guide in childhood. He had shown me not only how to be a good Christian but also how to look ahead in my life and search for the best and wisest course to follow. Now he was gone. Was it selfish of me to stay in school? Should I leave school and work in the fields to support Ngarnadji's children? The following morning when we went to class, some of my colleagues thought I was sick. Relatives from my village, like Djimadoum Ngadôg, Sangoum Yotôlmbaye, and Maïna Dômtiné, assumed that I must have heard from Massal some very bad news about my father's relatives. After dinner, they wanted to know what was going on with me since I had talked with her. Because they were relatives and close friends, I decided it would be safe to open my heart to them.

My three close friends and maternal relatives comforted me and cheered me up. They encouraged me to finish my academic year. In the second semester of that year, I applied for an internship at Coton-Chad manufacturing in Moundou. I was admitted to the mechanical department, where I was to learn how to operate and repair the machinery used to gin the cotton and press the seeds for oil. Other machines created soap from the oil. On my way to Moundou, I stopped by Béngamia to visit my cousin Ngarnadji's family and other

I was visited by maternal aunt Omyal Thamar.

relatives. Unfortunately, Ngarnadji's wife, Moueba, had taken her children to Bébôtô. My time in the village was very short, so I could not continue to Bébôtô to visit my nephew and nieces.

After a few days in Béngamia, I went to Moundou and presented myself to the head of the mechanical department. Then I was sent to the director of the oil and soap section to be trained by the mechanics. After two months of training, I left Moundou for N'djaména because our higher-level industrial technical classes were transferred there. New machinery had been sent from Italy to replace the school equipment destroyed by fighting in N'djaména, and upper-level students at Sarh were now to complete their training in N'djaména.

When the new classes started in N'djaména, my cohort was anxious. The four previous cohorts in this technical school had had difficulty succeeding in their graduation exams. In fact, few in the first three previous classes succeeded in their *baccalauréat*, but the year before we were qualified for the *terminal*, nobody at all succeeded on the *baccalauréat* exam.

That year, therefore, we were all in a great panic. Most of us wanted to transfer from our industrial school to one of the easier scientific schools. We did not have any hope of success in our program because we knew the value of our predecessors. They had been very intelligent students, and we knew them to be very hard workers, and yet they had failed. As our teachers explained, the reason our predecessors had failed was that the managers of the technical schools did not choose as exam questions the subjects taught by our instructors. The exam managers used to ask engineers (from Chad or foreign countries) who had not taught even one day in Chad to prepare the exam for them. Those engineers apparently just chose any book and prepared from it the exam subjects for the students.

Despite the disappointment of knowing that even good students often did not graduate, I was emboldened by many people and especially by my courageous close friends, Sangoum and Maïna. They had failed twice in their attempt to achieve the *baccalauréat* in the field of mechanical design. Their courage led me to study hard from the beginning of my courses.

35

A Rebel Rebels Against
Fellow Rebels

SUBLIEUTENANT JACQUE TÔLNGAR, a short and slim man, could not have been distinguished from the Gouranes, Habré's tribe, were it not for the Gor initiation marks on his face. Tôlngar was well known throughout the South for his courageous military actions when he was a rebel among the CODOs. This man defended his people of the South before the reconciliation by leading his CODO unit in attacks on the fighters, and then after the reconciliation, by attacking Koulangar's fellows as well as the fighters. Tôlngar would later become a man dangerous to his own people through his naivete.

Jacque Tôlngar was one of the last CODOs to rebel against his comrade CODOs after Major Sao, Chief Corporal Yondo, Captain (actually Lieutenant Colonel) Dingamadji, and few others during the time of Hissein Habré.

People like the late Sao of the Green CODOs and Yondo of the Red CODOs ran away from their bases, I have heard, because they had broken some regulation or rule laid down by the CODO leadership and were afraid of having to submit to punishment by the correctional brigade. (In the absence of jails among the mobile CODO units, "corrections" were generally 100 to 300 beatings with a cane of flexible, sun-cured wood.) Sao and Yondo then each created their own rebel movements in the South. Dingamadji — who studied physics in France and earned a degree in aviation mechanics — and other men were with their comrades in their CODO units and then suddenly decided to join Hissène Habré's forces, I was told. The fighters did not utilize Dingamadji and his comrades in direct fighting against the South, so by leaving the CODOs they were not put in the position of attacking the people that they had earlier defended.

Jacque Tôlngar, though, broke with the Neo-CODOs after Bégada and his own village of Bénjendouli had been attacked by fighters. What made Tôlngar mad was an incident involving the CODO advisor of war, then-Captain Guerngar, who was on patrol in that area. Probably a villager informed the fighters about Guerngar's presence in the area of Bégada. Eager to capture him, Habré's fighters of Doba came quickly and made a surprise attack on Bégada. Unable to face the large number of enemies and defend the village, Guerngar apparently was forced to retreat with his troops. One of his officers, unfamiliar with the area, ran down the wrong path. Instead of finding safety in the bush, he reached the village soccer field, where the enemies caught up with him in their Toyota. Because they were unable to fire their weapons accurately in the moving vehicle, the fighters ordered the driver to run the CODO down. Meanwhile Guerngar and the other officers and troops escaped to the southwest.

Jacque Tôlngar, who was on patrol in another area not far from his own native area, heard the noise of rifles from the direction of Bégada. He and his troops immediately ran toward the village to bring military assistance to Guerngar. By the time Tôlngar and his fellows arrived in Bégada, Guerngar had already left the village, and fighters had already accomplished their "mission" (burning down the homes and stealing the property of the villagers) and left the area.

When Tôlngar's troops arrived in Bégada, it was only some dead bodies that they saw. Nothing else remained of the village. Tôlngar himself, who discovered on the soccer field the body of Guerngar's officer, grew furious and said, "If we had had a brave officer here with his troops when the enemies came, our friends and villagers would not have lost their lives like this." Feeling resentful about the actions taken by his superior officer, Guerngar, Tôlngar did not return to the base. Instead, he began to patrol the area around his native village. And then, after some time, apparently he became so disgruntled with CODO leadership that he made contact with fighters for a possible reconciliation.

Ibrahim Itno, internal minister, who was on his "hunt" for people in Oriental Logon, agreed to come and meet Tôlngar in his own village, that is, in Béjendouli, for a reconciliation. During their few hours of negotiation, Tôlngar showed to the fighters and to the villagers present at the meeting the medal won by his uncle Rôbonat during the war against the French colonial government just before the independence of Chad. The show was followed by a spirited chorus of "*youh youh!*" made by some of the women of Béjendouli. Ibrahim Itno and his delegation went back to Doba after signing the agreement with Tôlngar and planned to come back the following day to meet Tôlngar to plan for a possible offensive against other Neo-CODOs. As it turned out, Itno intended finally to take Tôlngar's fellows to the North, to fight against rebels there, and to leave Tôlngar in the South to lead fighters against his former comrades.

The officers and troops at the Tôlngar's former Neo-CODO base heard about the negotiations conducted by Tôlngar and sent a unit to Béjendouli to arrest him. The unit arrived late in the evening in Béjendouli and could have arrested Tôlngar, but for some reason, it let him escape from its circle. That unit, as it made its way back to the base, then killed a retarded man in Babo. The following day, when Itno and his team of killers arrived in Béjendouli, they asked Tôlngar to take them to the areas of their enemies (that is, the Neo-CODO). Tôlngar apparently was now in the power of and under obligation to Ibrahim Itno and had to comply. He naturally wanted to protect his own people, the Gor Nangda, from the depredations of the fighters, so he proposed that the other Gor peoples, primarily the Gor Bod, should be attacked. Unfortunately, his plan later turned against the Gor Nangda whom he intended to protect.

Jacque Tôlngar welcomed the young men of his area who arrived on the second day of reconciliation meetings. He registered them as troops and then divided his followers into three groups. One group in arms had to stay with the young men who had just been registered. The second group had to take a group of fighters and lead them to Békôdô 1 and other villages, after crossing Béngamia, Békôï, and Bédio. The last group had to initiate the planned attack in Kokamti by crossing the following villages: Dokapti, Bélembikaré, Bélengardômti, and DôKôngô. Tôlngar and Ibrahim Itno led this group.

Tôlngar, who was very trusting and naïve, had instructed his men leading the second group not to attack his native area. Unfortunately, his men were not able to speak the language of the killers, nor had they the power to give them orders to attack or not. Unopposed by any clear instructions not to do so, fighters set fire on Béngamia, Békôï, and Bédio. Because Tôlngar's troops knew very well the areas in the region, they were able to lead the fighters stealthily by small paths to surprise Béngamia once again. The villagers of Béngamia and the surrounding region who had heard about the negotiations in Béjendouli thought nothing could happen to them during the following days, with their own man in so intimate a relationship with Ibrahim Itno. As a result, some of the people had come back home. Those people were horribly surprised by the fighters and by Tôlngar's followers. When the fighters suddenly appeared in the village, some of the people wanted to take the risk of running away. At least they had a chance of escaping or not fatally shot as they ran. On the other hand, Ndoyana and the other followers of Tôlngar, believing in their leader and trusting that his instructions to them would be followed, asked people not to run away. They assured the villagers that nothing was going to happen to them. The villagers trusted these men and surrendered themselves to the fighters. Once the fighters had gathered together all the villagers they could find in Béngamia, they opened fire on them. Tôlngar's fellows were not able to stop them. After the massacre, they did not know what to do with the bodies of their relatives that they had intended to defend. They had to continue on their mission to the other villages, such as Békôï and Bédio, where again many people were killed. In Békôdô 1 and 2, however, fewer people were killed because most people stayed away from the villages and remained in hiding in the bush.

Tôlngar had taken responsibility to attack the Gor Bod villages not near to his own Gor Nangda area but beyond them, from Békôdo 2 to Kou. Tôlngar now guided fighters — including Ibrahim Itno — from Béjendouli to Békôdô 2. Itno, whose intention was apparently to eliminate all the people from the South, did not make distinctions between the Gor Nangda and Gor Bod villages. Just after they passed Dokapti, they started attacking every village. The people of Bélembikaré, Bélengardomti, DoKôngô, and Kokamti were massacred by the fighters taking orders from Itno. Indirectly they were killed by the naïvité of Tôlngar.

The traditional healer, Baou Doumna, was lived in a location that seemed especially secure. Not only was his village geographically secluded from the others, but his family compound in particular was hidden by many mango and other trees. Nevertheless, even the healer was surprised by Tôlngar and the fighters. Baou Doumna had helped Tôlngar from time to time when Tôlngar was in the *maquis* by supplying food and the roots of trees. Not only that, but Tôlngar had used the healer's village also as his hiding place. Now this man, Baou Doumna, would find himself a prisoner of Tôlngar and Itno. He was arrested, tortured, and taken to DoKôngô, where Itno had established his temporary base and where he, Tôlngar, and the fighters holed up that night.

I suspect that Itno had found out from Tôlngar that Baou Doumna had protected the CODOs. That evening Itno had the healer brought to him and demanded that he answer his questions. At each question of Itno, the old man tried to answer, but before he could answer the question, the criminal Itno burned the old man's face, head, chin, or eyes with the scorching, burning end of his *drogue* (a marijuana cigarette), demanding that he tell the truth. It is always inhuman to see an old man treated this way. I do not know how Tôlngar himself felt while Itno was torturing Baou Doumna in his presence. Was not that the man who had fed Tôlngar when he was hungry? Was not that the man who had protected Tôlngar and his men from harm? Baou Doumna, who was finally released weak and sickly, returned to his village. He survived the ordeal and lived another fifteen years.

Habré was very smart to have sent all of Tôlngar's troops to the North and left him with only his bodyguards in Doba. A few weeks later, Tôlngar was sent to N'djaména, and while he was there, he visited Sanabé Abel. Abel asked Tôlngar about the situation in the Logon Oriental and told him directly what he had heard. If it was true, Sanabé said, and if Tôlngar saw himself as guilty of putting people in harm's way, he advised him to apologize deeply to those villagers who had suffered the loss of their loved ones and their homes. Tôlngar, however, denied doing anything wrong.

Tôlngar returned to Doba and continued helping fighters from time to time as they were sent on missions to hunt villagers in the region. Some months later he was sick. Some said he had been poisoned and that his health declined precipitously. As it was apparently a kind of sickness that the White medicine could not treat, Tôlngar was taken to his native village of Béjendouli.

As the condition of his health became increasingly desperate, Tôlngar was taken to different traditional healers to see if they could help him. None of them was able to give him hope. The last resort was to take him to Baou Doumna, who was famous for the power of his traditional medicine. On their way back to Béjendouli from a failed attempt to get help from another healer, Tôlngar's relatives stopped with him at house of Baou Doumna and asked him to please forgive what Tôlngar had done to him, so the healer would treat him.

Baou Domna approached the ox cart and pulled back a little bit the bed sheet with which Tôlngar had been covered. Baou Domna looked down at his face. Then he said to Tôlngar and to the dying man's relatives that he would have been able to find some tree roots to treat Tôlngar had his eyes not been burned. He said, "Since my eyes were burned, I no longer see the trees clearly and cannot get their roots to treat Tôlngar."

Baou Doumna's words broke Tôlngar's heart. At one time he had been like a son to the healer, and now there was nothing the old man could do for him. Tôlngar asked his relatives to cover his face again and take him back to Béjendouli. Some days or weeks later, Tôlngar passed away.

Epilogue

F IVE YEARS AFTER ESCAPING THE MILITARY and returning to high
school, I earned my degree, the Brévet d'Études du Premier
Cycle, in 1985. Five years later, I earned an industrial bacalauréat,
series F1, the equivalent of the college sophomore level of studies.

I taught physics and mathematics at the Lycée Adoum Dallah of
Moundou and at the same time worked as a mechanic at CotonChad,
1990–1991. A year later I was sent to Algeria, where I obtained a
Diplôme de Technicien Supérieur in 1994 at the Institut de Technolo-
gie d'Entretien Électro-Mécanique de Beaulieu, Algeria.

I escaped war-torn Chad in 1991, returned in 1994, escaped the
next round of war in 1995, and came to the United States in 1999 as a
United Nations refugee. I earned a bachelor of science degree in elec-
trical information engineering at the University of Northern Iowa.
Currently I am working as a chief mechanic at a manufacturing firm in
Iowa City, and am a master's degree candidate in Industrial Supervi-
sion and Management at the University of Northern Iowa. My wife
and I have two children.

Index